Kansas Gold

Historical Notes and Heritage Recipes from the First Fifty Years of the Kansas Wheat Commission

"Colorado may have its mountains, Minnesota its lakes, and California its seashore, but none can match Kansas on the beauty of its towering and stately elevators and its golden fields of wheat."
— *1967 Kansas Wheat Queen Miss June Inskeep, Cawker City, Kan.*

"It is our golden grain that is keeping millions from starvation."
— Myron Krenzin

KANSAS WHEAT COMMISSION

Copyright © 2007
Kansas Wheat Commission
Manhattan, Kansas

All rights reserved. No part of this book may be reproduced or transmitted in any form or by any means, electronic or mechanical, including photocopying, recording or by any information storage and retrieval systems, without prior written permission from the publisher.

ISBN-13: 978-1-56944-360-6
ISBN-10: 1-56944-360-2

Book written, edited and designed by Marsha Boswell in the United States of America. Recipe testing and food styling by Cindy Falk. Additional contributions by David Frey, Dusti Fritz, Steven Graham, Dana Peterson, and Adrian J. Polansky.

Printed for the High Plains Journal by Terrell Creative. Printed in China. Every reasonable effort has been made to ensure the accuracy of the information herein. However, neither the author, the editors, the publisher, nor the Kansas Wheat Commission is accountable for any errors or omissions that might have occurred.

Information about the Kansas Wheat Commission can be found at www.kansaswheat.org.

CONTENTS

5 **FOREWORD**
*Kansas Secretary of Agriculture
Adrian J. Polansky*

6 **Pre-1950s**
THE KANSAS WHEAT INDUSTRY

12 **1950s**
KANSAS WHEAT ACT PASSED BY LEGISLATURE, COMMISSION FORMED

32 **1960s**
NUTRITION EDUCATION IN OVERSEAS MARKETS

50 **1970s**
WHEAT CONSUMPTION REVERSES DOWNWARD TREND

68 **1980s**
ASIAN COUNTRIES BECOME TOP INTERNATIONAL MARKETS

90 **1990s**
GOVERNMENT BUYERS GIVE WAY TO PRIVATIZATION

118 **2000s**
WHEAT ACRES DECLINE IN THE NEW MILLENNIUM

140 **Post-2000s**
THE KANSAS WHEAT INDUSTRY LOOKS TO THE FUTURE

Kansas Wheat Commission, 2007. Front row, left to right: Mike Brown, Colby; Steve Clanton, Minneapolis; Ron Suppes, Dighton; Betty Bunck, Everest; Larry Kepley, Ulysses. Back row, left to right: Dean Stoskopf, Hoisington; Doug Keesling, Chase; Tom Morton, Oxford; Richard Randall, Scott City; and Jay Armstrong, Muscotah.

Kansas Wheat staff, 2007. Front row, left to right: Dana Peterson, producer policy specialist; Aaron Harries, director of marketing; Julie Winsor, financial and human resource specialist. Back row: Marsha Boswell, public relations specialist; Julie Owens, office manager; Dusti Fritz, chief executive officer; and Cindy Falk, nutrition educator.

SPONSORS

EXCLUSIVE
ORIGINAL RED STAR — A Tradition in Family Baking

GOLD LEVEL
Cereal Food Processors Inc.

Eversole Associates on behalf of The International Wheat Genome Sequencing Consortium

Farm Credit Associations of Kansas

High Plains/Midwest Ag Journal

In Memory of Jo Keesling, Past President of the Kansas Wheathearts

John Deere

Kansas City Board of Trade

College of Agriculture, Kansas State University — K-State Research and Extension

Louis Dreyfus

AM 580 WIBW

KAN

KBUF The Ag Leader

SILVER LEVEL
Kansas State University Department of Grain Science and Industry
MGP Ingredients, Inc.
Tom and Mary Morton

BRONZE LEVEL
AIB International
Kansas Farmer
Kansas Restaurant & Hospitality Association
Kansas State Bank
Kansas State University Department of Agronomy
U.S. Energy Partners LLC/White Energy Holdings

INDIVIDUAL LEVEL
Bruce and Barbara Dirks
David Frey
Dean and Mary Anne Stoskopf
Dennis and Judy Shirley
Dusti Fritz
Ehmke Seed
Eldon and Vickie Lawless
Forrest Chumley and Barbara Valent
Harvey Wood Jr.
Heartland Mill Inc.
In Memory of Dr. John & Annabel Shellenberger (by Margo S. Caley)
In Memory of John Bunck
In Memory of John Henry and Michael Dennis L'Ecuyer
In Memory of John Yost and Beverly Laskey
In Memory of Lynne and Hazel Russell
In Memory of Ray Applegarth
In Memory of Robert (Bob) Deyoe
Kansas Farm Bureau
Larry and Virginia Kepley
McClellan Farms - Bob & JoEva McClellan
Milton and Doris Giedinghagen
Richard and Glenda Randall
Stafford County Flour Mills
Steven and Cheri Graham
Charles and Lois Deyoe
Farmer Direct Foods

FOREWORD

By Kansas Secretary of Agriculture Adrian J. Polansky

Fifty years ago, visionary Kansas wheat farmers understood, as we do today, the critical need for industry research, education and promotion. The Kansas Wheat Commission has played a vital role in foreign market development, domestic consumption and pivotal research projects.

I have observed firsthand the benefits of Wheat Commission programs. The educational opportunities I experienced as a 4-H project winner provided the foundation for lifelong involvement in wheat-related issues and activities.

Leveraging USDA cooperative funding for foreign market development has been critical to the economic viability of Kansas wheat producers. As an officer of the Wheat Commission and U.S. Wheat Associates, I witnessed sales of Kansas wheat that would not have occurred without promotion activities.

Disseminating accurate information concerning the nutritional value of wheat and wheat products has protected our position in the domestic market. Research results from Kansas Wheat Commission-funded projects have been far-reaching. Varieties with important traits and advanced yields have had a profound impact, benefiting wheat producers' bottom lines.

The improved quality traits from those projects are equally important as we compete for a share of the world marketplace. The Hard White wheat program is a success story that will play an important role in the future, both in production and marketing.

Wheat producers have been able to position Kansas wheat as a reliable food staple by communicating with government and food industry officials from foreign lands through the International Grains Program at Kansas State University. These mutually beneficial international relationships are essential in our global marketplace, and they foster a greater understanding of diverse cultures.

As Kansas Secretary of Agriculture and a wheat producer, I am convinced that industry success in the future depends more than ever on an active and well-funded Kansas Wheat Commission.

Private and public funding for wheat research is not adequate, which makes funding through the Commission more vital than ever.

The need to enhance varietal traits for producers and consumers alike is absolutely critical to the future of the wheat industry. Biotechnology holds the key to successfully compete with other crops, food alternatives and cellulosic ethanol production. Wheat production and marketing have changed tremendously during the last 50 years. One thing that has not changed is the need for a well-funded and vibrant Kansas Wheat Commission.

Wheat commissioners from across the state have worked with Wheat Commission staff to serve producers and consumers for half a century. They will continue to move our premier Kansas industry into a successful future.

It has been an honor to be a part of the wheat industry and to be involved with the Kansas Wheat Commission over many years. This 50th Anniversary milestone is the perfect time to celebrate the Commission's many accomplishments and to rededicate ourselves to achieving the goals of those visionary Kansas farmers many years ago.

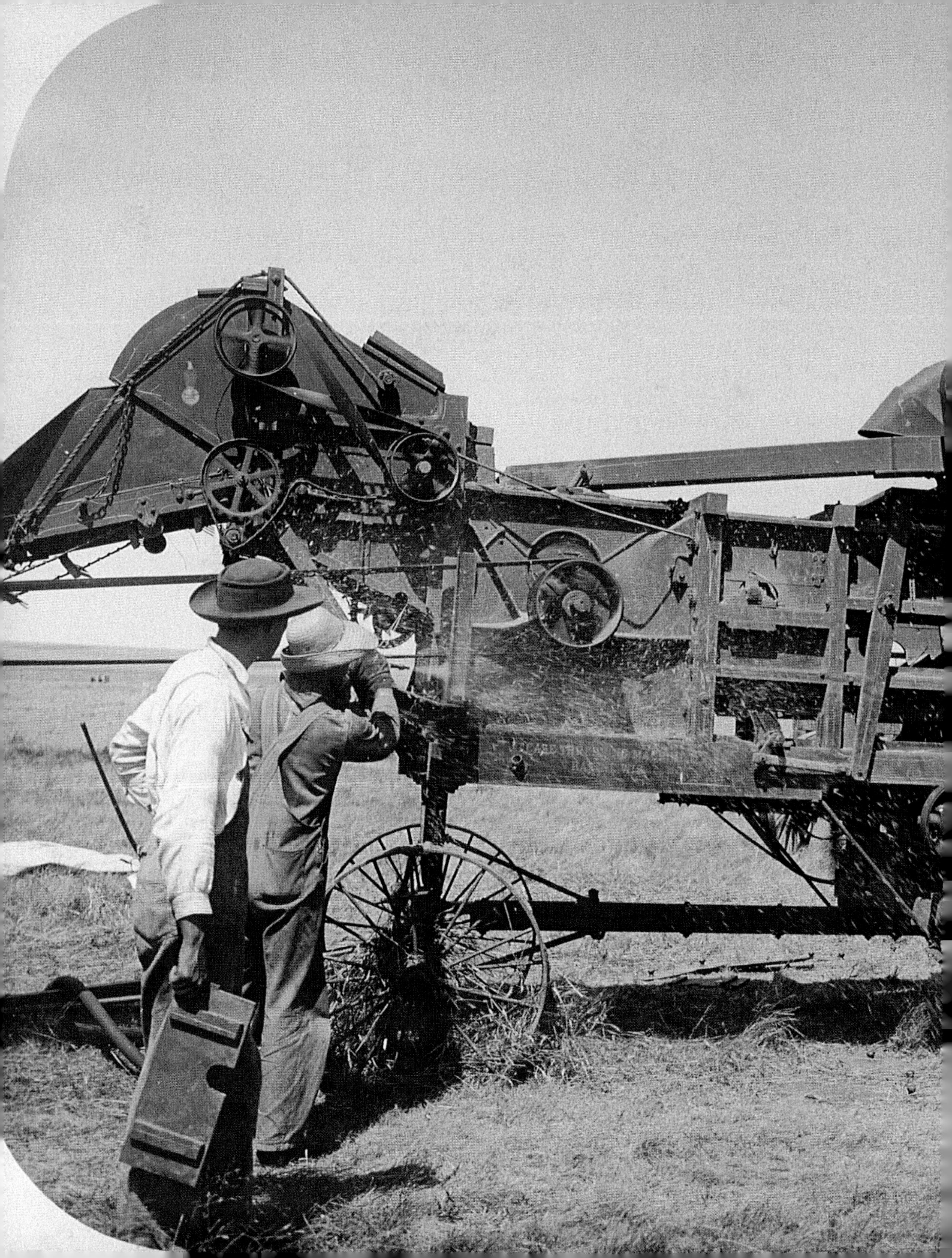

Pre-1950s

THE KANSAS WHEAT INDUSTRY

"Farming looks mighty easy when your plow is a pencil and you're a thousand miles from the field." — Dwight D. Eisenhower

Wheat is the most important crop in Kansas. It supports growers, their communities, and an array of industries, as well as feeding millions of people around the world. Kansas didn't become the "Wheat State" by accident. Settlers introduced numerous kinds of wheat, learned to grow them by trial and error, and suffered crop failures during many years. Today's growers, in contrast, have varieties adapted to Kansas; modern methods and machinery for producing the crop; and up-to-date information on cultivating the soil, protecting the plants against adverse conditions, and marketing the grain.

Most of the improved varieties and much of the modern technology for producing wheat in Kansas were developed at Kansas State University (KSU). These varieties became popular because they were productive, yielded high-quality grain, and resisted the pests and adverse weather that often damaged wheat in the state. Their annual contribution to Kansas agriculture amounts to hundreds of millions of dollars.

Introduction of Wheat in Kansas

The first wheat crop in Kansas was grown at the Shawnee Methodist Mission near Fairway in Johnson County in 1839. Production spread westward as the state was settled during the 1800s, but yields were low. The state's harvests didn't reach one million bushels until 1866 and 100 million bushels until 1914. Yields averaged less than 20 bushels per acre until 1914 and 30 bushels per acre until 1969.

Lack of suitable varieties was a major cause of low wheat production during the early years. Settlers mostly used familiar varieties they brought with them to Kansas from the eastern U.S. or Western Europe. Most of these wheats were ill adapted to the state.

Four introductions were particularly important for improving productivity of wheat in Kansas. The first was the well-known import of 'Turkey' Hard Red Winter wheat from the Crimea to south central Kansas by Mennonite settlers who arrived from the Ukraine in 1874. Both 'Turkey' wheat and the traditional production practices of the Mennonites were well suited to Kansas and often enabled them to successfully grow a crop when other settlers' crops failed.

M.A. Carleton, a graduate (B.S. 1887, M.S. 1893) and former faculty (1893-94) of Kansas State University, made two important introductions of 'Turkey'-type wheats. Carleton, a cerealist and plant explorer for the U.S. Department of Agriculture, introduced 'Crimean' and 'Kharkof,' Hard Red Winter wheats from Russia in 1900. 'Crimean' became the parent of the first improved wheat varieties developed by KSU. 'Kharkof,' being hardier than 'Turkey,' extended production of Hard Red Winter wheat throughout Kansas and into more northern states.

The fourth important introduction was 'Norin 10' by S.C. Salmon, also a graduate (M.S. 1913) and former professor (1913-31) at KSU. Salmon collected the semidwarf, or short, stocky wheats while serving as a crop consultant with the U.S. Army of Occupation in Japan in 1946. The International Maize and Wheat Improvement Center (CIMMYT) in Mexico used similar lines to create the varieties that started the Green Revolution in developing countries and are in the pedigrees of over 95% of the varieties grown in Kansas today.

1874 — 'Turkey' red wheat first planted in Kansas by Mennonite settlers.

1880 — 160,500 miles of railroad in the United States, an increase from only 30,000 miles of railroad in 1860.

1885 — Although wheat was well-established in the state, crops failed in 1885, 1886, and 1887, primarily from winterkill.

1890 — 40-50 labor-hours required to produce 100 bushels (five acres) of wheat with gang plow, seeder, harrow, binder, thresher, wagons and horses.

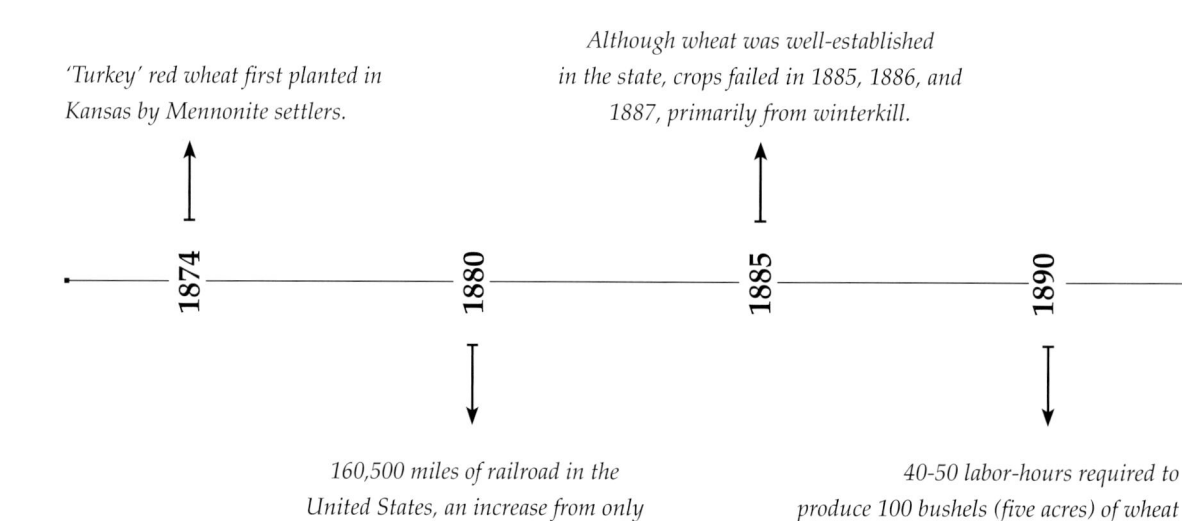

Early Varietal Development

Development of new crops for a region typically follows a sequence of evaluation of introduced varieties, selection of genotypes from the genetic diversity in introduced varieties, and hybridization to create new genotypes. Improvement of wheat at KSU followed the same course. Early researchers tested numerous varieties from around the world, selected strains from the best introductions to develop the first improved variety, and then crossed parents with desirable traits to create new varieties.

'Turkey' was first introduced in Kansas in 1874. By 1919, 'Turkey' occupied 98% of the state's wheat acreage and was the leading variety from 1880 to 1939. Incredibly, 'Turkey' was planted on over 1% of the state's acreage for 72 years, from 1880 to 1952. Although hard to find, 'Turkey' is still planted on small acreages today.

'Kanred' was the first Hard Red Winter wheat variety released by KSU in 1919, but 'Blackhull' and 'Tenmarq' were the first varieties to replace 'Turkey' as the leading varieties. 'Blackhull' was the leading variety from 1939 to 1941, and 'Tenmarq' from 1942 to 1944. Along with 'Turkey,' these two were the major varieties planted during the war years.

'Pawnee,' released in 1945, became the leading variety planted in Kansas by 1949 and continued its reign for seven years. 'Pawnee' was the first real departure in plant type from the earlier varieties, being noticeably earlier in maturity. This trait was readily accepted by Kansas farmers, because its early maturity allowed 'Pawnee' to escape the hot, dry conditions that are common in Kansas from mid- to late-June when wheat ripens. Pawnee was grown on over 1% of the state's acreage for 23 years.

(from "A History of Wheat Improvement at Kansas State University" by Gary M. Paulsen, SRL 136, March 2003, available at http://www.oznet.ksu.edu/library)

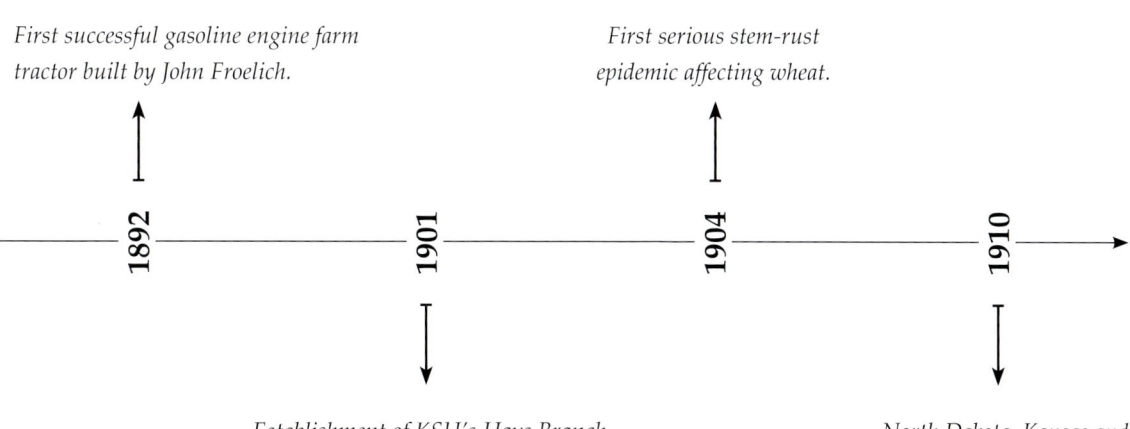

1892 — *First successful gasoline engine farm tractor built by John Froelich.*

1901 — *Establishment of KSU's Hays Branch Experiment Station expanded research with wheat to an area that was more representative of the major production regions.*

1904 — *First serious stem-rust epidemic affecting wheat.*

1910 — *North Dakota, Kansas and Minnesota are chief wheat-producing states.*

1930s and 1940s

The 1930s and 1940s were defining decades for the United States and its main source of national wealth: the farm. These two decades saw war and a severe economic depression and then transitioned to a time of post-war recovery and rapid technological advancements.

Kansas agriculture and the wheat industry were deeply impacted by the events of the 1930s or "Dirty 30s." Farming during this time could perhaps be remembered as the most difficult occupation. Producers were facing the worst and most prolonged drought of all time. The Great Plains region of Texas, Oklahoma, Kansas, Colorado, and Nebraska was most impacted, and the blowing dust from the region initiated the name the "Dust Bowl." By 1932, farm prices and income fell to the lowest level of the decade. "The Great Depression," the most devastating economic depression the United States has ever experienced, exacerbated the farm crisis. Consumers had no money to buy the crops and livestock that producers raised.

In addition to drought, producers faced crop disease. Leaf rust attacked the crop of 1935, which presented yet another obstacle in producing wheat and survival on the farm.

Toward the latter half of the decade, two significant events occurred that shined a ray of hope on agriculture in the Great Plains. In 1935 the federal government passed the Bankhead-Jones Agricultural Research Act, which more than doubled the federal support of research and extension work on the farm. Then, one year later, the Rural Electrification Act began improving the quality of life in rural America. The number of farms with electricity jumped from 13% in 1939 to 33% in 1940.

The 1940s can be remembered as a time of war and the economic and agricultural boom that followed. At that time, the United States was a net importer of wheat and feed grains of 91 million bushels. As the war ended, the agricultural boom began with technology. By

---

1916 — *Railroad network peaks at 254,000 miles; Rural Post Roads Act begins regular Federal subsidies to road building.*

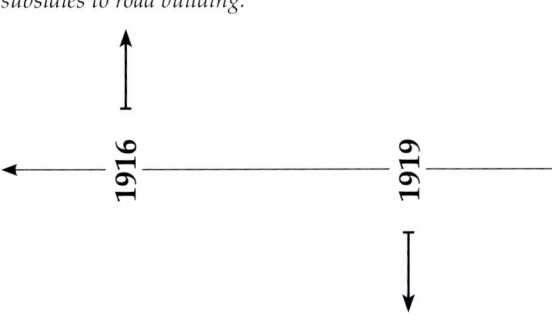

1919 — *K-State releases first Hard Red Winter wheat variety, 'Kanred,' from the pedigree of 'Crimean' from Russia.*

1928 — *Otto Rohwedder introduces his bread-slicing machine.*

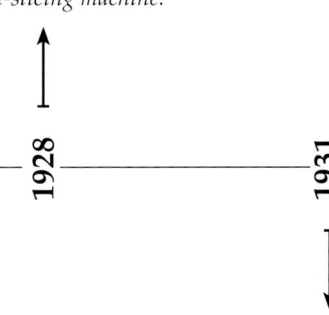

1931 — *Harvested acres: 13,623,000. Yield: record high 18.5 bushels per acre. Production: 251,885,000 bushels. Price: 33 cents per bushel, the lowest of record.*

1945, producers began to change from horses to tractors and to adopt technological practices. As a result, productivity per acre began to increase, and production surpluses began to rise.

Added production sparked added interest in agricultural exports. The United Nations began a Relief and Rehabilitation Administration, and the Food and Agricultural Organization General Agreement on Tariffs and Trade established working procedures to reduce tariffs between member nations. In addition, the United States assisted Europe in their post-war recovery.

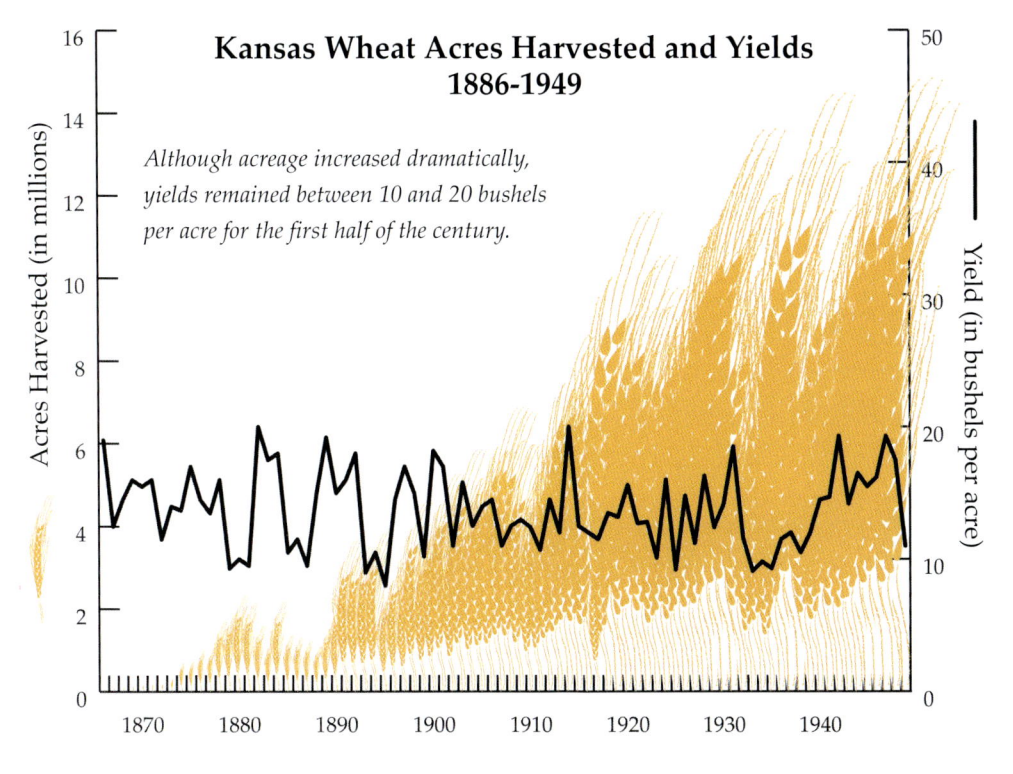

**Kansas Wheat Acres Harvested and Yields
1886-1949**

Although acreage increased dramatically, yields remained between 10 and 20 bushels per acre for the first half of the century.

Worst drought in U.S. history takes place in the Great Plains and covers over 75 percent of the country.

Second American agricultural revolution begins as producers change from horses to tractors; productivity per acre begins sharp rise.

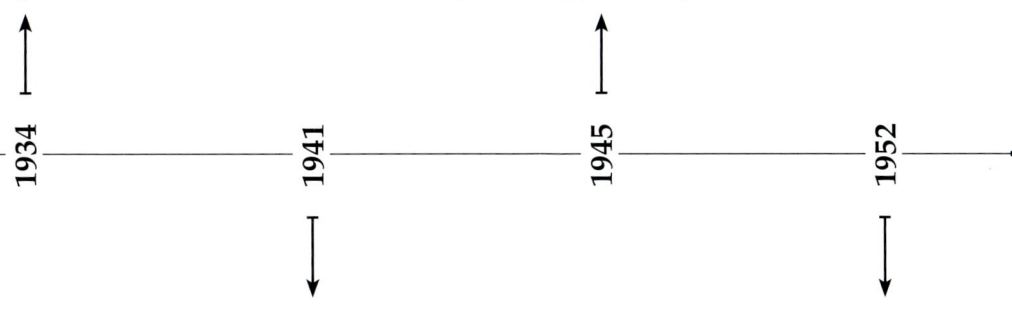

1934 — 1941 — 1945 — 1952

USDA publishes the first simple daily nutrition guide.

Official charter of the Kansas Association of Wheat Growers.

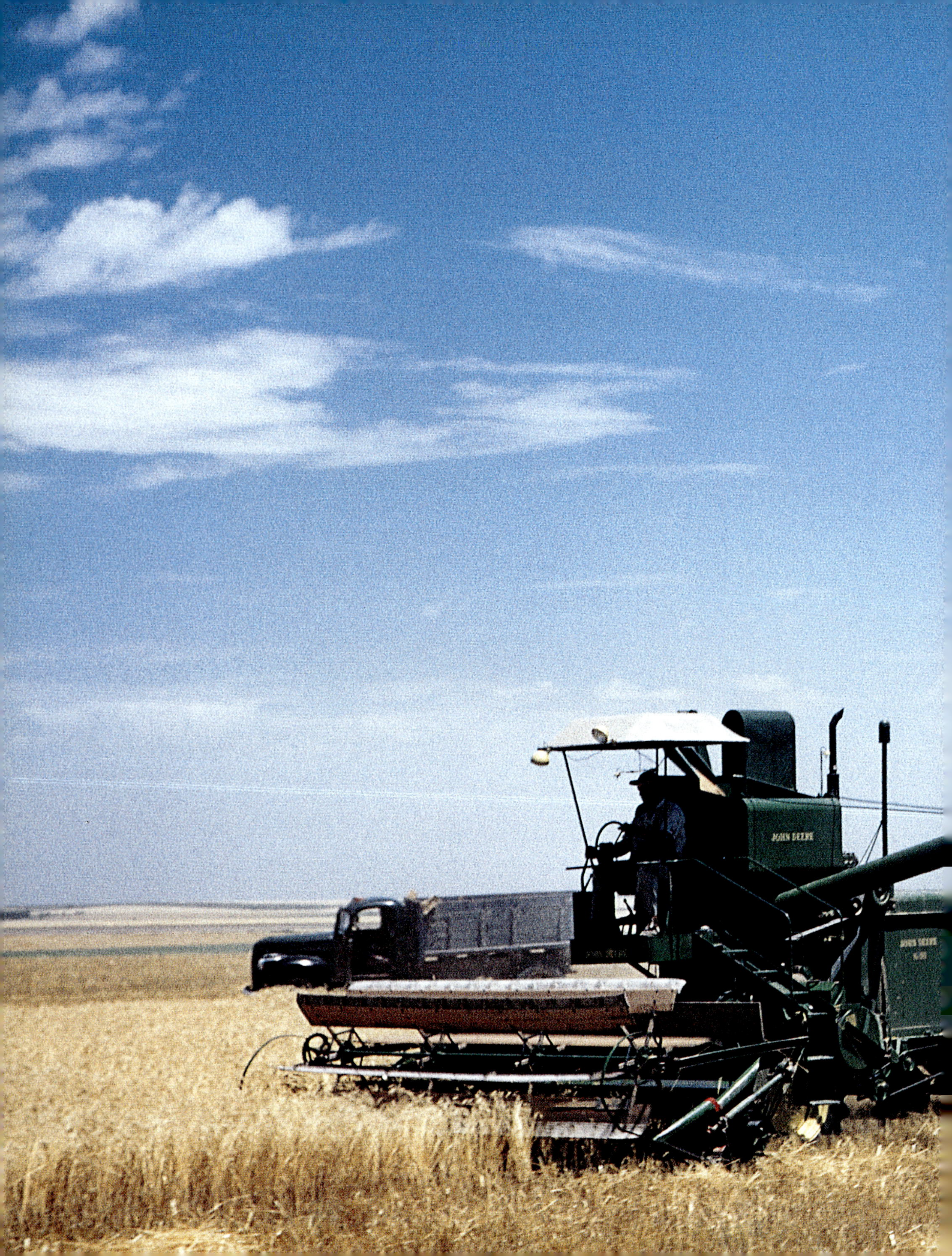
JOHN DEERE

1950s

KANSAS WHEAT ACT PASSED BY LEGISLATURE, COMMISSION FORMED

"The success of the Kansas wheat farmer does not only depend on his ability to raise good wheat, but also on his ability to merchandise it at home and abroad."
— W.W. Graber, first Administrator
of the Kansas Wheat Commission

In the early 1950s, the Kansas wheat industry was faced with increasing production, declining price, declining markets, and a constant reduction in Kansas wheat acreage allotments. It became very evident to wheat growers, the grain trade, and others interested in the Kansas economy and agriculture that wheat growers must improve their own positions, if they were to prosper and progress.

"From 1951 to 1957, the Wheat Growers introduced four wheat bills in the Kansas Legislature before one was finally passed and signed by Governor George Docking," wrote Graber.

It was through the efforts of the Kansas Association of Wheat Growers, and others interested in the welfare of the state's greatest single industry, that Senate Bill 396 passed.

The bill, known as The Kansas Wheat Act, was passed by the 1957 session of the Kansas Legislature and signed by Governor George Docking who appointed the first Kansas Wheat Commission.

"It was through the tireless efforts of Herb Clutter, Gib Egbert, Henry Parkinson, R.L. Patterson and others who persisted and finally won, that the Wheat Commission was created the last of April 1957. These men spent hundreds of dollars of their own money, and days and nights of time without remuneration, to accomplish this," wrote Graber in April 1987.

He continued, "However, the Legislature failed to make a funding appropriation to get the Commission off the ground. The Commission had 30 days in which to get organized, open and equip an office, hire personnel, print vouchers, and inform operators of elevators across the entire state to collect two mills on every bushel of wheat they purchased from producers."

The Commission held its organization meeting in Topeka, Kansas, on April 29, 1957, and elected officers.

The Kansas Wheat Commission was created to conduct a campaign of development, education and publicity and to find new markets for wheat and wheat products. An office was created at 201 West First Street, Hutchinson, Kansas, which opened July 1, 1957. The KWC was funded by a wheat assessment of 1/5 cent per bushel. Collections of the Kansas Wheat Tax were forwarded each day to the Treasurer of the State of Kansas in Topeka, where 80% of these collections were deposited in the Kansas Wheat Commission Fund, and the remaining 20% into the state's General Revenue Fund. The High Plains Journal from Dodge City was contracted to assist with publicity and disseminating information.

Market Development Activities

In August and September 1957 the KWC launched its first foreign market development work in cooperation with the Nebraska Wheat Commission and USDA Foreign

First Kansas Wheat Commission, 1957. Front row: R.L. Patterson, Oxford; Henry Parkinson, Scott City; G.W. Egbert, Ingalls; W.W. Graber, Administrator. Back row: Jim Petr, State Board of Agriculture (ex officio); Stanley Harris, Colony; Melvin Mustoe, Norton; Gerald Thompson, Makato; Byrd Hardy, Greensburg; Dr. John Shellenberger, Kansas State University (ex officio). Graber was originally appointed to the Commission, but resigned to accept the position as Administrator on May 23, 1958. Hardy was appointed to fill Graber's unexpired term.

Agricultural Service. The groups participated in the Anuga Trade Fair at Cologne, Germany, where exhibits were shown to promote goodwill and understanding, and ultimately, more use of Kansas and Nebraska wheat. In order to coordinate the foreign market development work of wheat commissions of Kansas and Nebraska, a Central Marketing Office was temporarily established in Lincoln, Neb.

Other fairs attended in the 1950s were the British Food Fair, London, England; a food fair in Vienna, Austria; the German Food Fair, Munich, Germany; the fair at Sao Paulo, Brazil; the Fine Foods Fair at Lausanne, Switzerland; and the Pacific Northwest Fair in Osaka, Japan.

Hard Red Winter wheat and its products were shown at these food shows in an effort to acquaint the wheat buyers in foreign countries with the quality characteristics of Kansas-grown wheat. Show visitors were given an opportunity to see, feel, and taste Kansas products.

These shows also provided an avenue to demonstrate the milling and baking characteristics. Thousands tasted doughnuts made from Kansas wheat and were impressed. A colorful brochure entitled *Wheat Unites the Nations*, printed in the languages commonly spoken in these areas, told the story of U.S. wheat in pictures and words.

The South American exhibits displayed bundles of wheat and wheat products. Bread and rolls were distributed to thousands at the Sao Paulo fair. The South American grain trade received much valuable information concerning U.S. wheat.

Munich Food Fair in Germany, 1957. A normal scene at the Hard Red Winter Wheat Doughnut Exhibit. Doughnuts at the rate of approximately 40,000 per day were served the fair-goers in London and Munich. Doughnut recipes on folders in the shape of a doughnut were given to fair-goers, telling these people how doughnuts can be made with Hard Red Winter wheat flour.

San Paulo, Brazil, Food Fair, 1958. Rolls, bakery products, and breads were served at the fair. The people liked what they tasted and saw. Interest in the American products immediately rose, and many questions were answered daily about U.S. products, concerning availability, cost, characteristics, processing, etc.

Great Plains Wheat Growers European Office, official opening, January 23, 1959. Front office interior scene, left to right, Henry Baehr, Assistant Agricultural Attache, Paris, France, who had been detailed from the Department of Agriculture to assist Mr. Bross in organizing the European Office; Miss Clementine Beverwijk, receptionist and stenographer; and Mr. Harvey Bross, European Representative for the Great Plains Wheat Growers European Office in Rotterdam, Netherlands.

Great Plains Wheat, Inc.

With the need for a more unified effort in foreign market development, the Great Plains Wheat Marketing Development Association organized on December 19, 1958. Its mission was to unite and coordinate the foreign market development efforts and funds of Hard Red Winter wheat producing states.

By 1960, the organization consisted of Kansas, Nebraska, Colorado, and later, North Dakota. Other Great Plains state wheat growers organizations joined as associate members. These included Oklahoma, Montana, and South Dakota. These states had not yet organized wheat commissions. The Great Plains Wheat Marketing Development Association organized with an office in Garden City, Kansas, and Clifford Hope as President. Hope had served as a Congressman and had been key in the organization of the National Association of Wheat Growers and the Kansas Association of Wheat Growers.

International Wheat Offices

Great Plains Wheat, Inc. identified foreign offices as one of its greatest needs. The Western Europe office organized to promote the use of U.S. wheat in the post-war recovery. This office was established in Rotterdam, Netherlands on January 23, 1959, under the leadership of Mr. Harvey Bross.

Jack Smith led the South American office in Lima, Peru. Three other international offices were located in New Delhi, India; Karachi, Pakistan; and Tokyo, Japan. Through these foreign offices it readily became apparent that several areas of the world were far behind the U.S. and Europe in nutrition education.

Foreign Nutrition Education

South America, India, and Pakistan were identified for the initial nutrition education programs. Nutrition education in Karachi, Pakistan, was desperately needed. Dire poverty, religious objection to red wheat, illiteracy, and lack of technical knowledge and equipment were challenges in this area.

Assistants that were native to Pakistan and India played a key role in research to better suit the tastes of the people. Arrangements with the Women's Christian College in Bombay, India, allowed the training of Indian people to cook with wheat. Mobile kitchens, which were mounted on trucks with loud speakers, projectors, screens, and other equipment, went into villages and cities and offered instruction on the streets.

Nutrition education programs were offered to native women in a college in Chile, to better qualify these people to work in the interest of more wheat consumption. There was great potential for increased consumption of wheat in many South American countries.

Through a study by Great Plains Wheat, needs in South America were identified as nutritional education, specifications, and other information about wheat shipments.

The wheat commissions and the American Federation of Millers cooperated jointly on nutritional education, and hired a nutritionist to assist with this education.

Additionally, research was conducted to show how Hard Red Winter wheat could be adapted to use in the chapatti, the most common use of wheat in Asian countries.

Surveys

In order to determine the needs of wheat-importing western European countries, the first buyers' survey was conducted in 1957. The survey also allowed producers to hear about problems in connection with wheat purchased from the United States. Dr. J.A. Shellenberger of KSU, and Graber were the Kansas representatives on this survey.

Japanese students eat bread in their school lunch program, a program carried on by the KWC through regional organizations of wheat groups, with the cooperation of the USDA Foreign Agricultural Service. School lunch programs were established in Japan to encourage bread consumption. In Tokyo, children were served a loaf of bread with butter, a bowl of vegetable soup, and dried skim milk.

Italian Pasta Delegation, October 1956. As a result of their visit, the Italians purchased huge quantities of U.S. wheat. Left to right: Dr. Antonio Perinetti, Italian Wheat Pool, Rome; Richardo Agnesi, Imperia, Italy; Professor Sabato Visco, University of Rome and Director National Institute of Nutrition; Professor Luigi Persico, Italian Milling and Baking School, Turin, Italy; Dr. Antonio Cocozza, Pugliesi Flour Mills, Bari; Miss Grace Lazzarino, Interpreter, University of Nebraska; Ing. Vincenzo Agnesi, Agnesi Wheat Mill and Pasta Company, Imperia, Italy; and Mike Dolbeau, student from France.

Results of the survey helped to chart future promotional work in these areas.

This initial survey was followed by a study of South America in the early part of 1958, and the Caribbean area in the spring of 1958. India and Africa were surveyed in 1959.

"We definitely need to merchandise wheat in Europe on a basis of milling and baking tests with a minimum of dockage, foreign material, and shrunken and broken kernels, if we are to maintain our position in that market. We are now offering recleaned wheat at the buyer's request. Work on protein analysis on export wheat is continuing," Graber wrote in 1960.

> "During our recent trip to the U.S., we were highly satisfied to visit the 'Land of Wheat,' also known as the world's Bread Basket, i.e., the State of Kansas."
> — *from the report by the Brazilian wheat team*

Foreign Trade Teams

The first foreign team brought to the United States was the Italian Pasta Delegation. The Midwest Research Institute was contracted to conduct an experiment on the blending of Hard Red Winter wheat with Durum wheat for use in the manufacture of pasta products. The members of the delegation visited the laboratory upon completion of the project to inspect and cook samples of the prepared blends. Members of the team were impressed with their results, and before their departure indicated they would recommend to the Italian government that U.S. Hard Red Winter wheat be used for blending with Durum wheat in the manufacture of their pasta products.

Other teams of wheat importers followed, and these trips provided one of the best methods of showing, firsthand, U.S. wheat production, merchandising, and handling to the foreign buyers. These teams were from Greece, Switzerland, Austria, Poland, the Philippines, Pakistan, Japan, Guatemala, Brazil and India.

The Indian visit resulted in the largest wheat transaction in the world. India purchased through PL480 over 487 million bushels of wheat to be delivered over a four-year period. Public Law 480, or Food for Peace legislation, originated in 1955 and transformed a temporary surplus disposal program into a major tool in the worldwide war against hunger.

By the end of September of 1959, 13 foreign trade teams had visited the Great Plains.

Marketing Kansas Wheat

The Kansas Wheat Commission and the Kansas State Board of Agriculture compiled and edited the booklet entitled *Marketing Kansas Wheat*. This was the first book about Kansas wheat published since 1920. The book was distributed to Extension people, libraries, schools, legislators, marketing people, the grain trade, USDA, millers and exporters.

> "Kansas and wheat are synonymous in the imagination of almost all persons who know that U.S. region, because when we refer to Kansas, we automatically think of wheat, and when we mention wheat, we always remember Kansas."
> – Correio Paulistano, July 27, 1959

Demonstration buses were used extensively in the Far East to educate native people on the use of U.S. wheat foods, and a similar program was undertaken in South America. A mobile kitchen, with loud speakers, and all of the necessary equipment was mounted on a truck. These vehicles, with the proper personnel, went from place-to-place where demonstrations were given on wheat foods.
Photo by Eugene Anthony from Black Star.

Mrs. Helen Asay, Home Economist in the Marketing Division of the State Board of Agriculture, shows Mrs. Gilbert Dreiling, a Topeka elementary teacher, kits of nutritional information. These kits were distributed to Kansas teachers and Home Economics Agents by the Kansas Wheat Commission and the Kansas State Board of Agriculture.
Photo from Division of Marketing, Kansas State Board of Agriculture, 1959

The demand for the publication, *Marketing Kansas Wheat* continued into the 1960s. Over 20,000 copies were distributed to key people interested in wheat in the United States and abroad.

"It is doubtful that any publication ever has given Kansas the publicity and captured the attention both in the United States and throughout the world that *Marketing Kansas Wheat* achieved," stated Graber.

Domestic Nutrition Program

The Kansas Wheat Commission and the Marketing Division of the State Board of Agriculture worked jointly on a Domestic Marketing and Nutrition Information program. Gary Rumsey, a graduate of Kansas State University, was employed to devote his time to this activity. The program utilized nutritional information, filmstrips, and educational programs originating from the Wheat Flour Institute and the Institute of Baking.

By 1958, information about the nutritional needs and requirements for Kansas school children was distributed to more than 7,000 teachers in Kansas. Over 5,000 filmstrips titled *Your Daily Bread* were distributed to schools in every state.

Nine hundred sixty-five kits of nutritional information were sent to home economists and home demonstration agents throughout the state for adult education. These kits pointed out the need for wheat products in a balanced diet. Wheat products had been sadly neglected. All of these groups welcomed this material and expressed the need for this information in Kansas schools.

One user of the materials stated, "The teachers have found the nutrition information interesting and informative. It is a helpful way of presenting materials to children."

In 1959, the human consumption of wheat in the United States rose one pound per capita. The 1959 KWC annual report states, "We feel we have had a part in stopping the decline of wheat consumption per capita in the United States — a decline which has been going on for 40 years."

The programs extended into schools in Missouri during the 1959-60 school year. Nearly 100,000 pieces of nutrition materials were placed in 50 of the largest school districts.

More than one million copies of the materials were distributed in the first two years of the program.

"This is a field (domestic promotion of wheat) which presents a tremendous challenge, for while it may not be as dramatic as foreign marketing work, and results may come slower, it is at the same time a more stable market, and the one with the highest dollar value for wheat producers," said Rumsey.

Information and Outreach

The High Plains Advertising Agency assisted the Wheat Commission with public relations work to producers by issuing a quarterly *Newsletter*. With 158,000 wheat producers, the cost of printing and mailing the *Newsletter* to all was prohibitive. It was sent to elevator operators and some farmers in each county, as well as others interested in wheat. Newspapers, magazines, radio, and television were also used to distribute information.

Booths and Fairs

The Kansas Wheat Commission exhibited at the Dodge City Fair, Belleville Fair, Iola Fair, Topeka Free Fair, and Kansas State Fair, Hutchinson. In 1959 the exhibit was mounted on a trailer to make it more mobile and available for fairs, conventions and meetings.

Small souvenir sacks of wheat were popular for conventions and meetings of various kinds. The printing on the sacks encouraged eating bread, "The Staff of Life" and told people about Kansas wheat and encouraged its use. Over 100,000 of these small wheat sacks were distributed throughout the United States and overseas.

One popular exhibit was the bread buffet exhibit that was set up for the national meeting of Home Economists in Denver. The exhibit attractively displayed 25 different kinds of bread. Visitors sampled some of the breads, received nutrition publications, and took with them new ideas about flour and bread uses. The wheat commissions of Nebraska and Colorado cooperated with this exhibit.

An exhibit on wheat at Kansas fairs was staffed by Gerald C. Fowler, Assistant Marketing Director for the Kansas Wheat Commission. Moving platforms and an automatic slide projector told the story of promotion of wheat at home and abroad.

Speakers on the program of the joint annual meeting of the Kansas Wheat Commission and Kansas Association of Wheat Growers covered a wide variety of subjects. Left to right, Dr. W. Dayton Maclay, director, Northern Utilization Research and Development Division Laboratory, Peoria, Illinois; Z. Arthur Nevins of Dodge City, representing Kansas Gov. George Docking; Clifford Hope, Garden City; J. Floyd Breeding, Congressman; R.L. Patterson, Oxford, KAWG President; G.W. Egbert, Ingalls, KWC Secretary-Treasurer. Nov. 17-18, 1958, Hutchinson, Kan. Photo by Ray Pierce, High Plains Journal, Dodge City.

Research

Research in the late 1950s included establishing a Wheat Reference Library at Kansas State University. Information on every segment of the wheat industry was collected and on file. This was the first comprehensive accumulation of this type of material ever to be undertaken.

Kansas State University, Manhattan, Kansas, conducted a research project using federal funds and matching wheat funds on bread flavor research. This was an effort to retain the aroma and taste of freshly baked bread. This work was under the direction of Dr. John Shellenberger. Retaining the characteristics of freshly baked bread would greatly increase bread consumption.

Another research project, conducted at Midwest Research Institute, Kansas City, Mo., was using low protein Hard Red Winter wheat flour mixed with Durum wheat flour for pasta, to create a cash market for low protein wheats, which posed a problem in 1959.

The Kansas Wheat Commission also helped secure 2,000 bushels of Commodity Credit Corporation wheat for research in cattle feeding at the KSU Hays Experiment Station and funded a study on the use of wheat in the manufacture of paper.

Congressmen encouraged partnering dollars through federal appropriations for basic research for new food and industrial uses.

New Wheat Food — Pilaf

Expanded wheat uses included Pilaf, a wheat food developed by the Western Research Laboratory in Albany, California. Testing was conducted by the Agricultural

Marketing Service of the United States Department of Agriculture. "If this wheat food receives a favorable response, it will be brought to the Midwest to a large city, where growers will have an opportunity to sell it to the public. If it passes this consumer test, it will be manufactured commercially and sold throughout the United States. The KWC will help in the promotion of this new wheat food."

Annual Convention

Annual conventions were held in Hutchinson in November 1958 and 1959. The purpose of the annual convention was to report to the Governor and the producers of Kansas the activities of the Commission, and to discuss new ideas and opinions concerning activities.

In 1960, Graber wrote, "More than 2,000 people attended last year's meeting. This is a decided increase over attendance during the past years, and shows the increase of wheat grower interest in solving his own problems."

The Future

In 1959, Graber wrote, "The Kansas Wheat Commission is about 18 months old at the time of this second annual meeting. Several projects have been undertaken and many more will be developed as time, funds, and personnel permit. Its future lies not only in the hands of the Commission, but with every person who has a stake in this great industry from the wheat producer on up. The Commission must work closely with the Kansas Association of Wheat Growers who can provide us with guidance and personnel in areas where we are limited. We solicit the suggestions of the grain trade, farmers, and everyone who has a genuine interest in the future of the wheat industry in Kansas."

In 1960, he wrote, "To predict the future of the work of the Kansas Wheat Commission would certainly be getting out on the far end of the limb. The work that needs to be done to promote Kansas wheat is almost unlimited."

**Retail Value of Loaf of Bread
1957-1959
Total Value 18.9 cents**

The contribution to retail value of a one pound loaf of white bread from each market segment

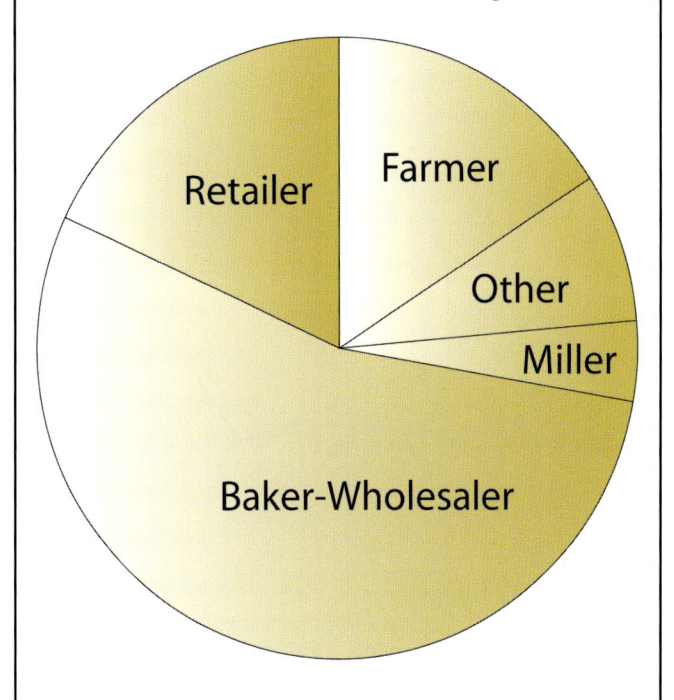

(Data from USDA Wheat Situation, Milling and Baking News, January 1, 1974)

Wheat Production and Varieties

Wheat producers annually harvested between 9.7 and 14.6 million acres of wheat during the 1950s, except for 1957 where Kansas recorded the lowest harvested acres since 1917, 5.27 million acres. The low production resulted from drought and inclement weather in addition to 4.25 million acres allotted to the Soil Bank Reserve. Production ranged from 100 million bushels in 1957 to the record production in 1952 of 307.6 million bushels.

Leading varieties in the 1950s were 'Wichita,' 'Pawnee,' 'Comanche,' 'Triumph,' 'Red Chief,' 'Kiowa,' and 'Ponca.' 'Wichita' replaced 'Pawnee' in 1955 as the state's most popular variety and remained the leading variety until 1959. 'Wichita' probably would have remained popular longer had it not been for an undesirable trait, shattering, which left four to five bushels per acre on the ground instead of in the combine. 'Wichita' was grown on at least one percent of the acreage for 30 years.

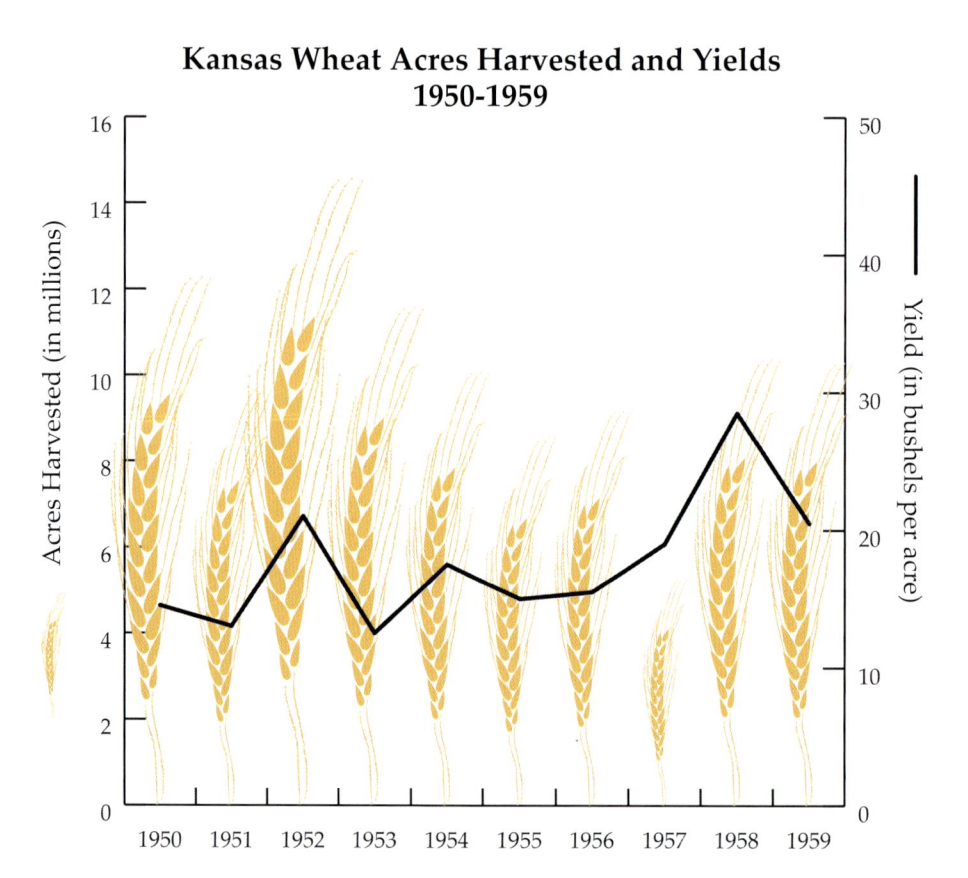

Kansas Wheat Acres Harvested and Yields 1950-1959

MRS. EISENHOWER'S BREAD

makes 3 loaves, 16 slices per loaf

ORIGINAL RECIPE OF PRESIDENT DWIGHT D. EISENHOWER'S MOTHER, IDA

ingredients
- 1 cake compressed yeast*
- ½ cup lukewarm water (110-115°F)
- ½ teaspoon granulated sugar
- ½ cup vegetable shortening
- ½ cup granulated sugar
- 1 beaten egg
- 1 ½ teaspoons salt
- 2 cups milk, scalded and cooled to lukewarm
- 7 ½ - 8 cups sifted bread flour

May substitute 2 ¼ teaspoons, or 1 package RED STAR® Active Dry Yeast

1 Dissolve yeast in lukewarm water, stirring in ½ teaspoon sugar. Let stand 5 minutes. Cream shortening with ½ cup sugar; add egg, salt, cooled milk, and yeast.

2 Stir in flour a little at a time until dough is stiff enough to knead. The less flour used the better the bread. Knead for 10 to 15 minutes, or until elastic. Place in greased bowl; cover and let rise until double. Punch down dough and let rise again until double.

3 Divide and shape dough in 3 greased 8 ½ x 4 ½ x 2 ½ -inch loaf pans. Cover with clean, damp towel. When double, bake in preheated 375°F oven 35 to 40 minutes, or until done.

Ida's note: *For whole wheat bread, use just enough white flour to handle when kneading.*

source: *Eisenhower Presidential Library and Museum, Abilene, Kansas.*

nutrition information *per serving (one slice): 112 cal, 3 g fat, 5 mg chol, 80 mg sodium, 18 g carbo, 0.5 g fiber, 3 g pro, 37 mcg folate.*

OVERNIGHT COFFEE CAKE

makes 20 servings

THERE IS SOMETHING ABOUT COFFEE CAKE THAT'S COMFORTINGLY OLD-FASHIONED.

ingredients
- 2 cups all-purpose flour
- 1 teaspoon baking powder
- 1 teaspoon baking soda
- 1 teaspoon ground cinnamon
- ½ teaspoon salt
- ⅔ cup margarine
- 1 cup granulated sugar
- ½ cup brown sugar
- 2 beaten eggs
- 1 cup low-fat buttermilk

topping
- ¼ cup brown sugar
- ½ cup chopped pecans
- 1 teaspoon ground cinnamon
- 1 teaspoon ground nutmeg

1 In small bowl, stir together flour, baking powder, baking soda, cinnamon, and salt. Set aside.

2 In a large mixing bowl, beat margarine with an electric mixer on medium speed for 1 minute. Add the granulated and brown sugars; beat mixture until blended. Add eggs; beat mixture until well combined.

3 At low speed, add dry ingredients (in 3 additions) alternately with buttermilk (in 2 additions); mix until thoroughly combined. Spread batter in well-greased 13 x 9 x 2-inch baking pan.

4 In small bowl, combine topping ingredients; mix with fork. Sprinkle topping over batter. Cover; refrigerate 8 to 12 hours, or overnight.

5 Bake coffee cake in preheated 350°F oven 40 to 45 minutes, or until tested done.

nutrition information *per serving (one serving): 197 cal, 8 g fat, 22 mg chol, 214 mg sodium, 29 g carbo, 1 g fiber, 3 g pro, 23 mcg folate.*

WHOLE WHEAT SUGAR COOKIES

makes about 36 cookies

A LONG-TIME FAVORITE COOKIE RECIPE MADE WITH WHOLE WHEAT FLOUR AND FLAVORED WITH CINNAMON AND ORANGE.

ingredients
- 2 cups whole wheat flour
- 1 teaspoon baking powder
- ½ teaspoon baking soda
- ½ teaspoon salt
- ½ teaspoon ground nutmeg
- ½ cup butter or margarine
- 1 cup granulated sugar
- 1 egg
- 1 tablespoon grated orange peel
- 1 teaspoon vanilla extract
- 2 tablespoons low-fat milk

topping
- ½ teaspoon ground cinnamon
- 2 tablespoons granulated sugar

1 Preheat oven to 375°F.

2 In small bowl, stir together whole wheat flour, baking powder, baking soda, salt, and nutmeg. Set aside.

3 In a large mixing bowl, beat butter or margarine with an electric mixer on medium speed for 1 minute. Add the sugar; beat mixture until combined. Stir in egg, orange peel, and vanilla; beat mixture until well combined.

4 Stir in the flour mixture and milk just until combined.

5 Shape into 1-inch balls and place on ungreased cookie sheet 2 inches apart. Flatten slightly with bottom of a glass dipped in topping mixture.

6 Bake cookies 8 to 10 minutes, or until golden. Transfer cookies to a wire rack to cool.

nutrition information *per serving (one cookie): 74 cal, 3 g fat, 13 mg chol, 59 mg sodium, 12 g carbo, 1 g fiber, 1 g pro, 1 mcg folate.*

PHOTO COURTESY OF THE WHEAT FOODS COUNCIL, WWW.WHEATFOODS.ORG

RYE KNOTS

makes 30 rolls

THIS DOUGH CAN BE USED FOR ANY SHAPE OR SIZE ROLL.

ingredients

- 2 packages RED STAR® Active Dry Yeast
- ½ cup lukewarm water (110-115°F)
- 1 ½ cups boiling water
- ¼ cup rolled wheat or rolled oats, dry
- ⅓ cup brown sugar
- 2 teaspoons salt
- 1 teaspoon anise seed
- ¼ cup vegetable shortening
- 3 tablespoons molasses
- 2 cups rye flour
- 2 tablespoons vital wheat gluten
- 2 ½ - 3 cups bread flour

note: For Heartland Mill rolled wheat flakes, go to www.heartlandmill.com.

1 Dissolve yeast in ½ cup lukewarm water; set aside.

2 In mixing bowl, pour boiling water over rolled wheat, sugar, salt, anise seed, shortening, and molasses. Cool to lukewarm (110°F). Stir in dissolved yeast.

3 Mix in rye flour and wheat gluten; beat until batter is smooth, about 2 minutes. Gradually add 2 cups bread flour. Cover; allow dough to rest 10 minutes.

4 Turn onto a floured board and knead in as much of the remaining flour to make a soft dough. Knead 8 to 10 minutes. Place dough in a greased bowl; turn to grease top. Cover; let rise until double, 50 to 60 minutes.

5 Punch down dough. Cover; let rise 30 minutes longer. Shape into knots: divide dough into 30 equal pieces; shape each into a strip about 9 inches long. Tie in loose knot, being careful not to stretch dough.

6 Place on greased cookie sheets. Cover; let rise until double. Bake in preheated 375°F oven 14 to 15 minutes. Cool on wire rack.

nutrition information *per serving (one roll)*: 92 cal, 2 g fat, 0 mg chol, 159 mg sodium, 17 g carbo, 1 g fiber, 2 g pro, 26 mcg folate.

MOUNTAINTOP BISCUITS

makes 12 (2 ½-inch) biscuits

A SIMPLE RECIPE THAT CAN BE PREPARED IN A MINIMUM OF TIME AND THEY'RE A MILE HIGH.

ingredients
- 3 cups all-purpose flour
- 2 tablespoons granulated sugar
- 4 ½ teaspoons baking powder
- ¾ teaspoon cream of tartar
- ¾ teaspoon salt
- ¾ cup vegetable shortening
- 1 beaten egg
- 1 cup low-fat milk

1 Preheat oven to 450°F.

2 Stir flour so it is not packed from being in container. Measure dry ingredients and level off. Sift flour, sugar, baking powder, cream of tartar, and salt into medium bowl.

3 Cut in shortening, with pastry blender or 2 knives (used scissors-fashion), until mixture resembles coarse meal.

4 Combine egg and milk; add to flour mixture all at once. Stir with fork just long enough to make a soft dough that forms a ball.

5 On lightly floured surface, knead lightly about ten times. Roll or flatten dough 1 inch thick using as little flour as possible. Cut straight down into dough with a 2 ½-inch biscuit cutter, being careful not to twist cutter.

6 Place 1-inch apart on ungreased cookie sheet. Bake 12 to 15 minutes.

nutrition information *per serving (one biscuit): 257 cal, 14 g fat, 19 mg chol, 557 mg sodium, 28 g carbo, 1 g fiber, 4 g pro, 50 mcg folate.*

DOROTHY'S DUMPLINGS

makes 12 dumplings

OLD-FASHIONED, FLUFFY DUMPLINGS ARE A TRUE COMFORT FOOD.

ingredients
- 1 cup all-purpose flour
- 2 tablespoons cornstarch
- 3 teaspoons baking powder
- ½ teaspoon salt
- 1 beaten egg
- ½ cup low-fat milk

1 In a medium bowl, combine flour, cornstarch, baking powder, and salt. Stir in egg and milk; mix just until the dry ingredients are moistened.

2 Drop batter, by rounded tablespoonfuls, onto boiling stew or broth. Cover tightly; boil gently 10 minutes, or until dumplings are fluffy and no longer doughy. For a tender dumpling, have the stew boiling and keep it covered constantly.

3 Serve immediately.

nutrition information *per serving (one dumpling): 55 cal, 1 g fat, 19 mg chol, 166 mg sodium, 10 g carbo, 0 g fiber, 2 g pro, 18 mcg folate.*

HOMEMADE NOODLES

makes 4 cups uncooked noodles

NOODLES, A LONG-TIME FAVORITE, ARE A HEALTHY, DELICIOUS ADDITION TO ANY MEAL.

ingredients
- 2 ½ cups all-purpose flour
- 1 teaspoon salt
- ½ cup cool water (68°F)
- 1 beaten egg

1 In medium bowl, sift flour and salt together. Beat together cool water and egg; stir into flour mixture until well combined.

2 Knead dough until smooth and elastic, about 5 to 8 minutes. Cover with a wet cheesecloth or towel for 30 minutes.

3 On a lightly floured surface, roll out into a thin sheet. With sharp knife, cut into ¼-inch strips, or use a noodle cutter. Separate noodles by lightly tossing with a dusting of flour.

4 Noodles may be used immediately or frozen in a sealed container or bag.

5 To cook fresh noodles, boil 10 to 12 cups water or broth; gradually add noodles. Cook, stirring occasionally, for 12 to 15 minutes.

variation: *Replace half of the all-purpose flour with whole wheat flour.*

nutrition information *per serving (½ cup uncooked noodles)*: 152 cal, 1 g fat, 27 mg chol, 300 mg sodium, 30 g carbo, 1 g fiber, 5 g pro, 63 mcg folate.

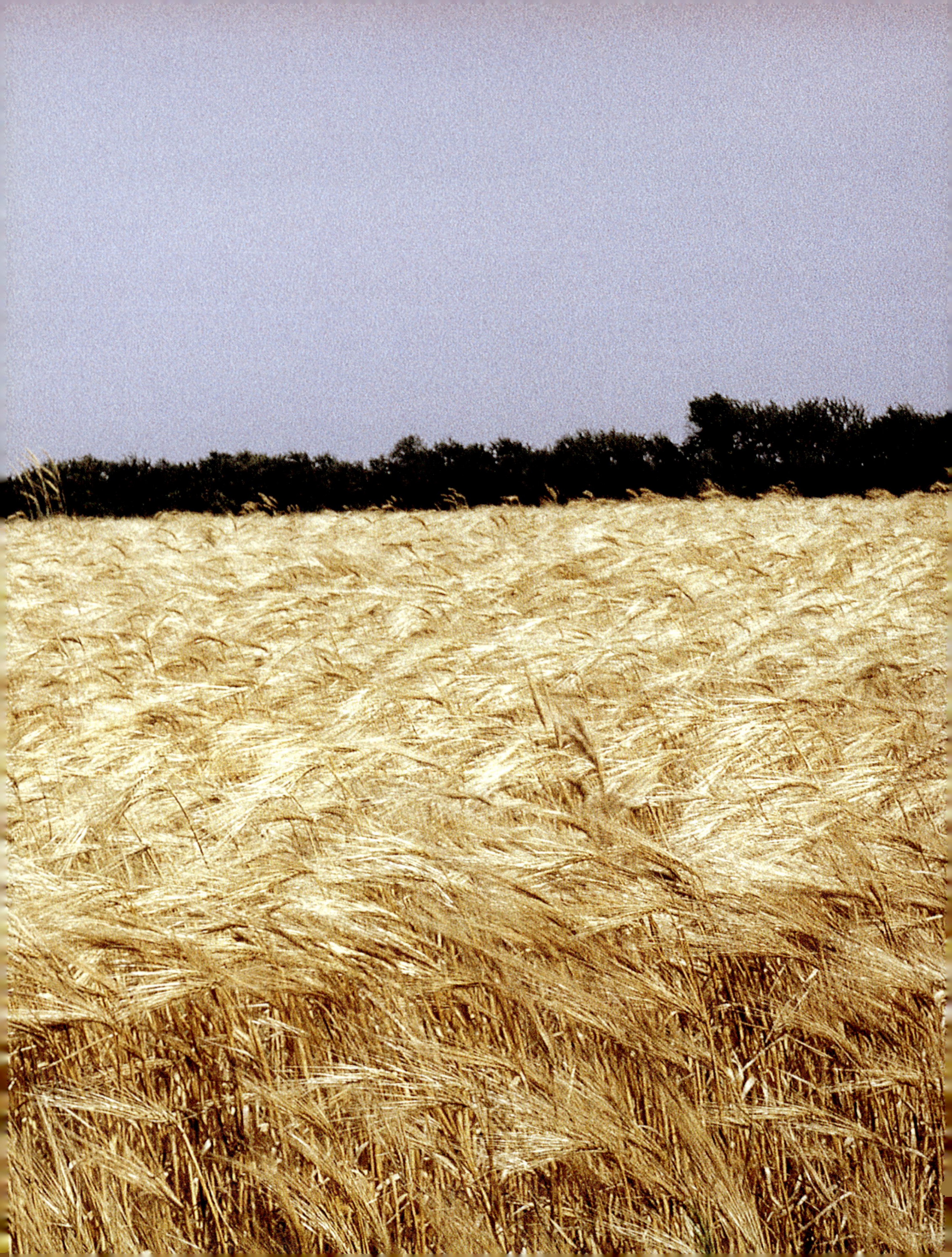

1960s
NUTRITION EDUCATION IN OVERSEAS MARKETS

> "Bread is life the world around, but in Kansas, bread is life and a lot more — it is the very core of our economy...We continue to maintain our position as the nation's leading wheat state."
> — Kansas Governor Robert B. Docking.

The average time to develop a new wheat variety is about 10 to 12 years. In 1962, the Kansas Wheat Commission initiated a continuing research project with the Departments of Agronomy and Grain Science at Kansas State University to develop Hard Red Winter wheat varieties with superior milling and baking qualities. This first Commission grant was $13,500 per year.

In 1964, over 1,000 samples of wheat were grown at the Hutchinson Experiment Field. These samples were selected on the basis of prior quality tests in the fourth and fifth year of the development cycle. Dr. E.G. Heyne, Professor of Plant Breeding in Kansas State University's Department of Agronomy worked with this varietal development.

Dr. E.G. Heyne, Professor of Plant Breeding, in Kansas State University's Department of Agronomy, at the Hutchinson Experiment Field. The first KWC research project was to develop Hard Red Winter wheat varieties with superior milling and baking qualities.

A second project was basic research by the KSU Food and Feed Grains Institute to break down the wheat into its various parts. This allowed finding new methods for processing wheat and new uses for food, feed, and industry.

The end use of wheat as food by the consumer was a third research project at KSU. The Department of Institutional Management looked for ways to encourage greater utilization of wheat products in quantity food preparation. Large quantity recipes for wheat flour, rolled wheat, bulgur, and other foods were developed. The Commission then tested the recipes in its test kitchen and then distributed recipe cards to consumers.

Information

In 1960, a quarterly newsletter, *The WHEAT GROWER from the Wheat State*, was sent to trade representatives, the Extension Service, and about 10,000 wheat growers in Kansas. The Commission's goal was to send the newsletter to every wheat producer in Kansas.

The Kansas Wheat Commission attempted to keep everyone who was interested in wheat informed of its activities through newsletters, news releases, radio, television, meetings, and through participation in conventions, conferences, and fairs. The Commission contracted with the High Plains Advertising Agency of Dodge City, Kan. for public relations services. The Kansas Association of Wheat Growers also promoted the work of the Commission.

By 1969, the Commission's newsletter was renamed, *The State of Wheat*, and was issued every two months.

Exhibits and Booths

Displays where people with special interests gathered proved to be one of the most effective ways to present information on wheat foods to segments of the American public. Numbers of people who gathered at the Commission displays and their requests for information on wheat foods showed that influential people, such as food editors, home economists, and school lunch personnel, were eager for information on wheat and wheat foods.

Kansas Wheat Commission personnel such as G.C. Fowler and Marcia Watt, facing the camera, sought to increase wheat usage through school lunch, new food products, and contacting those who feed the public.

Hundreds of thousands of pieces of literature were distributed annually.

When those attending the meetings would see the distinctive wheat displays and the name of the Kansas Wheat Commission, they would say, "There are 'The Wheat People.'" Crowds gathered around the Commission displays, asking their questions about wheat and requesting additional information.

Consumption of Wheat Foods

As in the 1950s, the Kansas Wheat Commission had a cooperative agreement with the Kansas State Board of Agriculture for development of a nutrition information program. The objective was to educate the general public about proper diets that included wheat foods, which were declining gradually from the American table. Marcia Watt, a home economist, worked with Extension home economists, demonstration agents, school lunch personnel, teachers, food editors, women's organizations, and others who had an interest in nutrition. Materials from the Wheat Flour Institute and the American Institute of Baking, Chicago, Ill., were purchased and distributed in Kansas, as well as other states.

For a Healthy Heart, Eat Bread

In 1964, Dr. Robert E. Hodges, M.D., Internal Medicine, Iowa State University, reported that the major changes in the American diet over the last 70 years were:

1. A slight decrease in supply of total calories per man per day;
2. A considerable decrease of total carbohydrates consumed, with a greater decline in supply of complex carbohydrate as flours, cereals, and potatoes, coupled with a dramatic increase in consumption of simple sugars and syrups; and
3. A slight increase of consumption of total fat with greater increase in the ratio of polyunsaturated to saturated fatty acids.

Research on the relationship between a healthy diet and heart disease prevention showed the beneficial role of complex carbohydrates. Studies indicated that carbohydrates might be the most important factor in dietary control of heart disease.

Every motorist could be a wheat foods booster with a "Serve Bread at Every Meal" bumper sticker attached to an automobile. The colorful 'little billboard' was part of the campaign of encouraging the American public to eat more bread…for better health…and better wheat markets.

A golden shower of wheat from the wheat fountain exhibit attracted many people interested in wheat to KWC exhibits and booths. The exhibit was unveiled to people outside the state for the first time at the National Restaurant Convention in Chicago.

The well-known wheat fountain exhibit was borrowed by the U.S. Information Agency and shown in Tanzania, Tunisia, and in the Congo. The fountain was supplied with Kansas wheat; however, visitors to the Tanzanian fair constantly took away handfuls of the grain. Had the fair lasted another few days, the fountain would have run dry.

One Slice of Bread

In March 1968, members of the Kansas Wheat Commission presented a resolution to Under Secretary of Agriculture Dr. John A. Scnittker, asking the government to institute a program to return "one slice of bread" to the American table. This slice of bread was removed in 1946, when the U.S. Government supported a public initiative to remove a serving of one slice of bread from the American table to save wheat for relief of famine in France and Italy. A result of this promotion was the introduction of a higher nutritional value bread in the 1970s.

Fortification of Wheat Foods

In January 1969, the United States Public Health Service reported that there were "very few" cases of actual hunger in the U.S. The report did find evidence of "widespread malnutrition." Malnutrition implies inadequate or improper diets. The Commission determined that consumers did not know what protein, calories, vitamins, minerals, and amino acids were necessary in a balanced diet. Suitable foods must be available to avoid malnutrition, and people must be inspired to eat them.

One solution was to fortify flour in bread and other bakery products with the necessary vitamins, minerals, and amino acid. By adding these needed items to food consumers already selected, the problem of malnutrition could be addressed. This resulted in a promotional campaign and tests of consumer acceptance of wheat products made from fortified flour.

Development of New Wheat Foods

Development of new wheat foods — Redi-Wheat, bulgur and rolled wheat — expanded domestic marketing efforts in the 1960s.

Redi-Wheat

Federal funds were secured in 1957 and development began at the Western Regional Research Laboratory, Albany, Calif. on canned wheat, wheat wafers, and other new food uses of wheat. The first of these to be developed was Redi-Wheat, which was introduced in the early 1960s. This processed, canned product was market tested and promoted by the Commission. At the World Food Fair, approximately 80,000 people tasted Redi-Wheat. They liked what they tasted, and a new market was developed. The Agricultural Marketing Service of the USDA market tested Redi-Wheat in Wichita in March 1961. The results of determining if Redi-Wheat had commercial potential were encouraging. The Commission worked with the Kansas Association of Wheat Growers to distribute Redi-Wheat.

Bulgur Wheat Foods

Redi-Wheat was the first step in development of bulgur, which essentially is dried and cracked Redi-Wheat. Bulgur was used in international food aid, domestic relief, and school lunch programs.

The Farmers Cooperative Commission Company of Hutchinson built a bulgur plant in the early 1960s to produce bulgur. Dried bulgur was processed and exported, creating a new market for wheat abroad. The Kansas Wheat Commission provided demonstrations at school lunch workshops and provided bulgur large quantity recipes. Bulgur was provided to school lunch programs in 22 states in 1962 and all 50 states in 1963. Survival wafers were made from puffed, dried bulgur with wheat owned by the Commodity Credit Corporation.

Government programs utilized hard red wheat, No. 2 grade or better, as a part of the stockpiling for Civil Defense.

Bulgur processors from all over the U.S. formed Bulgur Associates, Inc., in cooperation with Great Plains Wheat, Inc., to promote this product. Kansas Wheat Commission Administrator W.W. Graber resigned to serve as Executive Secretary of Bulgur Associates upon its organization on July 1, 1963. G.C. Fowler, a Commission employee since 1959, replaced Graber as Administrator.

Rolled Wheat

Rolled wheat, made from steamed, dried, and flattened wheat berries, was supplied to 70,000 school lunch programs in the nation. The Kansas Wheat Commission supplied large quantity recipes to those school lunch supervisors. During 1961, 100 million pounds of rolled wheat was consumed in this manner. Wheat was processed by a wheat rolling mill operation in Wichita, Kansas. The Commission programs resulted in establishment of new job opportunities, new industrial development, and a new outlet for wheat — all of which contributed benefits to the farm and to the Kansas economy.

Wheat Show and Awards

The Kansas Wheat Commission cooperated with the Kansas Association of Wheat Growers, 4-H, FFA, Extension, Kansas Wheat Improvement Association, and the grain trade in regional and state wheat shows. Winners of these quality and production competitions toured Texas Gulf ports to learn about grading, merchandising, and exporting of the wheat produced in Kansas. The goal was to stimulate interest in these facets of the supply chain and in the production of better quality milling wheat.

Utilization of Wheat

Federal funds were primarily used for the development of new industrial uses for wheat. Wheat starch was being used in the manufacture of paper. Wheat starch and wheat gluten were developed in synthetic fibers. Wallboard, insulating mate-

Kansas Wheat Commission booth at the National Association of Wheat Growers 1965 annual meeting, displaying new wheat foods, bulgur and rolled wheat, which were promoted for school lunch, institutional feeding, export aid, and domestic relief programs. Also a part of this booth was the Great Seal of the State of Kansas, made in wheat and wheat products, with the whole kernel wheat, bulgur, and semolina dyed the appropriate colors and applied to a wood background.

Wheat winners at the 1968 Kansas State Fair. (l-r) Thomas C. Roberts, President of the Kansas Wheat Improvement Association, which honored the Mill-and-Bake winner; John Polansky of Belleville, Mill-and-Bake winner; G.C. Fowler, KWC Administrator; Mrs. Shirley Brown of Leavenworth, Champion Bread Baker; Adrian Polansky of Belleville, 1968 Kansas Wheat King; Richard Stroade, Republic County Agent, Outstanding County Agent Award; and Joe J. Volmer of Parsons, Member of the Kansas Wheat Commission.

rial, oil drilling, and paper manufacturing offered great potential for industrial utilization.

Wheat Art

The art of making crafts out of wheat straw and wheat kernels became popular in the 1960s. While wheat art did not conceivably use much wheat in relation to the supply available, it provided a satisfying new art and craft. As wheat art spread, it helped to draw the attention to the wheat industry. The Kansas Wheat Commission printed instructions for these developing artists on how to make wheat art decorations.

Wheat Quality Survey

In 1962, the first wheat quality survey was conducted to determine the condition of the wheat as it came off the Kansas farm. The survey also included the cleanout (dockage) on the wheat when it arrived at the elevator, protein, sedimentation, and variety of the crop. This survey showed that 99.5 percent of all the railcars checked had less than 1.9 percent dockage, refuting the theory that all the dirt in export wheat comes from the wheat farmer.

Foreign Market Development

The success of the foreign marketing program was evident in 1960 when exports exceeded domestic consumption for the first time. Canada, Australia, Argentina, France, and Russia provided the greatest competition for U.S. wheat. The rise of economic agreements such as the European Common Market also had an effect on the demand. Portugal, Spain, Switzerland, and Austria entered the U.S. wheat market in the 1960s. Cash sales were also made to Spain, Italy, Libya, Nigeria, Japan, and the Netherlands.

Great Plains Wheat

Great Plains Wheat, Inc. continued to coordinate foreign market development efforts for wheat commissions of Kansas, Nebraska, Colorado, North Dakota, and South Dakota. GPW also played a roll in coordinating the efforts of states in finding uses and new markets for wheat. Initially, the headquarters office was in Garden City, Kansas, under the direction of Clifford Hope, and then later moved to Kansas City, Kan. A branch office was created in Washington, D.C., and in 1969, the Great Plains Wheat, Inc. headquarters moved to Washington, D.C.

Western Wheat Associates was the companion agency for wheat commissions of Washington, Oregon, and Idaho. Market development operations for both Western Wheat Associates and Great Plains Wheat were carried on in cooperation with the Foreign Agricultural Service of the USDA.

Top Markets for U.S. Wheat 1960s

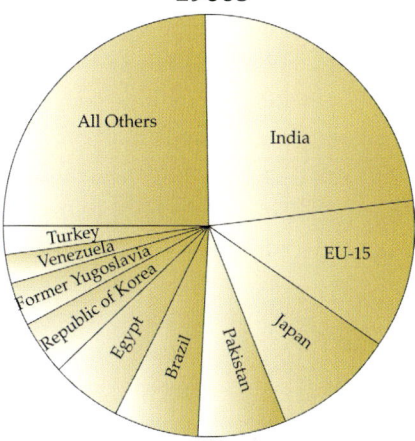

On a number of occasions, Great Plains Wheat cooperated with Western Wheat Associates in conducting the Asian wheat market development program under the combined name of Wheat Associates, U.S.A.

Foreign offices were established in Rotterdam, Netherlands; Rome, Italy; Lima, Peru; Tokyo, Japan; Karachi, Pakistan; Manila, The Philippines; New Delhi, India; Panama City, Panama; Caracas, Venezuela; Rio de Janeiro, Brazil; Republic of China; and Taipei, Taiwan.

Foreign Trade Teams

One of the greatest tools to influence foreign buyers was coordinating U.S. visits for teams of foreign millers, bakers, wheat importers, and government officials. Teams from Germany, Brazil, Southern Rhodesia, New Zealand, Japan, Republic of South Africa, Pakistan, Taiwan, Ecuador, Switzerland, the Netherlands, China, Venezuela, England, Southeast Asia, Peru, Belgium, Sudan, South Korea, Italy, West Germany, and other areas visited Kansas in the 1960s. Teams had the opportunity to inspect wheat available in Kansas; witness wheat production, handling, and marketing; inspect laboratories where cereal chemists worked with the grain; obtain information on bakery and retailing operations; and view Board of Trade activities. The teams also had the opportunity to visit the cereal complex at Kansas State University, including the world-famous milling and baking school. Kansas

A Japanese wheat buyer and KWC Administrator W.W. Graber ride a horse on a Kansas farm during the team's tour of the Wheat State.

U.S. Wheat Exports 1957-1970

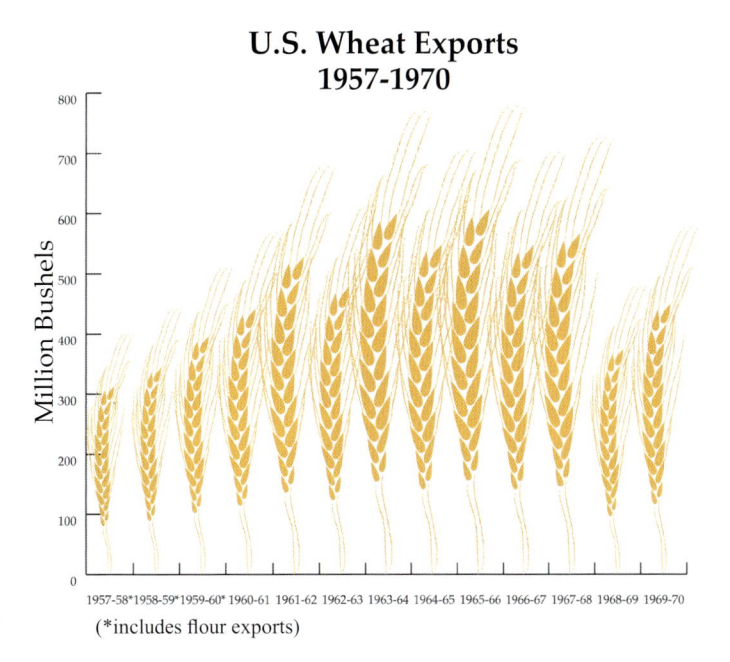

(*includes flour exports)

producers met with the teams to get acquainted and exchange ideas. The friendships that resulted from this exchange were an important part of developing these markets.

Foreign Nutrition Education

Home economists in Latin America, Japan, and southern Asia taught the value of a balanced diet featuring wheat foods, with a fleet of mobile units, ranging from three-wheeled cyclevans to large buses. They discovered that centuries-old diet habits could be changed.

In more advanced countries of Europe, where standards of living were similar to that in the U.S., market development was designed to prevent downward slips in per capita consumption and to recapture markets lost to competing wheat exporters. Following World War II, improvements in economic conditions in these countries resulted in a shift to more meats, fruits, and other products as consumption of cereal products lagged.

In countries where economies were less advanced, efforts to increase the use of wheat products were more successful. In Africa, particularly, there was a definite shift to cereal grains from the use of root crops, presenting great potential for rapid increase in the future.

> "We never were asked to buy U.S. wheat until representatives of your Kansas Wheat Commission came along."
> — G.A.D. Roberts of Causeway, Salisbury, Southern Rhodesia

A model kitchen was set up for the International Trade Fair at Tunis, Tunisia, including all-electric fixtures. During the fair, Anna Jane Baird demonstrated American baking with wheat foods.

Training Programs

Wheat growers directed educational and training programs for millers and bakers in many parts of the world. Technical assistance acquainted millers with the specific quality characteristics of U.S. wheat. Other training programs helped bakers turn U.S. wheat into high-quality products to increase consumer satisfaction, thus paving the way for increased demand for U.S. wheat. Examples of bakery training programs included schools for thousands of rural bakers in Japan; an international training program for South American bakers in Bogotá, Colombia; and a mobile unit designed to reach bakers throughout India.

Trade Fairs

Trade fairs and food fairs were attended in London, England; Munich, Germany; and Poznan, Poland. At these fairs, U.S. wheat, flour and finished products were displayed in the form of doughnuts, cakes, and breads. The fairs gave visitors the opportunity to feel, see, and taste U.S. wheat and wheat foods. Sandwiches debuted at the Food Show and Seminar in Tokyo, Japan in 1968. Japan was seen as a rapidly developing wheat market since per capita consumption of wheat foods in Japan had increased from 33 pounds to 70 pounds over the previous 20 years.

Kansas Wheat Test Kitchen Test, Taste and Tell

The Kansas Wheat Test Kitchen organized in 1963 under a contract with the Farmers Cooperative Commission Company of Hutchinson, one of the nation's producers of bulgur. The kitchen staff was responsible for (1) developing new recipes for rolled wheat, bulgur and flour; (2) testing recipes to assure that they would be acceptable products; and (3) releasing recipes through food editors and other interested groups.

A test panel of more than 100 homemakers from all over the state tested and evaluated the recipes. The panel furnished their findings on the ease of preparation, availability of ingredients, and assessment of the product after they had served it to their families. Recipes were produced for home use, and large quantity recipes were produced for use by school lunch programs and other institutional feeding groups and restaurants.

By 1966, the test kitchen personnel developed and tested recipes for wheat flour, semolina, cracked wheat, rolled wheat, bulgur, self-rising flour, and other forms of wheat. As a result, by the mid-1960s, there was an increase in demand for bread recipes. Homemakers, apparently seeking ways to economize on their grocery bills, began baking their own bread again. Consumers were also moving toward an age of new food combinations, for example, adding freeze-dried fruits to breakfast cereals.

Testing and informational campaigns were conducted in cooperation with USDA for

Wheat growers helped organize school lunch programs in Japan, southern Asia, and Latin America. Pilot programs were used as models for nationwide programs reaching millions of youngsters and eventually their parents. These school lunch programs were important in teaching the value of proper diets and sanitation and in encouraging school attendance. And they exposed a new generation to tasty and nutritious wheat foods.

Home economist Anna Jane Baird gave programs to a variety of audiences at the Kansas Wheat Commission's test kitchen in Hutchinson, Kansas. The kitchen staff was responsible for developing, testing, and releasing recipes for rolled wheat, bulgur, and flour.

In 1966, the annual award of Kansas Wheat Industry Man of the Year, made cooperatively by the Kansas Wheat Commission and the Kansas Association of Wheat Growers, recognized the work done in hybrid wheat development by Dr. Ronald W. Livers, right, of the Fort Hays Experiment Station, Hays. At the left is Anson Horning of Larned, making the presentation of an engraved plaque to Dr. Livers. Horning, a farmer, President of the National Association of Wheat Growers, and immediate Past-President of the Kansas Association of Wheat Growers, received the award at the 1965 Annual Wheat Meeting.

wheat foods growing in popularity, such as frozen bakery goods, partially baked frozen products, new cereal foods, health foods, and pre-mixes such as cake mix, biscuit mix, and bread mixes.

August, Sandwich Month

The Kansas Wheat Commission took part in the national observance of Sandwich Month, which was coordinated by the Wheat Flour Institute, Chicago in 1967. Press kits on Sandwich Month were distributed to 348 metropolitan daily newspapers over the United States. Many of them devoted full pages to the event, and almost all the papers devoted multiple columns.

Industry Promotion

"While Florida citrus growers contribute $7 million to promote their industry and Idaho potato growers spend $3 million, Kansas had only $400,000 in 1960 with which to promote its billion dollar wheat industry," as reported in an editorial released by the Kansas Press Service, Topeka, Kan. "Wheat means more to the economy of Kansas than any other single commodity or business. This year's wheat crop will bring nearly $500 million in new wealth to Kansas, not counting the income from milling, transportation, storage, baking, and processing, which would push this figure well over the billion dollar mark."

July, Kansas Wheat Month

In 1967, the Kansas Wheat Commission marked Kansas Wheat Month observances by presenting a copy of the Great Seal of the State of

1960s Wheat Awards

Kansas Wheat Queen

A Kansas Wheat Queen was selected each year to help in the promotion of wheat products. In addition to the honor of the title, the candidate also received a scholarship for college studies in wheat-related subjects and a wardrobe stipend.

1962	Carolyn Parkinson	Scott City
1963	Janet Herbin	Jamestown
1964	Carolyn Joyner	Freeport
1965	Nicki Mayrath	Dodge City
1966	Nancy Jo Atkinson	Udall
1967	June Inskeep	Cawker City
1968	Donna Lee Schippers	Oakley
1969	Sharen Stoecker	Oakley

Wheat Man of the Year

1965	Anson Horning	Larned
1966	Dr. Ronald W. Livers	Hays
1968	Carl A. Dumler	Russell
1969	Joe Berkeley	Dodge City

Kansas to Governor Robert Docking. The Seal was made out of wheat and wheat products, with whole kernel wheat, bulgur, and semolina dyed the appropriate colors and applied to a wood background.

For the 1968 celebration, the Kansas Wheat Commission promoted Wheat Month with placemats for use by Kansas restaurants, posters distributed by the Kansas Association of Wheat Growers, and a photography contest carried out by Kansas Wheat Improvement Association.

Wheat Production and Varieties

Throughout the 1960s, wheat production and yields were relatively uniform. Leading wheat varieties in the 1960s were 'Bison,' 'Triumph,' 'Wichita,' 'Kiowa,' 'Kaw,' 'Ottawa,' and 'Scout.' Notable pests included stem rust, Hessian fly and armyworm infestations. The 1967 crop had a record high average protein of 12.9%. The crop of 1969 produced a record yield, averaging 31 bushels per acre.

Observing July, Kansas Wheat Month, the Kansas Wheat Commission presented Governor Robert Docking a copy of the Great Seal of the State of Kansas, made with grains of wheat products. Making the presentation in the Governor's office were Miss June Inskeep, Kansas Wheat Queen, Carl A. Dumler, Commission Chairman, and Glenn A. Weir, Vice-Chairman of the Commission.

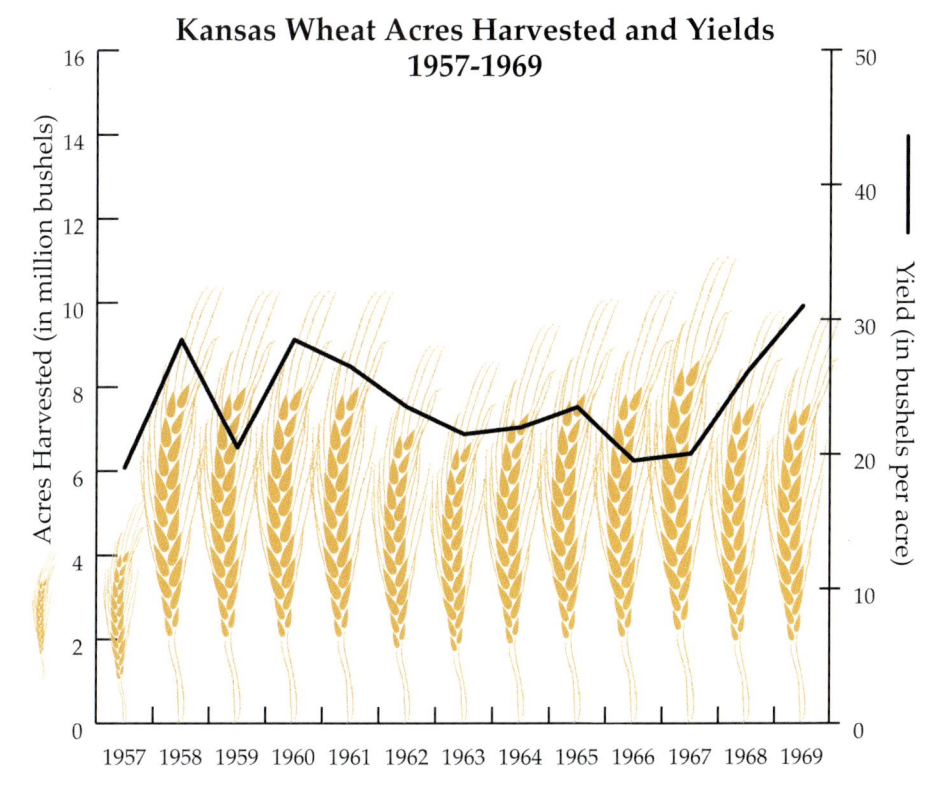

Kansas Wheat Acres Harvested and Yields 1957-1969

GLAZED MEATBALLS OR MEAT LOAF

makes 36 meatballs

CRACKED WHEAT IS WHOLE BERRIES THAT HAVE BEEN BROKEN INTO COARSE, MEDIUM, AND FINE FRAGMENTS. IT CAN EASILY BE ADDED TO MANY RECIPES. ADD CRACKED WHEAT TO TOP-QUALITY KANSAS MEATS FOR TASTY MEATBALLS OR MEAT LOAF.

ingredients
- 1 cup cooked cracked wheat
- 1 pound extra lean (9% fat) ground beef
- ½ pound lean ground turkey, sausage, or pork
- 1 (8-ounce) can tomato sauce
- 2 beaten eggs
- ½ teaspoon black pepper
- 1 ¼ cups packed bread crumbs (whole wheat)
- 2 teaspoons dried minced onion

glaze
- ½ cup ketchup
- 3 tablespoons molasses or brown sugar
- 1 teaspoon prepared mustard

1 To cook wheat, add ⅓ cup cracked wheat to ⅔ cup water and bring to a boil. Cover and simmer 12 to 15 minutes. Remove pan from heat; let stand covered 5 minutes.

2 Combine all ingredients; mix well. Shape into 1 ½-inch balls or shape in 9 x 9 x 2-inch baking pan. Spread glaze over top.

3 Preheat oven to 325°F. Bake meatballs 30 to 35 minutes. Bake meat loaf at 350°F 40 to 45 minutes, or until done.

note: *Sodium may be reduced by using ground beef instead of sausage. Reduced-sodium tomato sauce and ketchup may also be used.*

tip: *use food processor to make fine bread crumbs.*

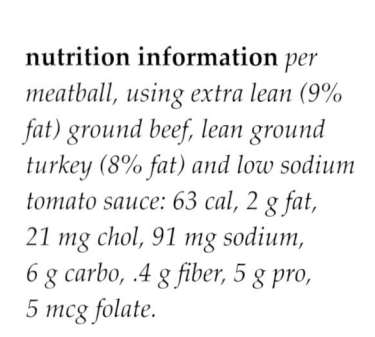

nutrition information *per meatball, using extra lean (9% fat) ground beef, lean ground turkey (8% fat) and low sodium tomato sauce: 63 cal, 2 g fat, 21 mg chol, 91 mg sodium, 6 g carbo, .4 g fiber, 5 g pro, 5 mcg folate.*

STIR AND DROP WHEAT ROLLS

makes 24 rolls

AN EASY ROLL RECIPE THAT CAN BE ENJOYED AT ANY MEAL.

ingredients

- 1 package RED STAR® Active Dry Yeast
- 1 cup lukewarm water (110-115°F)
- ¼ cup granulated sugar
- 1 teaspoon salt
- 1 beaten egg
- ¼ cup vegetable oil
- ½ cup cottage cheese, small curd, room temperature
- 2 ¾ - 3 cups bread flour
- ¼ cup rolled wheat flakes or quick-cooking rolled oats

note: *For Heartland Mill rolled wheat flakes, go to www.heartlandmill.com.*

1 In mixing bowl, dissolve yeast in lukewarm water. Add sugar, salt, egg, oil, and cottage cheese; mix well. Add 1 ½ cups flour and beat until smooth. Stir in rolled wheat or oats and enough additional flour to make a soft dough. Blend well.

2 Cover; allow to rise in bowl 1 hour. Grease two standard-size, 2 ½ x 1 ¼-inch, muffin pans. Stir down batter; fill muffin cups ¾ full. Cover loosely with plastic wrap that has been lightly coated with nonstick cooking spray. Let rise until almost double.

3 Bake in preheated 375°F oven 15 minutes, or until golden. Remove from pans and serve or cool on wire rack.

nutrition information *per serving (one roll): 96 cal, 3 g fat, 9 mg chol, 119 mg sodium, 14 g carbo, 1 g fiber, 3 g pro, 33 mcg folate.*

ROLLED WHEAT COOKIES

makes about 42 cookies

A POPULAR COOKIE RECIPE FROM 1966 USING ROLLED WHEAT FLAKES—WHEAT THAT HAS BEEN STEAMED, ROLLED, AND FLAKED. USING FRESH PECANS FROM SOUTHEASTERN KANSAS MAKES THIS A SCRUMPTIOUS KANSAS COOKIE.

ingredients
- 2 cups all-purpose flour
- 1 teaspoon baking powder
- 1 teaspoon baking soda
- ¼ teaspoon salt
- ¾ cup vegetable shortening
- 1 cup brown sugar
- 1 cup granulated sugar
- 2 beaten eggs
- 2 teaspoons vanilla extract
- 1 cup rolled wheat flakes or old fashioned rolled oats, dry
- 1 cup shredded coconut
- 1 cup Rice Krispies® cereal
- ½ cup chopped pecans or walnuts (optional)

1 Preheat oven to 350°F.

2 In a small bowl, stir together flour, baking powder, soda, and salt. Set aside.

3 In a large mixing bowl, beat shortening with an electric mixer on medium speed for 30 to 40 seconds. Add the brown and granulated sugars; beat mixture until combined. Add eggs and vanilla; mix 2 minutes.

4 Beat in flour mixture with a spoon. Stir in the rolled wheat, coconut, Rice Krispies®, and pecans.

5 Roll into 1 ¼-inch balls. Place on lightly greased cookie sheets. Flatten balls to 1 inch thick.

6 Bake 12 to 13 minutes, or until light golden brown. Let cool on cookie sheet for 1 minute. Transfer cookies to a wire rack to cool.

note: *For Heartland Mill rolled wheat flakes, go to www.heartlandmill.com.*

nutrition information *per serving (one cookie): 130 cal, 6 g fat, 10 mg chol, 70 mg sodium, 18 g carbo, 1 g fiber, 2 g pro, 13 mcg folate.*

COUNTRY FRENCH BREAD

A LIGHT BREAD WITH A VELVETY CRUMB AND CRISPY-CHEWY CRUST.

makes
2 loaves, 14 slices per loaf

ingredients
- 3 ¼ - 3 ½ cups bread flour
- 1 package RED STAR® Active Dry Yeast
- 1 ½ teaspoons granulated sugar
- 1 teaspoon salt
- 1 ¼ cups hot water (120-130°F)
- 1 ½ teaspoons cornmeal
- 1 egg white
- 1 tablespoon water

The key to crusty breads is steam in the oven. Create steam by placing a pan with 1½ cups boiling water on bottom rack 10 minutes before putting in the bread. Quickly close the door. Or, using a plant atomizer that has been used only for cooking purposes, spray the hot oven walls with a fine mist. Spray or brush cold water on the bread as well. Slash the loaves and quickly place them in the oven. Spray the loaves 3 times during the first 10 minutes of baking.

nutrition information *per serving (one slice): 60 cal, 0 g fat, 0 mg chol, 86 mg sodium, 10 carbo, 0 g fiber, 2 g pro, 31 mcg folate.*

1 Combine 1 ½ cups flour, yeast, sugar, and salt in a mixing bowl. Add water; beat on low until blended. Beat 3 to 4 minutes on medium speed. Stir in remaining flour to make a soft dough.

2 Knead dough 10 to 12 minutes or until soft and silky. Place dough in a greased bowl, turn to grease top. Cover; let rise in a cool (70°F) place until double (2 to 2 ½ hours). A cool rise results in the splendid flavor and character of the bread. Punch down dough, cover, and let rise again until double.

3 Punch down dough; divide in two equal pieces. Cover; let rest 10 to 15 minutes. Roll each portion into a 20-inch rectangle or the length of the baking sheet. Roll tightly from the long side and pinch to seal the side and ends. Smooth the loaf and taper the ends. Place loaves seam-side-down on greased baking sheets dusted with cornmeal. Cover; let rise until double.

4 Thirty minutes before baking, start method for creating steam and preheat oven to 400°F.*

5 With a very sharp knife, make 4 or 5 diagonal slashes on top of each loaf. Beat egg white and water together until frothy. Brush mixture over tops and sides of loaves. Bake 15 minutes, then reduce heat to 375°F and bake another 10 to 15 minutes, or until loaves are brown, crusty, and hollow-sounding when tapped on the bottom. Cool on wire racks.

BULGUR "SLOPPY" JOES OR CHILI

makes approximately 5 cups

BULGUR IS PARBOILED, DRIED AND PARTIALLY DEBRANNED WHEAT, RICH IN PROTEIN, THIAMINE, RIBOFLAVIN AND NIACIN, THE NUTRIENTS FOUND IN WHOLE GRAIN WHEAT.

ingredients
- 1 pound extra lean ground beef, pork, turkey
- ½ cup chopped onion
- ⅓ cup bulgur wheat, dry
- 2 teaspoons chili powder
- ¼ teaspoon black pepper
- 1 (14-ounce) can beef broth
- 1 (15-ounce) can tomato sauce
- 2 cups water (optional)

1 Brown meat in skillet with onion and bulgur; drain. Add chili powder, pepper, beef broth, and tomato sauce. Stir in water if making chili.

2 Cover; simmer at least 30 minutes. More water may be added depending on desired consistency. Serve on buns or in bowls.

nutrition information *per serving (½ cup Sloppy Joe mix using extra lean [9% fat] beef and fat free, no salt beef broth): 116 cal, 4 g fat, 17 mg chol, 330 mg sodium, 8 g carbo, 2 g fiber, 2 g pro, 12 mcg folate.*

CHAMPION REFRIGERATOR POTATO ROLLS

makes 2 tea rings or 36 rolls

A FAVORITE RECIPE TAUGHT TO MANY 4-H'ERS. USE THE DOUGH TO MAKE A VARIETY OF DINNER ROLLS OR SWEDISH TEA RINGS.

ingredients
- 1 package RED STAR® Active Dry Yeast
- ¼ cup lukewarm water (110-115°F)
- ⅔ cup vegetable shortening or butter
- ½ cup granulated sugar
- 2 teaspoons salt
- 1 cup hot mashed potatoes
- 1 cup hot potato water
- 3 beaten eggs
- 7 - 7 ½ cups bread flour*
- 1 teaspoon lemon peel

Half of the flour may be whole wheat flour.

1 Dissolve yeast in lukewarm water; set aside. In a large bowl, combine shortening, sugar, salt, potatoes, and potato water; cool to lukewarm.

2 Add yeast, eggs, 2 cups flour, and lemon peel; beat 2 minutes. Gradually add enough remaining flour to make a soft dough. Knead until smooth and elastic, 12 to 14 minutes.

3 Place dough in a greased bowl; turn to grease top. (Dough may be placed in a sealable bowl or bag and refrigerated 1 to 2 days. Punch down dough as necessary.) OR: cover dough; let rise in a warm (80°F) place until double. Punch down, cover, and let rise again.

4 Punch down dough, cover and let rest 10 minutes. Shape into a Swedish Tea Ring or rolls. Cover, let rise in warm (90°F) place until double.

5 For one tea ring, use half of the dough. Roll into 20 x 8-inch rectangle. Brush with melted butter. Sprinkle with mixture of ¼ cup granulated sugar and 2 teaspoons cinnamon. Roll, beginning with long side. Seal long edge. Place sealed edge down on greased baking sheet, forming a circle; seal ends. Using scissors, make cuts, ¾-inch wide, cutting almost through dough. Turn slices on sides, placing every-other-slice to the center of the tea ring. Cover; let rise until double. Bake in preheated 350°F oven 23 to 25 minutes, or until done. When cool, decorate with confectioners' icing, maraschino cherries and pecan halves.

nutrition information *per serving (Swedish tea ring): 198 cal, 7 g fat, 20 mg chol, 159 mg sodium, 31 g carbo, 1 g fiber, 4 g pro, 49 mcg folate. (dinner rolls): 153 cal, 5 g fat, 18 mg chol, 151 mg sodium, 23 g carbo, 1 g fiber, 4 g pro, 48 mcg folate.*

PHOTO COURTESY OF HOME BAKING ASSOCIATION

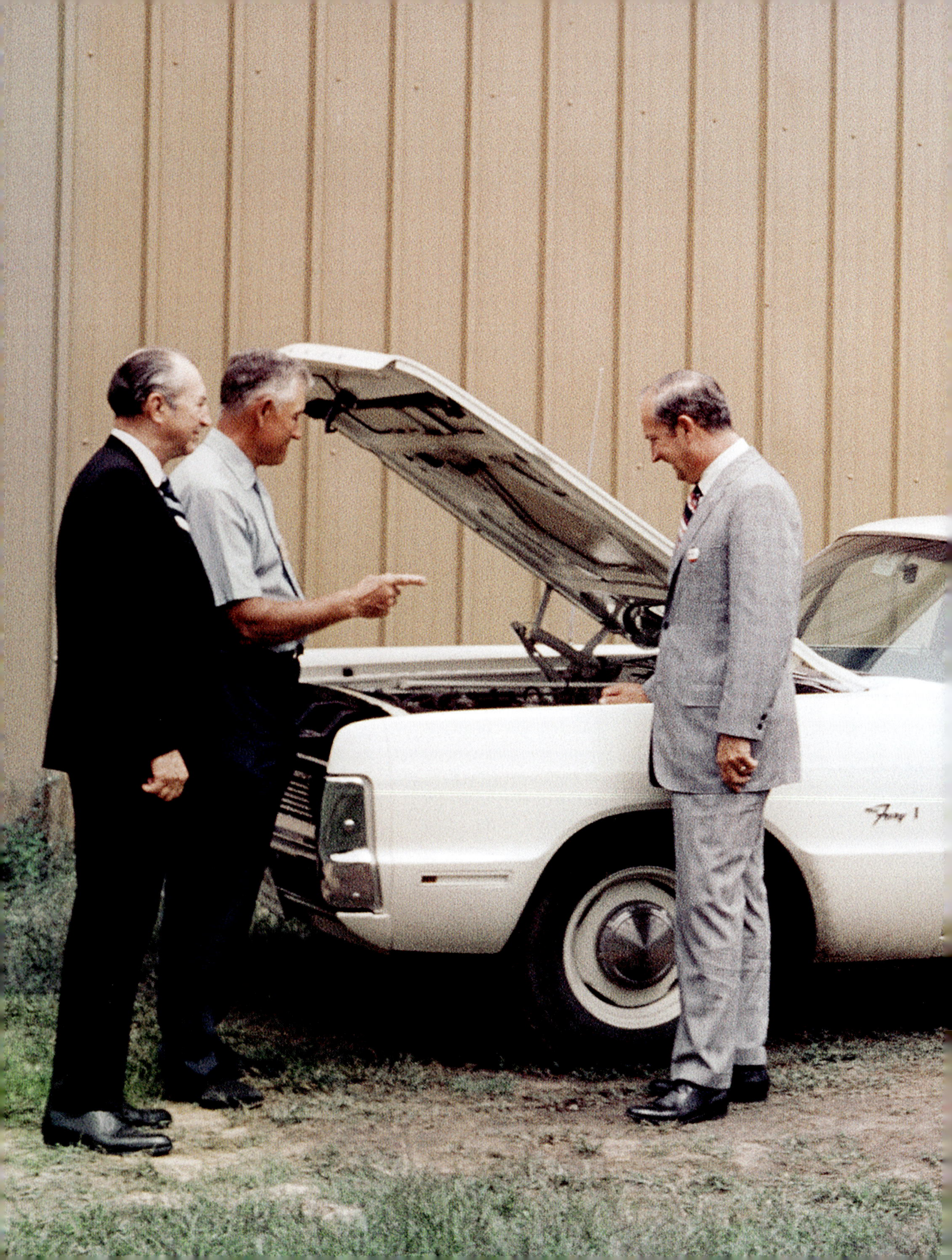

1970s

WHEAT CONSUMPTION REVERSES DOWNWARD TREND

"Just give the Kansas wheat farmer the cost of production and a little profit and he will bust his neck to feed the world." – Myron Krenzin, KWC Administrator, 1977

"Wheat vs. Pollution" Research

Research headlined the beginning of the decade of the 1970s.

Leading the exciting possibilities for new wheat uses was the use of alcohol made from wheat as a replacement for tetraethyl lead in gasoline and other motor fuels. The Commission proposed that it be required by Federal law that tetraethyl lead be eliminated from motor fuel formulation, and that grain alcohol be used as an additive. The Commission tested one of its cars on the wheat-alcohol-gasoline combination to determine the performance of this fuel and inspect the condition of the motor at the end of a normal use test.

Unfortunately, it was concluded that ethyl alcohol from wheat could not compete economically with ethyl alcohol produced from petroleum.

The "Wheat vs. Pollution" project of the Kansas Wheat Commission took the form of an experiment in which wheat alcohol was used as an additive to unleaded gasoline and a Commission staff car used to test the performance of the mixture. The staff car first was checked out on ordinary fuel in driving tests, and then was put on the road under normal driving condition with the alcohol-gasoline fuel. Change of carburetor jets was the only adaptation needed on the car for the new fuel.

Active interest in the wheat research under way at the Fort Hays Branch Experiment Station is shown above during an inspection tour of Kansas Wheat Commission-sponsored research at Hays.

Wheat for Feed

A program aimed at utilizing wheat for livestock feed was initiated at the Fort Hays branch of KSU. The research investigated how to utilize wheat in ruminant rations and developed new varieties of wheat specifically for feed use. Dr. Ronald Livers, wheat breeder, and John Brethour, animal nutritionist were partners on the project.

Kansas produced a record crop in 1971, which had a large impact on the wheat price. By having the ability to utilize the grain in feed, 287 million bushels of the surplus crop were used, and the stocks returned to normal in a short timeframe. In 1972 the Soviet Union started to purchase wheat, and with feed utilization of the '71 crop, the market could quickly and dramatically respond to this added international demand. If the wheat feeding project was responsible for only 10 cents per bushel of the increase, the return on investment in this project was $1,500 per dollar of investment.

Wheat Variety Study

Research initiated in 1962 continued on Hard Red Winter wheat varieties with superior qualities and genetically higher protein content, while retaining the good milling and baking properties. The project, under the direction of Dr. E.G. Heyne, KSU professor of plant breeding, included studies of protein levels, mixogram and baking results, as well as the genetic crossing of lines and agronomic characteristics. Dr. Heyne's research resulted in the wheat variety 'Eagle' that was released in 1970.

Wheat Streak Mosaic Research

In 1974, the Commission began battling wheat streak mosaic virus in Kansas wheat fields. The goal of a five-year contract with the Kansas Agricultural Experiment Station for $28,500 annually was to accelerate the development of wheat varieties with resistance to wheat streak mosaic, soil borne mosaic, and fungal diseases, such as leaf and stem rust. Dr. T. Joe Martin joined the Fort Hays Branch Experiment Station of KSU as a plant pathologist.

Wheat Breeding Research

Varieties with high yield potential and increased grain protein was the goal of a 1977 research project at the Fort Hays Experiment Station. The project would combine a number of selected wheat characteristics into varieties that most consistently produced the best possible yields in Kansas growing conditions.

Far-Mar-Co., Inc.

Wheat farmers throughout an eight-state area cooperatively owned Far-Mar-Co., a laboratory headed by Jimmy Dean. The goal of one research project with Far-Mar-Co. and the Kansas Association of Wheat Growers was to find new uses and processes that would enhance the price to the wheat producer. This project separated, with minimum damage, selected components of the whole wheat kernel. The results were excellent yields of vital gluten, starch, and bran-germ. This project resulted in a new process for wheat that was economically feasible.

New Food Studies

Working through the Food and Feed Grain Institute at KSU, KWC sponsored several projects to identify new foods. One project produced an instant whole wheat cereal using the whole wheat berry. Another project created bread, based on a whole wheat product rather than using combinations of wheat with other proteins. Work also began on the production of snack or convenience foods from wheat.

The Institute acquired extruders for the production of puffed snack foods. Two types of curl-type snack foods were prepared. The first was a caramel-flavored wheat curl, which resembled caramel popcorn, but with a crispier texture and no hulls. The other curl-type product was seasoned with butter, salt and a meat-flavoring agent. The snack food market was identified as huge potential for new products from wheat. Dr. Paul Seib headed these investigations.

Quantity Recipes

Through the Department of Institution Management at KSU, the KWC funded a project that investigated utilization of wheat products in quantity food preparation. This research resulted in recipes that minimized time-consuming steps, offered clear, easy-to-follow instructions, and were used by inexperienced cooks in food services where large numbers of people were fed.

New Loaf of Bread

Governor Robert B. Docking announced a project to provide a new, higher nutritional value bread. The project, developed from the Commission's "Eat One More Slice of Bread" program, debuted a new loaf of bread on the market, which was made from Blend A flour and contained added protein from wheat sources and essential minerals and vitamins. Blend A flour was a fortified wheat protein flour that did not use other products as protein boosters.

The Commission took on a project to find new uses and processes which would enhance the price of wheat for the producer. The objective of Far-Mar-Co. project was separation of selected components of the whole wheat kernel with minimal damage. Excellent yields of vital gluten, starch, and bran-germ were obtained.

International Day of Bread

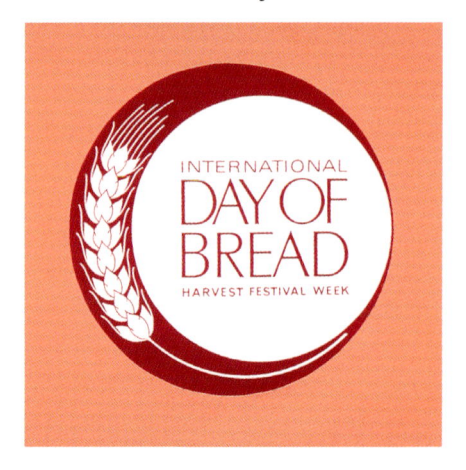

President Richard Nixon issued a national Proclamation setting aside a Day of Bread, and Kansas Governor Robert B. Docking proclaimed the Day of Bread observance for the State. The International Day of Bread was observed by Kansans at luncheon meetings October 28, 1969, and again October 6, 1970.

At the 1970 Day of Bread banquet in Kansas City, speaker Dr. Jean Mayer, consultant on nutrition to President Nixon and Professor of Nutrition at Harvard University, deplored the common idea that bread was fattening, and urged consumption of bread for better nutrition. He said, "Bread is still the Staff of Life. It is a low fat, low cholesterol food, and its consumption should be encouraged." He strongly urged including bread in the diet, and added, "We must convince the ladies that just looking at a slice of bread is not going to add pounds." Citing a "galloping increase in heart disease," in U.S. health statistics, Dr. Mayer said dietary changes, including increased consumption of bread, stood out as the best way of reversing that trend.

Telling the Story of Wheat

The story of wheat and wheat foods was told to the consuming public in a number of ways, including demonstrations, programs, exhibits, conventions, fairs, and publications. Anna Jane Baird appeared monthly on the Joyce Livingston Show, a morning television feature, where she demonstrated bread recipes during a 20-minute segment. The newest consumer program in 1970 consisted of cash prizes offered to Kansas School Food Service personnel for original recipes using wheat. The 12 winning recipes were distributed at the National School Food Service Convention in Boston.

"Breads Around the World" was the theme for 1970 exhibit and for Kansas Wheat Month in July. The exhibit, used at four national conventions, featured a revolving globe and a selection of foreign breads, each marked with the flag of the country of origin.

Commissioner Carl Dumler appeared on the "Over the Fence" show, taped in Washington and

A revolving globe, with examples of breads around the world, was featured at the School Food Service Convention in Boston.

used by 45 television stations across the nation. Dumler spoke of the work of the KWC in getting wheat food and nutrition information to the public.

A nine-pound loaf of bread was the main feature in 1975 exhibits and displays. It was designed to offset claims that the "high price" of wheat to the producer was responsible for the high cost of bread in the consumer market.

In 1978, the Kansas Wheat Commission initiated the Wheat Scoop, a news and information service directed to radio stations and newspapers throughout Kansas.

Great Plains Wheat, Inc.

Established in 1959, Great Plains Wheat operated in the highly competitive markets of Europe, Africa, the Middle East, Latin America, and the Caribbean area. GPW, with its home office in Washington, D.C., also maintained offices in Rotterdam, Netherlands; Caracas, Venezuela; and Rio de Janeiro, Brazil. In 1977, GPW opened a new Cairo, Egypt office to replace the former Middle East office in Beirut. An office was also established in Casablanca, Morocco.

The purpose of GPW was to make wheat from U.S. farms attractive to foreign buyers and users. GPW was funded through the state wheat commissions of the states (Colorado, Nebraska, North Dakota, Oklahoma, and South Dakota) it represented. The foreign market development activities of GPW were performed in cooperation with the Foreign Agricultural Service of the USDA. During the first 15 years of GPW's existence, U.S. wheat exports grew by more than 80% from a level of 613 million bushels in 1959 to 1.1 billion bushels in 1975.

The grain industry was dominated by government buying offices, which were extremely price conscious. The role of GPW expanded to include technical assistance and trade servicing as a vehicle for establishing and continuing good relations between farmers and the foreign government wheat buyers.

In order to more fully expand this new phase of wheat promotion into the areas of Asia and Oceania, the KWC appropriated funds to become a full member of the other producer-funded wheat marketing association, Western Wheat Associates, Inc. For this purpose, the Commission approached the 1979 Kansas legislature and received an increase in the 22-year old mill levy, raising the levy from 2 to 3 mills per bushel.

1974-75 Kansas Wheat Queen Carla Jo Lawless of Galva, holds a loaf of bread containing 50 cents worth of wheat.

European Economic Community Price Slashing

GPW acted as a voice for all U.S. wheat producers in filing a protest under the Fair Trade Act and against the European Economic Community (EEC) wheat sales practices. The lawsuit brought official U.S. government recognition of the harmful influence that EEC price slashing had on U.S. wheat prices. Kansas Congressman Dan Glickman testified on behalf of GPW arguments, and as a result, the U.S. Government vowed to never allow foreign subsidies to again significantly harm U.S. markets for wheat.

U.S. Wheat Marketing Conference

Nearly 200 people from 13 countries attended the U.S. wheat marketing conference for Latin America in 1979. Participants included government buying officials, grain traders, flour millers, and related industry professionals. This was one of the many market expansion programs that Great Plains Wheat conducted through international offices.

First Brabender report launched, 1978. (l-r) James Shaver, Martha Brabender, George Voth, and Governor Bennett.

Top Markets for U.S. Wheat 1970s

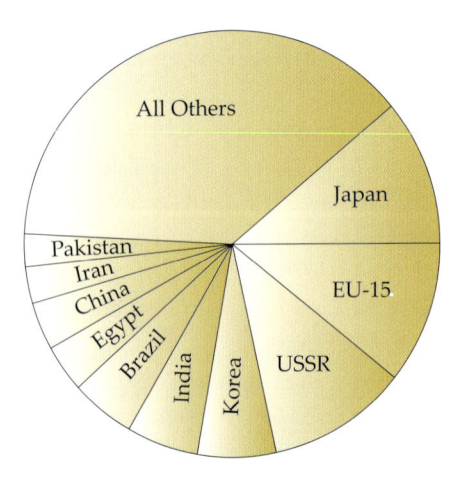

Brabender Study

In November 1977, two Kansas Wheat Commissioners, James Shaver and Marvin Koch traveled to Europe and investigated the sprout damage problem there. These two commissioners visualized a new potential market for Hard Red Winter wheat and began contacting European millers and laying the groundwork for a significant research study that was to be called the Brabender study.

The objectives of the Brabender study were to educate European millers on the quality of Hard Red Winter wheat as a blending wheat, as it had little or no sprout damage. KWC wanted to establish the reputation of Hard Red Winter wheat in Europe as a good baking wheat. Initially the research was going to be performed in the United States. However, for increased acceptance of the study, it was decided to have the research performed by the Brabender Corporation, a German company that manufactured wheat-testing equipment.

The findings were significant and resulted in a 30% blend of U.S. Hard Red Winter wheat with European supplies. European bakers found many improved characteristics, specifically dough quality, protein content, and loaf volumes.

Trade Teams

Wheat industry teams from overseas who visited Kansas in the 1970s included teams from Japan, Caribbean, India, Germany, the Netherlands, Central America, China, Portugal, Colombia, Taiwan, France, United Kingdom, South Africa, Algeria, Ecuador, Switzerland, European Economic Community, Indonesia, Brazil, Iran, the Benelux countries, Chile, Thailand, Soviet Union, Peru, Italy, Scandinavia, Zambia, Cameroon, Cyprus, Malaysia, Poland, Finland, Jordan, Bolivia, Morocco, Romania, Pakistan, and others.

China Reopens the Door

In 1979, the first U.S. agricultural team to visit China since normalization of diplomatic relations included representatives of U.S. wheat producers. The People's Republic of China purchased U.S. wheat for the first time since 1974. The volume they bought more than made up for the slack Soviet purchases in fiscal year 1979, and kept export demand at a high level.

U.S. Wheat Exports 1970-1980

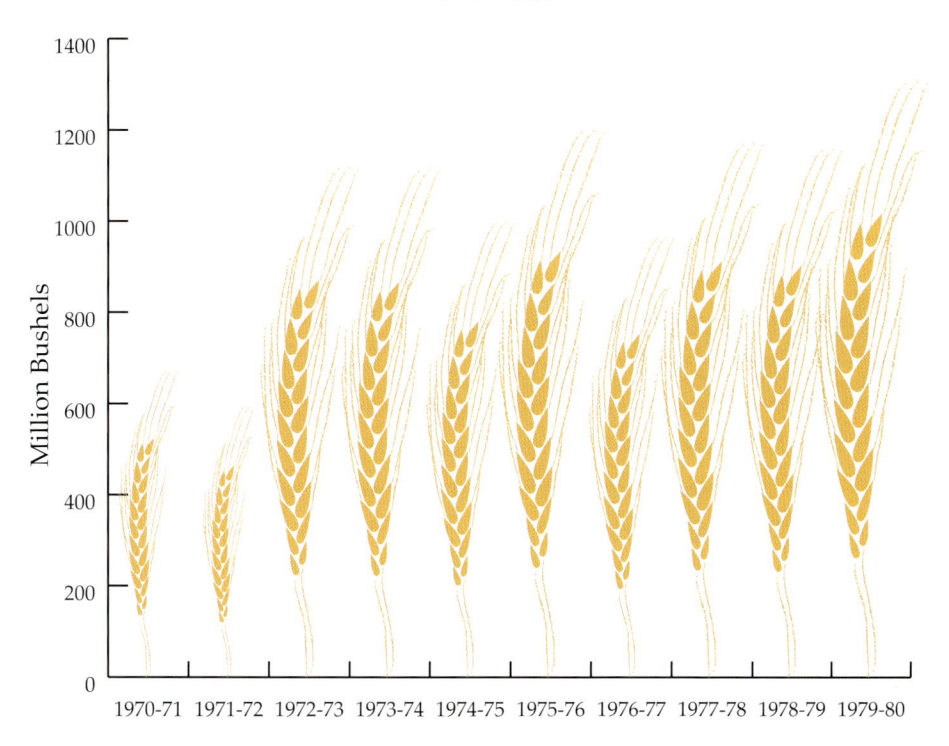

This mobile display was used to educate the public about wheat during the 1974 centennial.

The "Eat the basic 4 foods every day" emblem was designed by the Food Council of America. Since color was the "in" thing in the early 1970s, the Commission featured the new Nutritional Awareness emblem on the "July Is Wheat Month" placemats, as well as a focal point in exhibits. This "Basic 4" design was created to promote better nutrition.

International Grains Program

In 1978, the International Grains Program (IGP) was formed in the Grain Science Department of Kansas State University. The purpose of the IGP was to educate foreign millers, bakers, government buyers, and other visitors about wheat, corn, grain sorghum, and soybeans.

Wheat Marketing Field Day

An annual field day focused on such vital topics as the importance of research in wheat production, protein testing, proper storage, and finding and developing marketing opportunities for Hard Red Winter wheat.

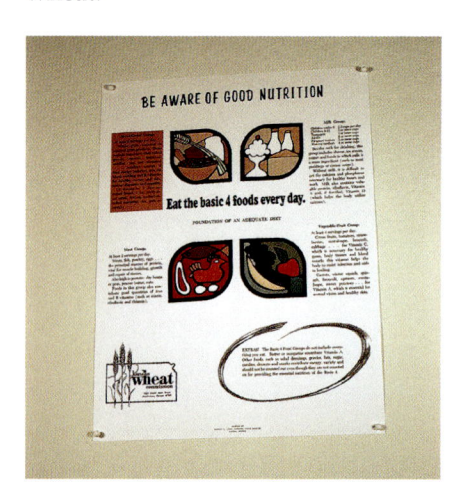

Transportation

KWC joined other states in successfully protesting rate increases by the nation's railroads. The protest resulted in a savings to Kansas wheat farmers of approximately $3 million in transportation costs.

Centennial Year of Introduction of Turkey Wheat

1974 was an especially significant year for Kansas and the wheat industry. It marked the 100th anniversary of the introduction of 'Turkey' red wheat by Mennonite immigrants to Kansas. This introduction paved the way for Kansas' inevitable first place role in Hard Red Winter wheat production.

The 1974 recipe book, *Century of Wheat Recipes*, celebrated the centennial of the introduction of 'Turkey' Hard Red Winter wheat into Kansas and the beginning of our great wheat industry.

Recipe Booklet

The 1970-71 family-sized recipe booklet was notable and used a round mod-green design. It contained recipes and a short horoscope for each of the 12 months. It generated much interest, and many people returned to Commission exhibits for additional copies.

Creation of the Wheat Foods Council

The Wheat Foods Council was formed in May 1972 at a meeting in the Kansas Wheat Commission test kitchen in Hutchinson. Home economists from Texas, Colorado, South Dakota, Nebraska, and Kansas shared the domestic promotion activities undertaken in the various states. Their collective purpose was to promote the use of more wheat and wheat foods and to establish a connection with allied groups. The group agreed to work on programs in which all the states could participate.

A "Bake and Take" program was decided upon for promotion in each state. The campaign would encourage women to bake a product and take it to someone's home.

Kernel Beard and the Stucky Points System

In 1973-74, a new diet program was introduced. The system used simplified values called nutrient points. It was produced out of concern over the elimination of bread from diets as a result of food faddism, misinformation, or the simple convenience of cutting out bread servings to save calories. Good nutrition means bread and wheat foods should be included in the diet with full knowledge of their nutritional value. The system used a perky Kernel Beard as an emblem and was developed by the Kansas Wheat Commission under the direction of Mrs. Virginia Toews Stucky, registered dietician and KWC consultant on nutrition. A series of booklets on the diet control system were made available to the public. The Kernel Beard Stucky Point System was easy to teach and used by people of all ages and on any dietary restriction.

Gold Certificate Award

In 1975 the KWC designed the Gold Certificate Award to draw attention to attractive service of tasty bread by Kansas restaurants. For those who featured bread, the KWC administered a pat on the

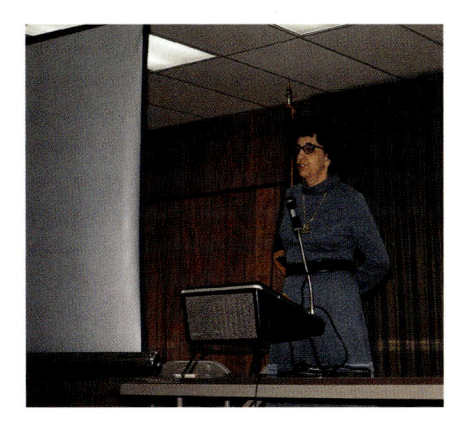

The Wheat Foods Council was formed in May 1972 at a meeting in the Kansas Wheat Commission test kitchen in Hutchinson. The purpose of the group was to promote the use of more wheat and wheat foods, and to establish a liaison with allied groups.

Mrs. Virginia Toews Stucky was the originator of the nutrition point diet system and the Kernel Beard books and pamphlets used in the diet control program, which gave bread its proper place in the diet.

A successful program for increasing the use of wheat foods domestically was the annual Sandwich Contest and Sandwich Month. All over the United States, food editors of publications and broadcasting studios were busy telling homemakers and those who serve large numbers of people about new combinations of ingredients for sandwiches. Besides being attractive and tasty, all the sandwiches met nutrition requirements. The Staff of Life, bread, was the main ingredient in these sandwiches.

back with an award in the form of a gold certificate. The Gold Certificate Award listed the restaurant or organization and the Commission's commendation for serving excellent bread in an appetizing manner.

Prominent Leaders

During the 1970-71 year, Carl A. Dumler, Russell, served as President of the Board of Directors of Great Plains Wheat. Aaron E. Hawes, Larned, was Chairman of the important Foreign Marketing Committee; Lawrence E. Brenan, Dodge City, was on the Wheat Advisory Committee; and A. Rex Cozad, Norcatur, served as Chairman of the Transportation Committee.

In 1974, Florence E. Dumler, Russell, was appointed to the KWC and was the first woman to be a member of a state wheat commission in the United States. Mrs. Dumler was first appointed to the Commission to fill the unexpired term of her late husband, Carl A. Dumler. Mrs. Dumler served as Vice Chairman of KWC and was elected Secretary of Great Plains Wheat for the 1975-76 year.

1970s Wheat Awards

Kansas Wheat Queen

1970	Kathy Berger	Bucklin
1971	Evelyn Ebright	Lyons
1972	Sheri Henderson	Lakin
1973	Vera Jean Gill	Harper
1974	Andrea Polansky	Belleville
1975	Carla Jo Lawless	Galva
1976	Elaine Dick	Buhler
1977	Becky Herman	Garden City
1978	Nancy Dible	Oakley
1979	Renae Kilian	Russell

Wheat Woman of the Year

1971	Anna Jane Baird	Hutchinson
1973	Fredia Worthington	Burrton
1974	Carol Torline	Spearville

Wheat Man of the Year

1974	Dr. Wayne E. Henry	Hutchinson
1976	Prof. Arlin B. Ward	Manhattan
1977	Earl Hayes	Stafford

Commission Personnel

Through the 1970s, there were several changes in Commission personnel. G.C. Fowler, Administrator, took a leave of absence and later passed away. Myron Krenzin, Assistant Administrator, served as Acting Administrator during Fowler's absence. Creel Brock of Stafford was named Administrator in mid-1970.

Brock resigned his position on October 1, 1974, and at that time Commissioner A. Rex Cozad of Norcatur, resigned as Commissioner and was employed as Administrator. The Governor appointed Dennis Shirley, also of Norcatur, to complete Cozad's Commission term. In 1978, David Frey was hired as Public Relations Assistant.

Wheat Production and Varieties

Favorable weather resulted in production through the first four years of the century with leading yields and a record average of 37 bushels per acre in 1973. Short rainfall in the spring coupled with wheat streak mosaic virus in 1974 escorted several lower production years with weather, disease, production and harvest problems.

Leading varieties in the 1970s were 'Scout,' 'Eagle,' 'Triumph,' 'Centurk,' 'Sage,' and 'Parker.'

The District 4-H Wheat Show in Salina drew 75 physical samples and 107 Mill and Bake entries. Winners included (left to right) Lori Shoemaker, Narka, Champion, Physical Samples, and Charles Odgers, Sublette, Champion, Mill and Bake. Kansas Wheat Queen Andrea Polansky is at center. To the right are Dean Stoskopf of Hoisington, Reserve Champion, Mill and Bake; and Frank Scheuerman, Narka, Reserve Champion, Physical Sample.

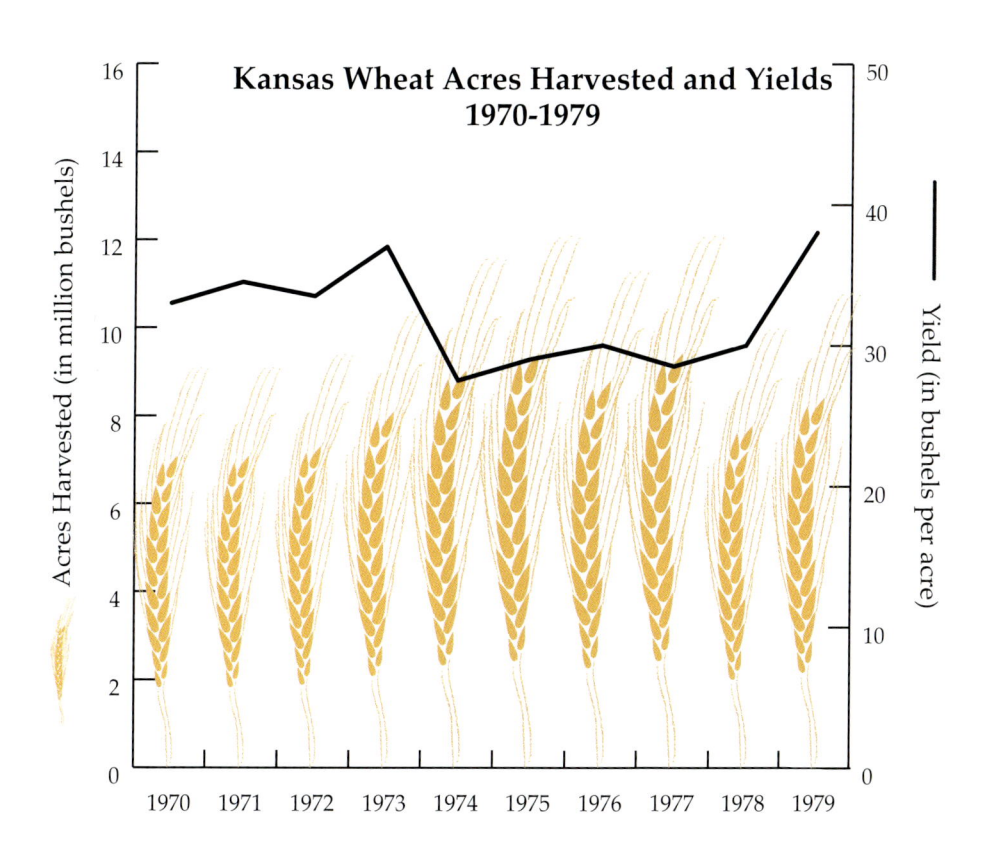

Kansas Wheat Acres Harvested and Yields 1970-1979

WHEAT DILL BUNS

makes 24 buns

THESE BUNS HAVE A DELIGHTFUL LIGHT TEXTURE AND GOOD FLAVOR. THE SPECIAL INGREDIENT IS DILL WEED.

ingredients
- 2 packages RED STAR® Active Dry Yeast
- 2 cups whole wheat flour
- 2 teaspoons dried dill weed
- ¼ cup granulated sugar
- 2 teaspoons dehydrated minced onions soaked in 1 tablespoon water
- 2 teaspoons salt
- 2 tablespoons margarine or butter
- 2 beaten eggs
- 1 (16-ounce) carton small curd cottage cheese, room temperature
- ½ cup hot water (120-130°F)
- 3 ½ - 4 cups bread flour

1 In large mixing bowl, combine the yeast, whole wheat flour, dill weed, sugar, onion, and salt. Add the margarine, eggs, and cottage cheese.

2 Add the water; beat at medium speed 2 minutes, scraping bowl often.

3 Stir in 1 cup bread flour, mixing well. Gradually add enough of the remaining flour to form a soft dough.

4 Knead 10 to 12 minutes or until smooth and elastic. (Dough should be slightly sticky). Place in greased bowl, turning to grease top. Cover; let rise in warm place until double.

5 Punch down dough; cover, let rest 10 minutes. Divide dough in half; cut each half into 12 pieces. Shape each in a smooth ball. Place on greased baking sheets. Flatten to form a bun. Cover; let rise until double.

6 Bake in preheated 400°F oven 10 to 12 minutes, or until golden. Remove from pans and cool on wire rack.

nutrition information *per serving (one bun): 150 cal, 3 g fat, 21 mg chol, 286 mg sodium, 25 g carbo, 2 g fiber, 7 g pro, 53 mcg folate.*

GLAZED RAISIN LOAF

makes 1 large loaf, 16 slices

THIS RECIPE WAS TAKEN FROM A POPULAR 1973 KWC BOOKLET, "RECIPES FROM THE KERNEL."

ingredients
- 1 cup raisins
- 1 cup cool water
- 1 package RED STAR® Active Dry Yeast
- ¼ cup lukewarm water (110-115°F)
- ½ cup low-fat buttermilk
- ¼ cup granulated sugar
- ¼ cup margarine or butter
- 1 ¼ teaspoons salt
- 2 beaten eggs
- 3 ¼ - 3 ½ cups bread flour
- Confectioners' icing (optional)

1 Soak raisins in cool water for 5 minutes; drain well. Dissolve yeast in lukewarm water. Heat buttermilk slightly (90-100°F).

2 In mixing bowl combine yeast, buttermilk, sugar, margarine, salt, and eggs; stir in 2 cups of flour; beat well. Add raisins and enough remaining flour to make a soft dough. Knead until smooth and elastic about 10 to 12 minutes. Place dough in lightly greased bowl, turning dough to grease entire surface. Cover; let rise until double.

3 Punch down dough. Round into a ball. Cover; let rest 10 minutes. Roll out to a 9 x 12-inch rectangle. Roll up as for jelly-roll; seal edges and ends. Place in greased 9 x 5 x 3-inch loaf pan. Cover; let rise until almost double, about 1 hour.

4 Bake in preheated 375°F oven 30 to 35 minutes, or until done. If crust browns too fast, cover with foil last 5 to 10 minutes of baking. Turn out of pan and cool on rack. If desired, when cool, drizzle confectioners' icing on top.

nutrition information *per serving (1 slice): 176 cal, 4 g fat, 27 mg chol, 229 mg sodium, 31 g carbo, 1 g fiber, 5 g pro, 56 mcg folate.*

PEANUT BUTTER NUT BREAD

makes 1 loaf, 16 slices

A GOLDEN RECIPE FROM THE PAST BUT STILL A CROWD PLEASER.

ingredients
- 1 cup low-fat buttermilk
- ¼ cup Grape-Nuts® cereal
- ¾ cup brown sugar
- 1 cup quick-cooking rolled oats, dry
- 1 teaspoon baking soda
- ½ teaspoon baking powder
- ½ teaspoon salt
- 1 ¼ cups all-purpose flour
- 1 beaten egg
- ¼ cup smooth peanut butter
- ¼ cup coconut
- ¼ cup chopped pecans
- ¼ cup melted margarine or butter

1 In mixing bowl, stir together buttermilk, Grape-Nuts®, brown sugar, and oats; soak 1 hour.

2 In small bowl, stir together soda, baking powder, salt, and flour. Add to soaked ingredients. Stir in egg, peanut butter, coconut, pecans, and melted margarine or butter. Mix together with spoon until well blended. Place in lightly greased 8 ½ x 4 ½ x 2 ½-inch loaf pan.

3 Bake in preheated 350°F oven for 1 hour or until toothpick inserted in center of loaf comes out dry. Cool for 10 minutes. Remove from pan and continue to cool on wire rack.

nutrition information *per serving (one slice): 177 cal, 7 g fat, 14 mg chol, 245 mg sodium, 25 g carbo, 1 g fiber, 4 g pro, 28 mcg folate.*

CRANBERRY GRIDDLE CAKES

makes about 2 dozen griddle cakes

AS STATED IN THE 1977 PANCAKE-SHAPED BOOKLET, "GOOD ANY TIME... OF THE YEAR!"

ingredients
- 1 ½ cups all-purpose flour
- 2 tablespoons granulated sugar
- 1 tablespoon baking powder
- ¾ teaspoon salt
- 1 beaten egg
- 1 cup low-fat milk
- 3 tablespoons vegetable oil
- ¾ cup diced, jellied cranberry sauce

1 In medium bowl, sift together flour, sugar, baking powder, and salt. In second bowl, combine egg, milk, and oil. Add liquid ingredients all at once to flour mixture and stir until mixture is smooth. Gently stir in cranberry sauce.

2 Pour about 1 tablespoonful batter on hot greased griddle. Cook until golden brown on both sides, turning when uncooked side has a bubbled surface. Turn only once. Serve hot.

nutrition information *per serving (one griddle cake): 68 cal, 2 g fat, 9 mg chol, 112 mg sodium, 11 g carbo, 0 g fiber, 1 g pro, 13 mcg folate.*

WHEAT PASTRY

makes 1 double crust pie or 2 single shells

A PERFECT PASTRY RECIPE THAT COULD HOLD ANY TYPE OF FILLING. A FAVORITE RECIPE DEMONSTRATED BY KWC HOME ECONOMISTS IN 1978 IN THEIR POPULAR PIE PROGRAMS.

ingredients
- ¾ cup vegetable shortening or ⅔ cup lard*
- 1 cup whole wheat flour
- 1 ¼ cups all-purpose flour
- 1 teaspoon salt
- 4 - 5 tablespoons ice water

*Do not use oil in crust.

1 Cut shortening into whole wheat flour, all-purpose flour, and salt with pastry blender or 2 knives until particles are size of small peas. Sprinkle in ice water, a small amount at a time, tossing with a fork until all flour is moistened and pastry cleans side of bowl. (If dough is still dry, add a small amount additional ice water. Flour differs in absorption.)

2 Gather pastry into a ball. Divide in half. Shape each half into a flattened circle on lightly floured pastry cloth. Roll pastry; fold in half. Place in pie pan; unfold and ease into corners of plate pressing firmly against bottom and side.

3 For baked shells, prick bottom and sides with fork. Bake in preheated 450°F oven about 8 to 10 minutes.

nutrition information (⅛ of one crust): 146 cal, 10 g fat, 0 mg chol, 146 mg sodium, 13 g carbo, 1 g fiber, 2 g pro, 18 mcg folate.

SPLIT LEVELS

makes 20 bars

THE POPULARITY OF THE SPLIT-LEVEL HOME DESIGN MAY HAVE DECREASED SINCE THE 1970'S, BUT THE POPULARITY OF THESE BAR COOKIES HAS NOT.

ingredients
- 1 cup semisweet chocolate morsels
- 1 (6-ounce) package cream cheese
- ⅓ cup evaporated milk
- ½ cup chopped pecans
- ½ teaspoon almond extract, divided
- 1 ½ cups all-purpose flour
- ½ teaspoon baking powder
- ¼ teaspoon salt
- ¾ cup granulated sugar
- ½ cup margarine or butter

1 Combine chocolate morsels, cream cheese, and milk in saucepan. Melt mixture over low heat, stirring constantly. Remove from heat and stir in pecans and ¼ teaspoon almond extract. Set aside to cool.

2 Combine flour, baking powder, salt, sugar, margarine, and ¼ teaspoon almond extract. Beat at low speed until fine particles are formed. Press half of the mixture in greased 9 x 9-inch pan. Spread chocolate mixture on top.

3 Top with remaining crumbs. Bake in preheated 375°F oven approximately 30 minutes, or until tested done. Cool; cut into bars.

nutrition information *per serving (one bar): 198 cal, 12 g fat, 11 mg chol, 108 mg sodium, 21 g carbo, 0.5 g fiber, 2 g pro, 17 mcg folate.*

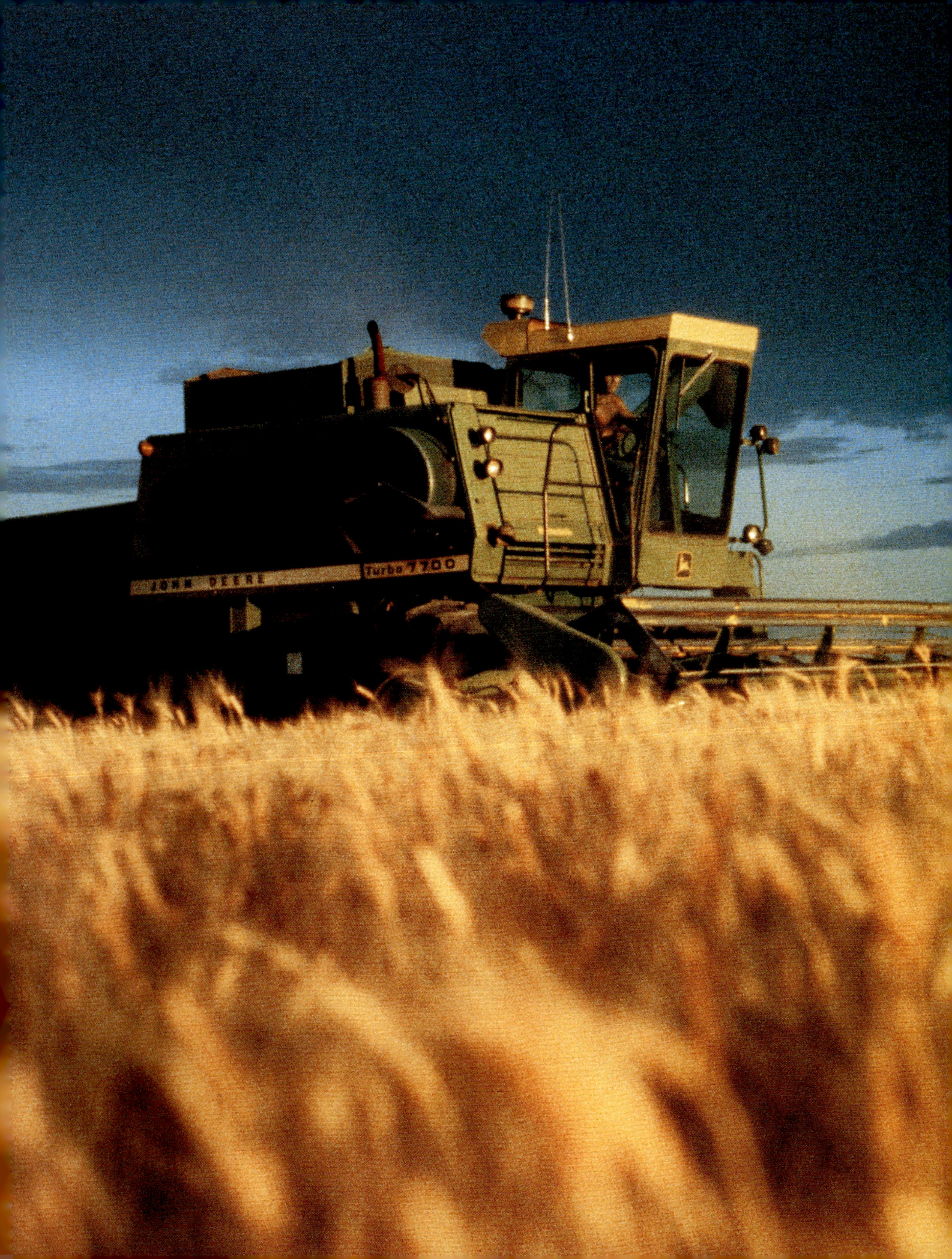
JOHN DEERE
Turbo 7700

1980s

ASIAN COUNTRIES BECOME TOP INTERNATIONAL MARKETS

> "Our commitment to represent the interests of Kansas wheat producers in the world of market development remains our foremost responsibility. This is the reason the Kansas Wheat Commission exists."
> — Steven M. Graham, KWC Administrator, 1984

In January of 1980, after years of planning, the two international U.S. wheat promotion organizations disbanded and formed a new organization with a unified purpose — U.S. Wheat Associates. Western Wheat Associates had operated primarily in Asia, and Great Plains Wheat had operated over the rest of the world.

The January 1980 USSR grain embargo severely impacted export markets for Kansas wheat. Additionally, the 1980 harvest was the largest wheat harvest to date.

In 1982, the Kansas Wheat Commission celebrated its 25th anniversary.

In April 1984, the KWC moved to Manhattan to operate closer to overseas wheat buyers who visited the milling and baking capital of the world.

1984 marked the beginning of a steady increase in wheat consumption patterns, affected by increased ethnic products and an increase in meals eaten away from home.

The "Speak for Wheat" spokespersons program was initiated in 1986. These volunteers shared information about wheat with audiences throughout the state.

Photo by Leon Sowers, Murdock, Kansas, First Place, 1987 Kansas State Fair entry

Research Projects

Research projects in the 1980s included the economics of on-farm storage, wheat for alcohol, and non-baking utilization of vital wheat gluten.

Research also provided a cost and benefit analysis of cleaning market wheat. The project examined the profitability of cleaning wheat at a Kansas country elevator. The results showed it to be profitable and were distributed throughout the United States. The Commission continued supporting the germplasm bank that contains the largest collection of wild wheats used to breed new lines of Kansas wheat with resistance to diseases. The Wheat Quality Council continued to conduct milling and baking tests on all varieties developed.

Hard White Wheat

In 1987, KSU released for seed increase a Hard White winter wheat variety. A Hard White Winter Wheat Task Force, made up of representatives from the Kansas Wheat Commission, Kansas State University, Kansas Association of Wheat Growers, Kansas Crop Improvement Association, and private wheat seed companies, met regularly to plan the production, distribution, and marketing of what was to become a new class of U.S. wheat. The KWC had funded development of Hard White varieties since 1981.

Hard Red Winter Wheat Variety Development

Although variety development takes 10 to 13 years, the KWC invested in this long-term research to produce new varieties with better milling, baking, and agronomic qualities for Kansas producers.

By 1987, two KSU Hard Red Winter varieties, 'Newton' and 'Arkan,' had each provided more than $12 million to Kansas farmers. 'Arkan,' released in 1984, was shown by milling tests to be a hard wheat, but appeared by kernel shape to be a soft wheat. This dilemma resulted in additional research for more objective tests for distinguishing between hard wheat and soft wheats.

'Norkan' and 'Dodge' were also being planted by Kansas farmers by the fall of 1987. In 1988, KSU's crop variety review board recommended for release the variety 'Karl.' It too was developed with funding by the Commission. 'Karl' was proposed as an eventual replacement for the state's most popular variety at the time — 'Arkan.'

Variety development also focused on producing varieties for target markets and the foods they eat in those markets. Some of these targets were Chinese noodles, pasta, and

Joe Martin explains Hard White wheat research at KSU's Fort Hays Experiment Station.

oriental noodles from HRW instead of traditional rice.

Additionally, international breadmaking was a focus with diverse bread-type products being made by various importing countries. Specifically, the Brabender wheat blending study of the earlier decade lead to variety development for HRW to improve milling and baking quality in blends in Europe.

Domestic Market Development

The U.S. Surgeon General Dr. C. Everett Koop called wheat-based foods an inexpensive, non-fattening approach for improving the American diet. He said, "Wheat-based foods can be an individual's best one-stop source of carbohydrates, fiber, protein, Vitamin B, and important trace minerals. Wheat foods are abundant and inexpensive, yet they are not fattening. You can't ask for much more than that." (Wheat Industry Council Press Release, Sept. 8, 1982)

Wheat Foods Council

Commissions from five states were instrumental in forming the Wheat Foods Council in 1972. And by the 1980s, membership had expanded to twelve full members and two associate members from nine states.

The KWC made significant contributions to the WFC in 1988-89 by providing financial support and in-kind contributions from staff services. At this time, the WFC did not have its own staff. Instead, members worked together to formulate programs and activities for the Council. They also volunteered to carry out the actual programming and promotional activities. Wheat producer groups funded ninety-nine percent of the budget. Kansas

WFC Officers in 1985 were (front l-r) Sheila Alexander, Oklahoma Wheat Commission; Judi Adams, North Dakota Wheat Commission; (back l-r) Sharon Patterson Davis, Kansas Wheat Commission; and Mary Anne Greeland, Oregon Wheat Commission.

An early group of spokespersons toured the General Mills flour mill in Kansas City as part of their training program. Commissioner Joe Berry (left) and his wife Geneva, traveled with the group.

Spokesperson Joyce Besthorn demonstrated cooking techniques for wheat and wheat related foods at the 1988 3i Show. Programs devoted to women's interests were first added to the 3i Show in 1980. The art of making yeast bread in a food processor, use of convenience breads, and other timely ideas were also presented.

Wheat Commission Nutritionist Sharon Davis was elected Chairman of the Wheat Foods Council in 1988 and served a two-year term.

Per Capita Consumption

1984 marked the beginning of a steady increase in wheat consumption. American consumers were dining out more and consuming a lot more fast foods that were served on buns. The increased availability of ethnic variety products like pizza, sandwiches, tortillas, pasta, ethnic variety breads, crackers, and cookies also made an impact. Most importantly was the changing attitude toward carbohydrates and fiber as being necessary parts of the diet.

Spokespersons

In 1986, KWC Nutritionist Sharon Patterson Davis started the new "Speak for Wheat" spokesperson program. Twelve "Speak for Wheat" volunteers shared information about wheat around the state through food preparation demonstrations and talks about nutrition, wheat marketing, and wheatweaving. The founding volunteers were Joyce Besthorn, Claflin; Cynthia Falk, Onaga; Joyce Banbury, Russell; Pam Turner, Stafford; Lynnea Huffman, Pratt; Karen Schulteis, Harper; Melanie Eddy, Syracuse; Sherry and Shonda Leighty, Ulysses; Nadine Griffin, Abilene; Linda Jaynes, Weir; and DeAnn Dail, Sylvan Grove.

SunnyWheat Bread

In November 1989, SunnyWheat Bread was declared the official state bread. The Kansas Restaurant Magazine for food editors statewide featured Kansas wheat products. "Celebrating Kansas Wheat" was exhibited at the Celebrate Kansas Food Expo, Kansas Restaurant Show, Kansas School Food Service, National Restaurant Show, Kansas State Fair, and 3i Show.

U.S. Wheat Associates

Kansas financed both U.S. wheat promotion organizations, Great Plains Wheat and Western Wheat Associates, and in January 1980 they merged into one worldwide organization, United States Wheat Associates, Inc. Member states of USW were Kansas, Colorado, Idaho, Minnesota, Montana, Nebraska, North Dakota, Oklahoma, Oregon,

South Dakota, Texas, Washington, and Wyoming. Support from USDA's Foreign Agricultural Service gave a two-to-one match to the producer dollar.

USW conducted over 320 programs in 96 countries around the world from its 12 foreign offices and two domestic offices in Washington, D.C. and Portland, Oregon. These offices were located in Rotterdam, Netherlands; Casablanca, Morocco; Cairo, Egypt; Mexico City, Mexico; Santiago, Chile; Singapore, Malaysia; India; Manila, Philippines; Taiwan; Tokyo, Japan; Korea; and Hong Kong. An office in Bejing, China opened in 1983. By 1989, USW had 16 offices. Unfortunately, demonstrators firebombed the Seoul, Korea office, and the June 1989 massacre at Tiananmen Square caused the temporary abandonment of the Beijing office.

A study by Chase Econometrics, an independent research firm, found that each dollar contributed by producers for market development purposes returned $100 of additional income from wheat sales to the grower and $133 to the U.S. economy.

Kansas wheat producer Adrian Polansky of Belleville served as chairman of U.S. Wheat Associates for 1985-86. Polansky traveled to more than 30 countries as the producers' international wheat market development representative, encouraging others to buy U.S. wheat.

Kansas Wheat Commission hosted the USW summer board meeting in Manhattan in 1986. The board accepted Arizona as the sixteenth state member and toured the International Grains Program and American Institute of Baking.

Trade teams from all over the world traveled to Kansas in the 1980s to learn about Kansas wheat and the U.S. marketing system.

KWC Nutritionist Sharon Davis and Kansas Wheat Commissioner Kent Eddy, Syracuse, introduce Sunny-Wheat Bread at the Kansas Restaurant Association convention.

Loo Kai Soon, U.S. Wheat Associates/Singapore, demonstrates how to make Asian noodles from Kansas flour to Sharon Davis, KWC Nutritionist.

Individuals and groups from more than 66 countries visited Kansas during the decade.

In May 1981, the sixth "Buy American" mission from the Taiwan government toured the United States, buying $12 million worth of HRW wheat while in Kansas. They also renewed a grains contract with the U.S. signaling their intent to buy 12 million tons of grain from the U.S. in the next five years. The Taiwan Buying Mission continued to make Hard Red Winter wheat purchases on an annual basis.

International Markets

In 1980, President Carter placed a grain embargo on the Soviet Union, canceling contracts for the sale of 17 million metric tons of U.S. wheat, corn, and soybeans. The embargo was in response to Soviet military action in Afghanistan. The Soviet Union was the top market for U.S. Hard Red Winter wheat at the time.

This decrease in demand coupled with a record crop of 420 million bushels in the summer of 1980 plummeted the price of Hard Red Winter wheat. For price sensitive buyers like the People's Republic of China, this moved their purchases from Soft Red Winter wheat when HRW was not much higher in price than Soft Red Winter wheat.

By 1981, India once again became a net wheat importer, purchasing 600,000 tons of Hard Red Winter wheat. This came after five years of net exports from India. Previously, in 1975, India was America's biggest customer of wheat. Improved agricultural practices, irrigation, semi-dwarf varieties, and favorable weather meant that India became a net exporter of wheat from 1976 through 1980. By 1981, stocks were too low to keep pace with consumption.

The Trincomalee Flour Mill in Sri Lanka, which opened in 1981, was the world's largest flour mill under one roof. Previously a large flour importer, Sri Lanka became an importer of up to 800,000 tons of wheat annually.

Iraq emerged as a large buyer of U.S. Hard Red Winter wheat in 1983, and Japan was consistently a top market of U.S. HRW throughout the 1980s. In May 1988, a protocol was signed between U.S. Wheat Associates and the USSR Ministry of Grain Products. The USSR was the largest buyer of HRW in 1988 and the second largest buyer of all U.S. wheat.

Scab Scare

Wheat scab, a fungus that causes a reduction in both yield and quality, showed up in the 1982 crop.

It was not so much scab itself, but a 1982 *Wall Street Journal* article,

People's Republic of China Ministry of Commerce officials study flour packages at the General Mills plant in Kansas City.

which resulted in great concern from traditional export customers of winter wheat. At one time during the uncertainty of the summer, customers from Europe, South America, the Middle East and Asia were not buying HRW wheat. Even after the USDA confirmed only minor danger, some traditional customers avoided purchasing any of the 1982 HRW crop.

In September 1982, the Soviets would accept no tolerance of scab-damaged kernels. This was especially concerning since the Soviet Union was the largest market for U.S. HRW. In November, representatives from HRW wheat states and USW met with Soviet embassy officials in Washington to discuss wheat quality. A Soviet grain delegation toured the U.S. and Kansas evaluating the scab issue. They signed an agreement to accept a workable wheat scab tolerance level. By December, the Soviets re-entered the U.S. wheat market after nearly a one-year absence and bought U.S. HRW with a scab tolerance of .3 percent.

WETEC

In 1984, the U.S. and Chinese governments entered into a textile dispute that cost U.S. wheat farmers approximately $1.2 billion. To avoid future problems, the wheat states formed the Wheat Export Trade Education Committee (WETEC) to inform people of the importance of wheat exports to the U.S. economy. China became the third largest buyer of U.S. HRW, and was the largest buyer of all U.S. wheat by 1989.

USW Special Projects

USW special projects included bakers' training facilities in Nigeria and the Philippines, milling facilities in Brazil and the People's Republic of China, a wheat research institute in Taiwan, special bread research in southern Asia, a mill management seminar in the Middle East, wheat quality and flour testing lab in India, a resource center in Iraq, baking equipment in Korea, as well as consulting services to flour mills in various areas of the world.

Additionally, the KWC donated three specially designed experimental mills to the CERTREM milling and baking school in Brazil.

South American flour millers agreed to establish a Flour Millers Association to serve the entire continent. USW had been working toward this establishment for some time.

Kansas Wheat Commission Chairman Adrian J. Polansky and State Secretary of Agriculture W.W. (Bill) Duitsman discuss the upcoming tender with the head of the Taiwan delegation.

(bottom) Governor John Carlin signs papers of cooperation and friendship with the official delegation from the Republic of China (Taiwan).

Happy 50th Anniversary, Kansas Wheat Commission!
by Steven Graham
KWC Staff, 1980-1995
KWC Administrator, 1981-1995

It is truly an honor to share a few thoughts on the 50th anniversary of the Kansas Wheat Commission. Wheat producers were leaders in developing the concept of self-funded research and market development organizations, not only in the United States but in the world. Wheat producers, through their wheat commissions, went "global" many years before the rest of society recognized the need. In fact, wheat producers and their staff were often in countries before formal diplomatic relations were established. The story of the Kansas Wheat Commission and other commissions should be told and retold, because it has been an earth breaking story of vision, leadership, persistence, and success.

The Kansas Wheat Commission allows producers to do what one producer would like to do but cannot by him or herself — and that is to develop new wheat varieties, create new uses for wheat, and market the proper class of wheat to the end users who need it, whether in the U.S. or around the world. The Kansas Wheat Commission was an "information organization" long before anyone coined the term. Information about the newest varieties of wheat, the newest uses of our Kansas wheat, the quality of the year's crop, and the supply and demand picture is all necessary for communicating with producers, purchasers, and users of our Kansas hard wheat.

I was associated with the Kansas Wheat Commission from 1980 to 1995, and it was a wonderful part of my life. KSU Milling Professor Arlin Ward introduced me to Administrator Myron Krenzin who, along with Chairman Adrian Polansky (our current Kansas Secretary of Agriculture) and the other six commissioners, hired me to be Assistant Administrator. As I reflect on that 15-year period, I have come to the realization it was a time of many exciting events.

The funding of the first official research to create Hard White wheat started soon after I came to the commission. The International Grains Program, under the direction of Dr. Charles Deyoe, conducted its first official short course in 1981 and developed an array of information to share with wheat buyers worldwide through wheat team visits, short courses, and international consulting trips.

The Wheat Foods Council came to be a force in promoting healthy, wheat-based diets in the U.S. We saw wheat consumption move to some of the highest levels in years. U.S. Wheat Associates, fresh off the merger of Great Plains Wheat and Western Wheat Associates, pulled together a very talented staff under the leadership of Winston Wilson, and this staff created a formidable array of programs in the world's wheat markets. In 1984, at the urging of commissioner Dennis Shirley, the Commission moved its office to Manhattan, to be closer to many of its Kansas partners in wheat research and promotion.

I also recognize my tenure at the Kansas Wheat Commission was dominated by "Wheat or Grain Boards" in nearly every country of the world. Countries large and small had Boards which did the purchasing of wheat for their flour millers. This was often done under the guise of controlling the price of flour and/or bread. Thus, maintaining good relations with the Wheat and Grain Board leaders was essential to sales of U.S. wheat. One wrong misstep and they could be purchasing wheat from our competitors. We came close to disaster several times over the years.

Probably the best story to illustrate this point occurred in 1982. That year the Kansas wheat crop experienced a wet spring just before harvest, which resulted in scabby kernels and a small amount of vomitoxin. The Russian wheat buyers, who had a zero tolerance for scab and vomitoxin, announced they would not buy any U.S. wheat. This would have been a disaster for Kansas, because Russia was the world's top wheat buyer at the time and purchased mainly Hard Red Winter wheat — the class of wheat grown in Kansas.

U.S. Wheat Associates' staff convinced the Russian wheat buyers to come to the United States and bring some grain scientists along to talk with our scientists. The Kansas Wheat Commission was asked to organize visits with Kansas producers, traders, wheat millers, and scientists who would explain how they were dealing with the crop and why it was usable, with the proper precautions, in the eyes of the U.S. wheat industry. The pressure was on. One very prominent U.S. flour miller leaned over to me during a meal event with the Russians and said, "This is very important to the industry. You better not blow it." I whispered back, "I know. Why do you think we invited you?" He got the point. We were successful in encouraging the Russians to specify some minimums in their contracts for scabby kernels and vomitoxin and their purchases resumed.

Funding research into new wheat and wheat products, conducting market development work in the U.S. and around the world, and promoting the use and sale of Kansas wheat takes many partners. In Kansas, we have the Kansas Association of Wheat Growers, Kansas State University, the International Grains Program, the American Institute of Baking, and the USDA Agricultural Research Service's Grain Marketing and Production Research Center. In the U.S., we have the other wheat commissions, the National Association of Wheat Growers, the Northern Crops Institute, the Wheat Marketing Center, the Wheat Quality Council, and the Wheat Foods Council. Globally, there is U.S. Wheat Associates with its headquarters in Washington, D.C. and offices worldwide.

Upon further reflection, I see the Kansas Wheat Commission is first and foremost about maintaining positive human relations — by generating a flow of products and information and getting them to the right people — at all levels of the wheat industry. The wheat industry people I have been privileged to know over the years are many and varied.

Writing this piece has made me think of many friends and their wonderful influence on my life. Some memories cause sadness, as I remember good friends who have passed on. Others bring smiles, such as the time David Frey and I took Fernando Coutinho (pictured below, on right), the president of the Brazilian Wheat Board, on our Commission staff's progressive Christmas dinner, going from house-to-house. We did not make a fuss that he was with us and simply treated him as one of us. He talked about this experience for years afterward and thanked us for opening our homes and treating him as a true friend — which he was.

Wheat is the "Staff of Life." I know that my life has been blessed by working for the wheat producers of Kansas and the Kansas Wheat Commission. Happy 50th Anniversary!

Pictured at the K-State Union are Steven Graham, KWC Administrator; Gloria Parenté, Graduate Student in Grain Science from Brazil; and Fernando Coutinho, President of the Brazilian Wheat Board.

Additional projects included an activity with the American Institute of Baking, duplicating conditions in Southeast Asian bread production to demonstrate the quality of products from U.S. wheat. The Chinese-American Flour Mill in Beijing, the largest project undertaken by USW to date, was completed in 1985. Finally, new lab equipment was donated to the Korean Baking School and China Wheat Products Research and Development Institute in Taiwan to train bakers with U.S. wheat.

Korea

During the 1988 Seoul Olympic games, USW, in cooperation with 1,000 small bakeries, introduced new baked goods to Koreans. The project, which was supported by Targeted Export Assistance funds from USDA/FAS, involved a Korean national media campaign, bakery fairs, and displays in the cooperating bakeries. By the end of the year, monthly sales of new bakery items had gone from half a million dollars to $4 million. U.S. market share in Korea was 85 percent.

During the 1988 Seoul Olympic games, U.S. Wheat Associates, in cooperation with 1,000 small bakeries, introduced new baked goods to Koreans. The project involved a national media campaign, bakery fairs, and displays. Monthly sales of new bakery items increased from $0.5 million to $4 million.

Top Markets for U.S. Wheat 1980s

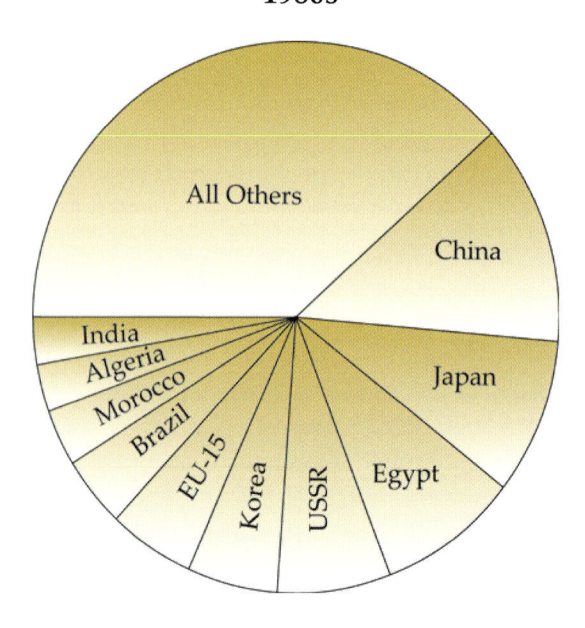

Taiwan

In 1981, nearly 650 Taiwanese attended a three-day Baked Wheat Foods and Sandwich Exhibition, sponsored by U.S. Wheat Associates and the American Trade Center in Taipei. The turnout far exceeded attendance projections.

Pakistan

The Pakistan Institute of Baking was established with the signing of a Memorandum of Understanding between USW and the University of Agriculture in Faisalabad, Pakistan. It was the first bakers training facility of its type ever established in Pakistan.

Average per capita wheat food consumption in Pakistan was double that of the United States, and the population growth rate exceeded three percent. In December 1989, USW, using milling consultants from KSU, organized a series of well-attended flour milling seminars. The Pakistan government turned wheat purchasing over to the milling companies.

Wheat Industry Promotion Council

To better coordinate activities, research and special projects, the Texas, Oklahoma, Colorado, Nebraska and Kansas wheat commissions formed an informal organization in 1984 called the Wheat Industry Promotion (WHIP) Council. Meetings were held semi-annually to address problems of regional interest and determine action. The WHIP Council showed a marked interest in the International Grains Program in Manhattan.

Wheat Grading Standards

Wheat producers supported changes to wheat grading standards where dockage would be measured to the nearest 0.1 percent and protein on a constant 12 percent moisture basis. The Federal Grain Inspection Service put these two new procedures into effect on May 1, 1987, as well as the section of the Grain Quality Improvement Act that forbids recombining dust, dockage, and foreign material once it is removed from grain.

Transportation

The movement of grain from farm gate to end use customer became increasingly more expensive. Some rail systems that were deteriorated in condition closed. As the shipping rates often meant the difference

U.S. Wheat Exports 1980-1990

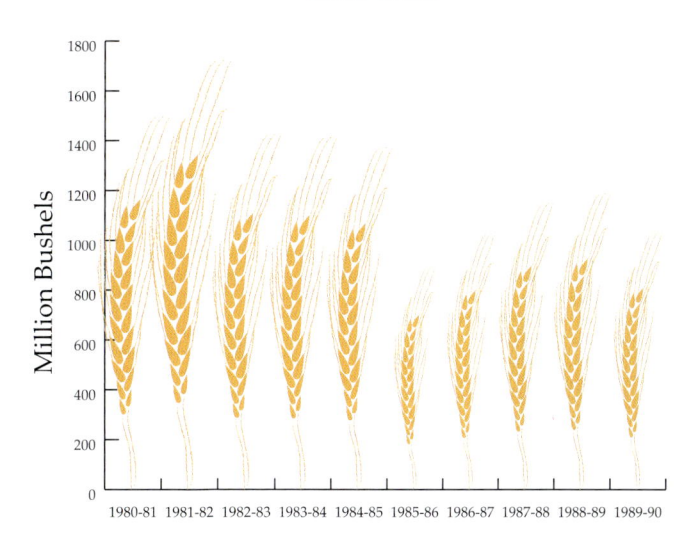

between the sale of U.S. wheat and the sale of a competitive country's wheat, KWC funded research on rail deregulation.

Wheat Quality Contests

KWC continued with their Grain Marketing Study Tour for State Fair Best of Wheat award winners, variety booth winners, state 4-H wheat project winners, and state FFA crops judging contest winners. They toured industry locations in Manhattan, Kansas City, and the Texas Gulf ports.

Agriculture Council of America

Kansas Wheat Commissioners served on the board of the Agriculture Council of America, and Adrian Polansky served as chairman. The ACA, representing hundreds of farm organizations and agribusinesses, was promoting the idea of a

The KWC worked with the Kansas Association of Wheat Growers to perform tests at elevators across the state during the 1985 harvest. The KWC provided a protein analyzer that Howard Tice, KAWG executive director, used to educate farmers about wheat quality. Through this project, 977 samples were tested at 22 locations. Tom Roberts, executive director of the Wheat Quality Council, also used the protein analyzer when evaluating wheat samples at county fairs.

stronger agriculture to urban America. The theme was "American Agriculture: we can turn the tide!" and emphasized the over-riding benefit of a strong export program. Agricultural exports counter the tide of imports that generate a variety of negative impacts on our economy — impacts felt, if not always realized, by the urban consumer.

Kansas Gold on Television

The 1980s brought on an ambitious public relations project designed to promote the state's biggest asset: Kansas Gold. The KWC produced a series of television public service announcements (PSAs) extolling the virtues of Kansas, the Wheat State, and presenting Delos Smith Jr., a professional actor and Hutchinson native. This was the Commission's first television undertaking, and the PSAs were broadcast free of charge by participating television stations.

"It is our golden grain that is keeping millions from starvation," said Myron Krenzin, KWC Administrator.

More Television Programming

Educating the general public about wheat, its uses and its importance through the television increased through the 1980s.

A Norwegian film crew filmed the 1982 wheat harvest in Kansas for school television in Scandinavia and other parts of Europe. Their half-hour documentary depicted life on the Great Plains and was used as an educational tool.

Two photojournalists from a French magazine, a television crew from NBC, and an economic reporter from Japan traveled to Kansas to understand Kansas agriculture.

A 1986 public service announcement emphasized that Kansas, the Wheat State, should be known for its delicious breads. Radio and television ads sponsored by the Wheat Industry Council through 1985 and 1986 encouraged the public to "Eat Wheat, America."

A television public service announcement distributed across the state in June 1988 featured a variety of wheat foods and reminded people that "wheat goes from field to flour to food" and that wheat is "Good for Kansas, good for us."

Levy Changes

The early 1980s saw several changes to the wheat promotional levy. After years of recognized increase in international marketing needs the State Legislature increased the Kansas wheat promotional levy authority to ten mills per bushel effective June 1, 1982. The Kansas Legislature set the levy authority maximum at 10 mills; however, at that time, the commissioners levied four mills. Declining acreage and production through the mid-1980s decreased income 37 percent from 1984 to 1987. The four-mill levy was replaced by the seven-mill assessment on June 1, 1988. The additional funding was to be used to aggressively promote Kansas wheat, to continue supporting U.S. Wheat Associates to market U.S.

1980s Wheat Awards

Kansas Wheat Queen
1980	Laurie Green	Ludell
1981	Kelli White	Kingstown

Wheat Man of the Year
1980	Myron Krenzin	Hutchinson
1981	William Morand	Hutchinson
1983	Harland Priddle	Topeka
1984	Fritz Gwin	Beloit
1985	**Wheat Couple of the Year**	
	Ken & Betty Goertzen	Haven
1986	Adrian Polansky	Belleville
1987	Tom Roberts	Manhattan
1988	Gary Gilbert	Clay Center
1989	Joe Jagger	Minneapolis

Wheat Woman of the Year
1988	Sharon Davis	Manhattan
1989	Joyce Besthorn	Claflin

wheat around the world, for more research into new food and nonfood uses of wheat, and for more education about the nutritional value of wheat foods.

Personnel

KWC Administrator Myron Krenzin went to work as a Marketing Specialist with U.S. Wheat Associates in the European office in Rotterdam, Netherlands, in January 1981.

Assistant Administrator Steven Graham was promoted to Administrator, and David Frey became Assistant Administrator.

Long-time KWC Nutritionist Anna Jane Baird retired in January 1983.

Kansas Secretary of Agriculture Sam Brownback, ex-officio member of the Kansas Wheat Commission, receives an appreciation award from KWC Chairman Adrian Polansky.

New Building

The KWC moved to Manhattan on April 30, 1984 to have closer contact with more overseas wheat buyers who came to Manhattan, the milling and baking capital of the world. Manhattan was home to Kansas State University Grain Science and Industry Department, International Grains Program, American Institute of Baking, USDA Grain Marketing Research Laboratory, and the Wheat Quality Council.

The Kansas Wheat Commission office was moved to the new building in Manhattan on April 30, 1984. The move was made to place the Commission in closer contact with more overseas wheat buyers who came to Manhattan, the milling and baking capital of the world.

The Kansas Wheat Commission celebrated the International Day of Bread on October 5, 1984, with an open house at the new Manhattan office. Governor John Carlin cut a symbolic loaf of bread to stress the importance of wheat to the Kansas economy and to the well being of people around the world.

International Day of Bread

Governor John Carlin proclaimed October 5, 1984 as the Day of Bread in Kansas. The Commission celebrated the International Day of Bread with an open house for more than 230 people at the new Manhattan office. Governor Carlin cut a symbolic loaf of bread to stress the importance of wheat to the Kansas economy and to the well being of people around the world.

Wheat Production and Leading Varieties

Wheat production in the early 1980s was quite variable as 1980 and 1983 proved to be record crops. Diseases take-all root rot and Fusarium head blight (wheat scab) affected the 1982 crop. The Acreage Reduction and Payment in Kind Programs brought abandonment to all-time highs. The decade ended on a sour note as weather variability impacted the development of the crop and the largest abandonment since 1952 was recorded at 28.2%. Leading varieties in the 1980s were 'Newton,' 'Larned,' 'Tam 105,' 'Hawk,' 'Arkan,' 'Eagle,' and 'Scout'/'Scout 66.'

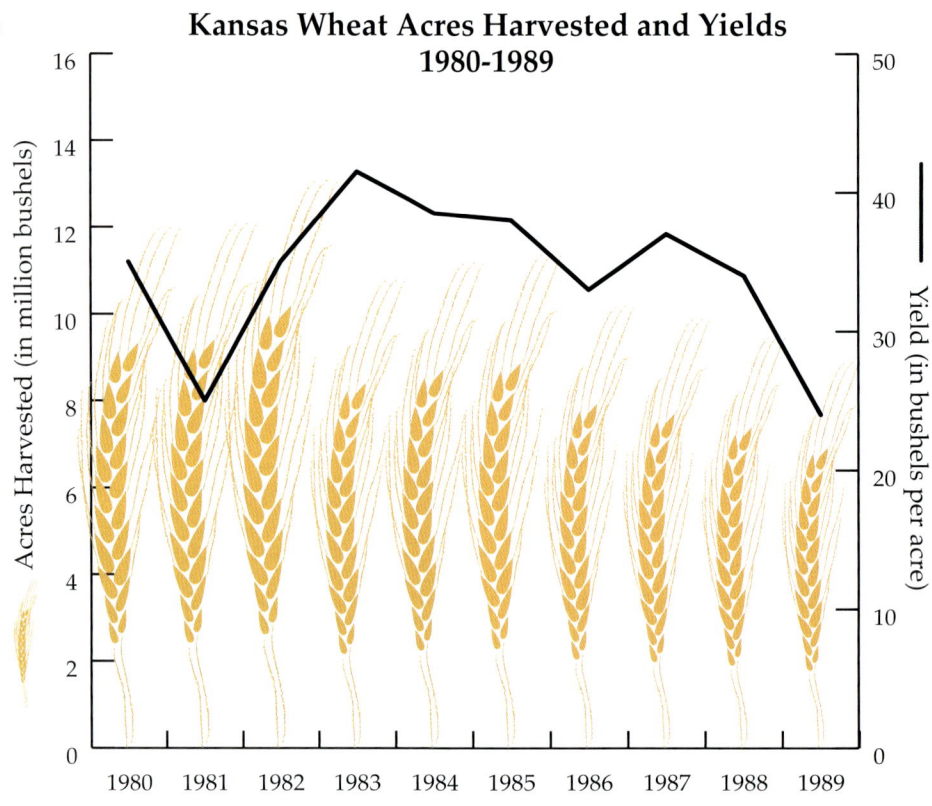

**Kansas Wheat Acres Harvested and Yields
1980-1989**

PORTUGUESE SWEET BREAD

makes 2 loaves, 20 slices each

FROM THE POPULAR "ETHNIC IS NOW" BOOKLET, A COLLABORATIVE PROJECT WITH KSU BAKING SCIENCE DEPARTMENT, NATIONAL ASSOCIATION OF WHEAT GROWERS, AND THE WHEAT FOODS COUNCIL.

ingredients
- 2 packages RED STAR® Active Dry Yeast
- 1 ¼ cups warm water (110-115°F), divided
- ¾ cup granulated sugar
- ⅓ cup nonfat dry milk powder
- 5 ½ - 6 cups bread flour
- 1 teaspoon salt
- 3 beaten eggs
- ½ cup butter
- ¼ cup dried currants (optional)
- 1 egg
- 1 tablespoon water

1 In a large bowl, dissolve yeast in ¼ cup of the water. Sprinkle 1 teaspoon of the sugar on top; let stand 5 minutes.

2 Stir in remaining 1 cup water, sugar, dry milk, and 2 ½ cups of the flour. Beat 2 minutes. Add salt, 3 eggs and butter; blend well. Add remaining flour a little at a time until a soft dough forms.

3 Knead 10 to 12 minutes by hand or with dough hook. Place in greased bowl; turn to coat. Cover, let rise until double. Punch dough down. Divide into two equal pieces. Cover; let rest 10 minutes.

4 Braided Loaf: If desired, knead currants in one half. Cover; let rest 30 minutes. Divide dough into three equal parts; roll into 14-inch ropes. Lay ropes side-by-side on greased baking sheet. Starting in middle, braid. Pinch ends; turn under and pinch to seal.

5 Cover; let rise until double. Using a pastry brush, cover entire surface with egg wash (1 egg and 1 tablespoon water beaten together).

6 Bake in a preheated 350°F oven, 30 to 35 minutes, or until tested done. Loosely cover loaves with aluminum foil the last 10 to 15 minutes to prevent over-browning.

nutrition information *per serving (one slice): 113 cal, 3 g fat, 28 mg chol, 92 mg sodium, 18 g carbo, 0.5 g fiber, 3 g pro, 40 mcg folate.*

PHOTO COURTESY OF THE HOME BAKING ASSOCIATION

KANSAS STATE CROWN BREAD

makes 18 servings

A SIGNATURE BREAD OF KANSAS STATE UNIVERSITY, MANHATTAN, KANSAS. THIS POPULAR RECIPE WAS PRINTED IN THE KANSAS WHEAT COMMISSION'S 25TH ANNIVERSARY RECIPE BOOK IN 1982.

ingredients
- 2 packages RED STAR® Active Dry Yeast
- ½ cup lukewarm water (110-115°F)
- ¾ cup lukewarm milk (95°F)
- 3 tablespoons granulated sugar
- 3 tablespoons vegetable shortening
- 1 ½ teaspoons salt
- 1 beaten egg
- 3 ¼ - 3 ½ cups bread flour
- ¼ cup pecan pieces
- ¾ cup granulated sugar
- 1 teaspoon cinnamon
- 3 - 4 tablespoons butter or margarine, melted
- 5 - 7 whole maraschino cherries
- Whole pecans (optional)

1 In mixing bowl, dissolve yeast in water. Add milk, sugar, shortening, salt, and egg. Stir in 2 cups bread flour and beat 2 minutes. Gradually add enough of the remaining flour to form a soft dough.

2 Knead until smooth and elastic, 10 to 12 minutes. Cover; let rise until double. Punch down dough; cover, let rest 10 minutes.

3 Grease with shortening or coat with nonstick cooking spray the bottom and sides of a tube cake pan. Sprinkle pecan pieces in bottom of pan. Mix together ¾ cup sugar and cinnamon. Divide dough into 18 equal pieces. Form each piece into a uniform roll. Lightly coat each roll with melted butter or margarine and roll in cinnamon-sugar mixture. Arrange twelve rolls on the outside and six rolls in the middle of the pan. Cover; let rise until double.

4 Bake in preheated 350°F oven 40 minutes or until done. Tent top with foil if necessary to prevent over-browning.

5 Let cool in pan 30 minutes before removing. Remove from pan placing upright. Place maraschino cherries on top in the space between rolls and decorate with whole pecan pieces.

nutrition information *per serving (one roll): 191 cal, 6 g fat, 18 mg chol, 204 mg sodium, 30 g carbo, 1 g fiber, 4 g pro, 58 mcg folate.*

WHOLE WHEAT CHOCOLATE SHEET CAKE

makes 24 servings

A WHOLE WHEAT VERSION OF THE TRADITIONAL FAVORITE FIRST PRINTED IN 1988. THIS PHOTO AND RECIPE APPEARED IN THE NATIONAL SCHOOL FOOD SERVICE AND NUTRITION MAGAZINE.

ingredients
- 2 ½ cups whole wheat flour
- 1 cup granulated sugar
- 2 teaspoons ground cinnamon
- ¼ cup baking cocoa
- 1 cup water
- ½ cup vegetable oil
- 1 ½ teaspoons baking soda
- 1 cup low-fat buttermilk
- 2 beaten eggs
- 1 teaspoon vanilla extract

icing (optional)
- ¼ cup baking cocoa
- ½ cup butter or margarine
- ⅓ cup low-fat milk
- 3 cups confectioners' sugar
- ½ cup chopped pecans (optional)

1 Preheat oven to 350°F. Mix flour, sugar, and cinnamon together in large bowl. Bring cocoa, water, and oil to boil. Pour over flour mixture and mix 1 minute, scraping bowl. Dissolve soda in buttermilk, adding to mixture in bowl along with eggs and vanilla. Mix additional 2 minutes.

2 Pour into greased and floured 10 x 15 x 1-inch jelly-roll pan. Bake 20 minutes, or until done.

3 Icing: Bring cocoa, butter, and milk to a boil. Remove from heat and beat in sugar and pecans. Frost cake while warm.

tip: To cut calories, omit icing. Just before serving, sift on confectioners' sugar.

nutrition information: *(one serving without icing): 129 cal, 5 g fat, 18 mg chol, 96 mg sodium, 19 g carbo, 2 g fiber, 3 g pro, 8 mcg folate. (one serving with icing): 215 cal, 9 g fat, 29 mg chol, 98 mg sodium, 32 g carbo, 2 g fiber, 3 g pro, 8 mcg folate.*

PITA BREAD

makes 12, 6-inch pitas

THERE IS NOTHING MORE REWARDING THAN MAKING PITA BREAD. A FAVORITE RECIPE IN THE "ETHNIC IS NOW" RECIPE BOOKLET.

ingredients
- 1 tablespoon RED STAR® Active Dry Yeast
- 1 cup lukewarm water (110-115°F)
- 1 tablespoon olive oil
- 1 cup whole wheat flour
- 1 teaspoon salt
- 2 cups all-purpose flour
- Cornmeal
- Wheat Germ

nutrition information *per serving (one pita): 123 cal, 2 g fat, 0 mg chol, 196 mg sodium, 24 g carbo, 2 g fiber, 4 g pro, 60 mcg folate.*

1 In large mixing bowl, dissolve yeast in ½ cup water. Stir in remaining ½ cup water mixed with oil. Vigorously stir in whole wheat flour, salt, and all-purpose flour to form a soft dough.

2 Turn dough onto floured surface. Knead dough about 10 minutes or until elastic, adding only enough flour to manage the dough. Place dough in greased bowl. Cover, let rise at room temperature until double, about 1 ½ hours.

3 Punch down dough and roll into long cylinder on lightly floured surface. Cut into 12 equal pieces.

4 Form each piece into a smooth ball. Cover, let rest 5 minutes.

5 With rolling pin, roll each ball out on lightly floured surface, flipping circles and using just enough flour to keep it from sticking. Make rounds as even and flat as possible, about 6 inches in diameter and ¼-inch thick.

6 Sprinkle cornmeal or wheat germ on baking sheet to prevent sticking. Place 3 to 4 pitas on each baking sheet. Move oven shelf to lowest position and allow pitas to rest while oven preheats to 500°F.

7 Work quickly so heat is not lost placing baking sheet on bottom oven rack. Bake 1 ½ minutes without peeking. Dough will begin to puff up. Continue baking 1 to 2 more minutes. (Little browning will occur since there is no sugar in the recipe.)

8 Remove from oven and cool on rack. Cut each pita in half. Eat fresh with a variety of fillings, or package and store in refrigerator or freezer.

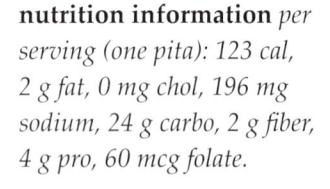

PIONEER BREAD

makes 2 loaves, 20 slices each

THIS POPULAR RECIPE WAS PRINTED IN THE KANSAS WHEAT COMMISSION'S 30TH ANNIVERSARY RECIPE BOOK IN 1987. IT WAS ALSO SELECTED TO APPEAR IN THE 2005 KANSAS GETAWAY GUIDE.

ingredients
- ½ cup yellow cornmeal
- ¼ cup brown sugar
- 2 teaspoons salt
- ¼ cup vegetable oil
- 1 cup boiling water
- 2 packages RED STAR® Active Dry Yeast
- ½ cup lukewarm water (110-115°F)
- 1 cup cool water
- 1 cup whole wheat flour
- ½ cup rye flour
- 4 - 4 ½ cups bread flour
- Yellow cornmeal

1 In a large mixing bowl, combine cornmeal, brown sugar, salt, and oil with 1 cup boiling water. Dissolve yeast in ½ cup lukewarm water. Mix cool water into cornmeal mixture; stir in yeast. Beat in whole wheat and rye flours, mixing well. Gradually stir in enough bread flour to make a moderately soft dough.

2 Turn dough onto lightly floured surface and knead until smooth and elastic, using only enough additional flour to handle the dough. Knead dough 10 to 12 minutes.

3 Place dough in a greased bowl, turning to grease top. Cover; let rise in warm (90°F) place until double, about 1 hour. Punch dough down and divide into 2 pieces.

4 Shape each piece into round loaves. Place in greased 9-inch pie plates or cookie sheets that have been sprinkled with additional cornmeal. Cover; let rise until almost double.

5 With a very sharp knife, gently make 4 slashes in the top of each loaf in a tick-tack-toe pattern; only about ⅛ to ¼-inch deep.

6 Bake in preheated 375°F oven 30 to 35 minutes, or until golden and loaf sounds hollow when tapped. Remove from pans after 5 minutes and cool on rack.

nutrition information *per serving (one slice): 88 cal, 2 g fat, 0 mg chol, 118 mg sodium, 16 g carbo, 1 g fiber, 2 g pro, 31 mcg folate.*

Bread machine recipes for Pioneer Bread are available at www.kswheat.com.

MICROWAVE SPICE CAKE

makes 20 servings

THE MICROWAVE OVEN WAS A POPULAR METHOD OF COOKING IN 1989 WHEN KWC HOME ECONOMISTS DEVELOPED THIS AROMATIC TREAT.

ingredients
- 1 ½ cups boiling water
- 1 cup quick-cooking oats, dry
- ½ cup margarine or butter
- 1 cup brown sugar
- ½ cup granulated sugar
- 2 beaten eggs
- 1 ½ teaspoons vanilla extract
- 1 ⅓ cups all-purpose flour
- 2 teaspoons ground cinnamon
- 1 teaspoon baking soda
- ½ teaspoon salt
- ½ teaspoon ground nutmeg
- Whipped topping (optional)

1 Combine boiling water and oats; set aside. Cream margarine or butter, brown sugar, and granulated sugar together until light and fluffy. Add eggs, beating well. Blend in vanilla and oat mixture.

2 In small bowl, sift together dry ingredients; add to creamed mixture. Blend at low speed until moistened, then beat at medium speed 2 minutes.

3 Pour into ungreased 11 x 7 x 2-inch microwave-safe baking dish. Microwave uncovered on MEDIUM (50 percent power) 8 minutes. If microwave shelf does not rotate, give dish a half-turn every 3 to 4 minutes. Microwave on HIGH 7 to 8 minutes or until toothpick inserted in center comes out clean. (Microwave ovens vary in power; therefore, cooking time may vary.)

4 Let stand on a flat, heat resistant surface to insure that the bottom will be completely baked. To serve, top each piece with a dollop of whipped topping.

nutrition information *per serving: 150 cal, 5 g fat, 21 mg chol, 177 mg sodium, 25 g carbo, 1 g fiber, 2 g pro, 15 mcg folate.*

FOOD PROCESSOR QUICK BURGER BUNS **makes** 8 buns

ONE OF THE RECIPES FEATURED IN THE POPULAR EDUCATIONAL PROGRAM, "FRESH BREAD THE PROCESSOR WAY," PRESENTED IN 1988 BY THE KANSAS WHEAT COMMISSION.

ingredients
- 3 cups all-purpose flour (may be part whole wheat)
- 2 tablespoons granulated sugar
- 1 teaspoon salt
- 1 package RED STAR® QUICK-RISE™ yeast
- 3 tablespoons margarine, cut into pieces
- 1 cup warm water (90°F)

Log on to www.kswheat.com for additional food processor recipes including Rye Buns and Pita.

1 In food processor bowl with dough blade in place, combine for 10 seconds the flour, sugar, salt, yeast, and margarine.

2 Begin processing on HIGH speed, pouring 1 cup warm water steadily through tube. When dough forms a ball, stop adding water. Entire 1 cup may not be needed. Process an additional 60 seconds to knead the dough.

3 Take dough out, knead a few strokes to form a smooth ball, cover and let rest 15 minutes. Grease cookie sheet. Divide dough into 8 equal pieces and shape into buns. Let rest 5 minutes and flatten slightly. Cover; let rise in a warm place (90°F) until double.

4 Bake in preheated 400°F oven 12 to 15 minutes.

nutrition information *per serving (one bun): 219 cal, 4 g fat, 0 mg chol, 334 mg sodium, 39 carbo, 1 g fiber, 5 g pro, 93 mcg folate.*

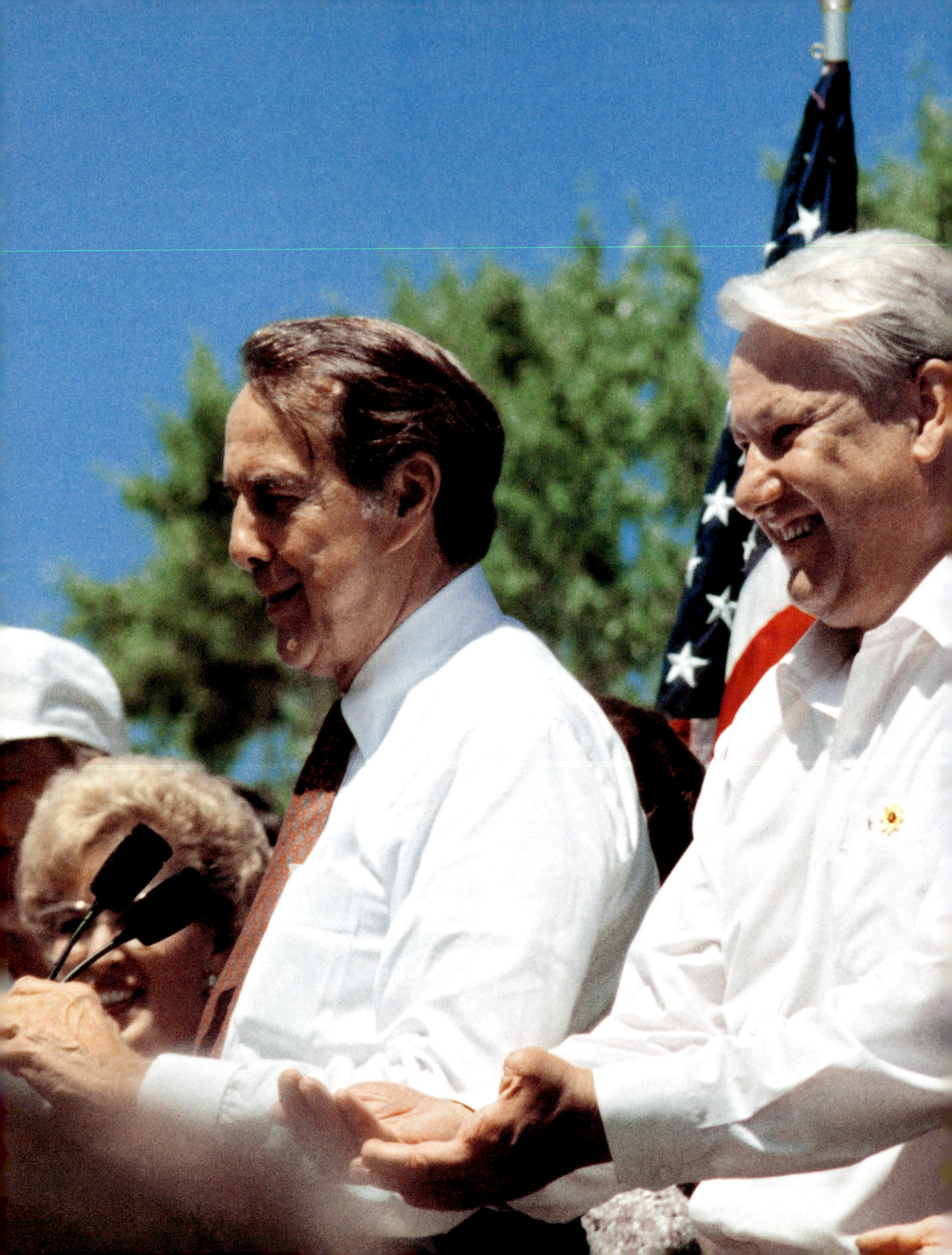

1990s

GOVERNMENT BUYERS GIVE WAY TO PRIVATIZATION

"Foreign government buyers are phasing out and private traders are now doing the purchasing. As a result, new buyers need education, but are also becoming more quality-minded."
— Jack Staatz, KWC Chairman, 1993

The drought-reduced crop of 1989 resulted in a huge reduction in Kansas farm income as well as reduced collections to the Wheat Commission. Commissioners reduced the fiscal year 1990 budget by a third, nearly $600,000, and as a result, the newsletter and other educational projects were temporarily suspended. The Commission became a partial member of U.S. Wheat Associates for the first time ever and postponed continuance of several research projects for a year. This trend was reversed for the wheat harvest of 1990, which was a record 472 million bushel harvest.

The summer of 1993 will be remembered for extensive rainfall and flooding that caught the state in mid-harvest. Early wheat was of excellent quality, but wheat of later harvest saw reduced test weights, protein levels and quality.

When Russian President Boris Yeltsin visited the farm of Greg and Sandy Rau in June 1992, representatives of Kansas agriculture, including Kansas Senator Bob Dole and the Kansas Wheat Commission, provided a barbecue for the delegation. The Kansas Wheat Commission provided whole wheat buns made at the Friendship House in Wamego.

The late 1990s saw several years of yields per acre in the high 40s with a record state average yield of 49 bushels per acre in 1998. The wheat crop of 1997 came out of dormancy early and a late freeze hit it hard although ideal weather allowed it to develop into over 500 million bushels. Weather continued to afflict wheat production as hail and harvest rains arrived at inopportune times.

U.S. Wheat Associates

U.S. Wheat Associates continued as one of the KWC's main priorities through the 1990s. Seventeen state wheat commissions contributed to its market development work with more than 300 projects in 140 countries. These activities focused on providing information to international customers to increase their knowledge of how to buy wheat in the U.S. marketing system and how that wheat can be used for the intended product. The Foreign Agricultural Service matched producer investment in USW by nearly $3 for every $1 producers invested. Joe Berry, Lenora, Kan., served as Chairman of the board in 1996-97.

The Japanese Food Safety Team was one of many trade teams that traveled to Kansas to learn about U.S. wheat and the U.S. wheat marketing system.

Top Markets for U.S. Wheat 1990s

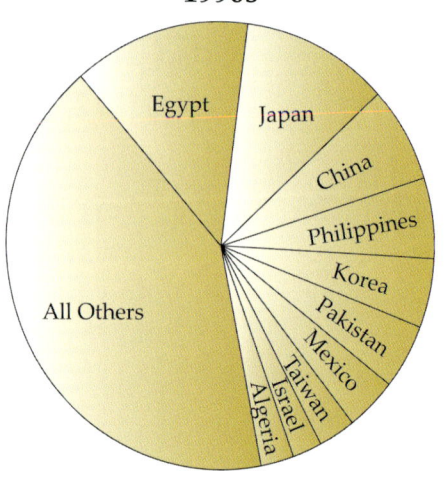

When the Karnal bunt situation panicked many international buyers in 1996, U.S. Wheat Associates distributed to its international offices survey data from the Kansas Department of Agriculture that showed no Karnal bunt existed in Kansas and other plains states.

Vietnam saw its first delivery of commercially purchased U.S. wheat since the United States lifted its 19-year trade embargo in 1994. Even before the trade ban was lifted by the United States, USW was working to develop a market for U.S. wheat in Vietnam.

In March 1998, USW began breakthrough contacts with the embargoed market of Cuba. KWC and USW donated flour to a relief organization in Cuba.

Trade Teams

Trade teams representing the top wheat-buying nations brought an average of nearly 250 trade team visitors and short course participants to

Kansas each year. They toured KSU's Department of Grain Science and International Grains Program facilities, the American Institute of Baking, the Federal Grain Inspection Service, the Kansas City Board of Trade, farms, grain elevators, mills, bakeries, and grain export handling facilities.

Trade teams from nearly 50 different countries visited Kansas in the 1990s.

Notably in 1992, Nigeria lifted its ban of wheat imports, which allowed USW to build the relationships with wheat buyers from this region. Another notable event in 1992 included Russian President Boris Yeltsin's visit to a Wichita farm for a Kansas barbecue.

International Grains Program

Kenyan millers attended a wheat procurement short course at the International Grains Program. The U.S. wheat market share in Kenya grew from five percent to more than 70 percent. Two millers who attended the course said, "If we had not attended the short course in Kansas, we would not have even attempted to buy U.S. wheat on our own. With the training we received, we were able to work through all the details and buy a 25,000 metric ton shipload of Hard Red Winter wheat." They later purchased more wheat.

World Trade

January 1, 1994 saw the North American Free Trade Agreement (NAFTA) implemented and the U.S. wheat industry split over imports of Canadian wheat into the United States. Processors and some of the trade were urging increased imports while producers cried foul. Eventually, Canadian wheat imports into the United States were capped at 1.5 million tons per year. The KWC secured reports under the Freedom

U.S. Wheat Exports 1990-2000

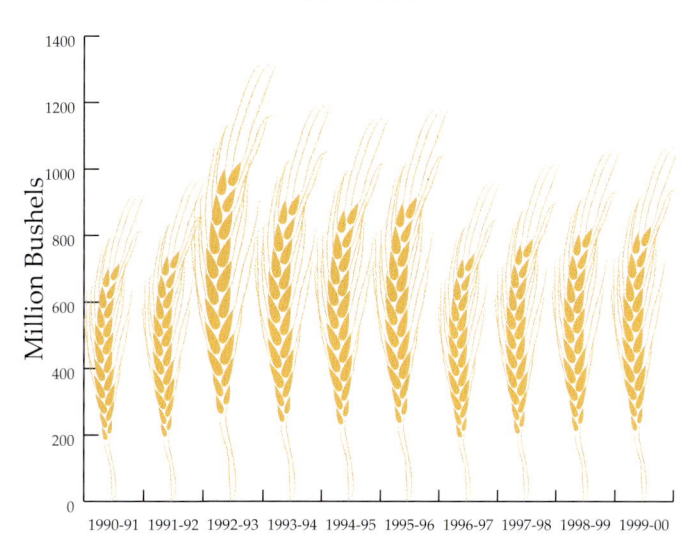

Agriculture Secretary Dan Glickman met with Egyptian wheat buyers and processors in Cairo, Egypt. The KWC co-sponsored the American Quality Wheat logo program, which appeared on products containing at least 80 percent U.S. wheat. Packages featuring the logo could be seen in nearly every grocery store in Egypt.

of Information Act that helped lead to the requirement of end-use certificates on any imported Canadian wheat.

Additionally, the General Agreement on Tariffs and Trade (GATT) came under the World Trade Organization, and more countries privatized importing functions.

Wheat Foods Council

KWC Nutritionist Sharon Davis served as the Wheat Foods Council's interim director in 1990. The Council exhibited and distributed educational and promotional information at a number of national conferences. In January 1991, Judi Adams, M.S., R.D., became the Council's first director. Adams assumed her duties at the Council's newly established national office in Denver, Colorado.

The WFC made significant progress in realizing funding from the entire wheat foods industry in the early 1990s. Previously funded only by state wheat producer organizations, in 1992, additional funding from the Millers' National Federation, the Independent Bakers, producer groups, the National Pasta Association, and the American Bakers Association produced a larger budget. In 1996-97, KWC Communications Specialist Susan L'Ecuyer served as Chairman of the Wheat Foods Council.

New Dietary Guidelines

The Food Guide Pyramid, which replaced the Basic Four Food Wheel, illustrated the USDA's 1990 Dietary Guidelines and their recommendations that Americans eat six to 11 servings of breads, cereals, rice, and pasta each day. Because Americans averaged only four servings of grain products daily, the guidelines could have a dramatic effect on the domestic market. If Americans achieved even the minimum six servings, producers would sell an additional 300 million bushels of wheat. That's almost one entire Kansas wheat crop, or an extra $1 billion.

WFC Gallup Poll

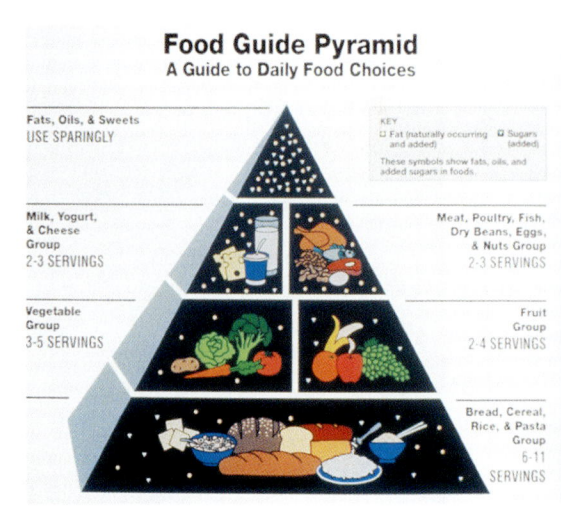

To help focus and direct its educational program, the WFC contracted with the Gallup Organization to conduct a poll, testing consumer knowledge of nutrition and wheat foods. The 1991 poll revealed that 49 percent of Americans did not know white bread was a wheat food, and another 48 percent thought that oatmeal was a wheat food. The poll also revealed that two-thirds of Americans were unaware of the new dietary guidelines. As a result, only 15 percent of the respondents said they needed to eat more grain foods. The task appeared to be a basic one: teaching the public what grain foods are, why they are important to a balanced diet, and what constitutes a serving.

Subsequently a 1993 Gallup poll revealed that 93 percent of all Americans weren't getting enough bread, and 50 percent of those surveyed mistakenly believed bread is fattening. The 1995 poll found that familiarity with the Food Guide Pyramid had doubled, from 27 percent in 1993 to 56 percent in 1995.

You're not getting enough.

U.S. Wheat Flour Disappearance, 1964-2005

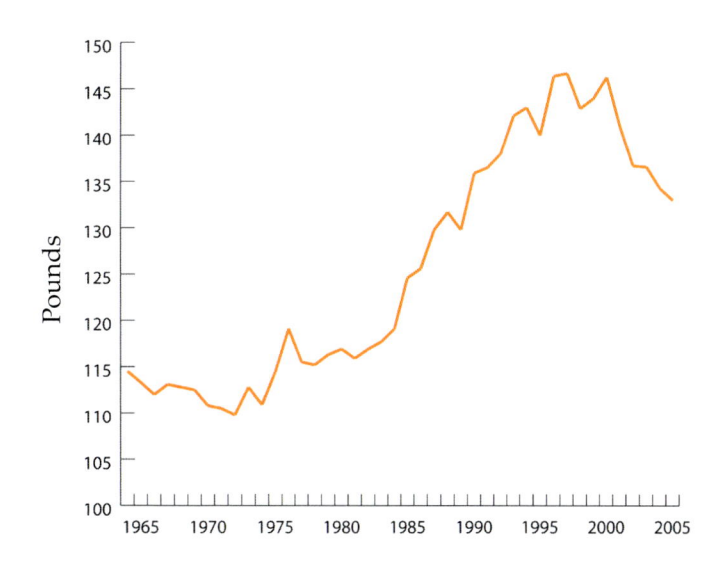

Per Capita Consumption Increasing

In 1993-94, *Milling & Baking News* credited the Wheat Foods Council, for its work to increase consumption.

"Efforts on the part of grain-based foods to bolster consumption center on the activities of the Wheat Foods Council, where wheat farmers, millers, bakers, and other wheat foods sectors come together in a unified effort to spur consumption," the magazine said. "This program may claim a measure of credit for spreading the word about what it takes to increase consumption amidst growing recognition of the importance of wheat foods to a healthy and value-driven diet."

In the 1990s, tortillas made from wheat flour were the fastest growing bread product in the world and the fastest growing bakery product in the United States.

KWC Home Economist Cindy Falk presented many programs on bread machines during the Kansas State Fair and at other exhibits.

School Meals to Comply with Dietary Guidelines

WFC met with USDA on adapting school menus, as wheat consumed in school meal programs was about 16.5 million bushels. In 1994, President Bill Clinton signed the "Better Nutrition and Health for Children Act," which required that by the 1996-97 school year, the country's 95,000 school meal programs must meet the federal nutrition guidelines reflected in the Food Guide Pyramid. During this time, almost 25 million children ate lunch and five million children ate breakfast at school each day. Under the new program, children would be well on their way to getting a daily average of six to 11 servings of grain-based foods that would increase wheat usage to 30 million bushels.

Fastest Growing Wheat Food: Tortillas

In the 1990s, tortillas made from wheat flour were the fastest growing bread product in the world and the fastest growing bakery product in the United States. In the U.S., there were 70 billion tortillas consumed in 1997, and 45 billion of them were flour tortillas. By partnering with the Tortilla Industry Association, the Wheat Foods Council developed a nutrition information project targeted at Hispanic consumers in the U.S., as well as consumers in Central and South America.

Bread Machines

The 1990s brought on the introduction of bread machines. Tips for bread machine use and recipes for the machines were introduced into the 1992 recipe book. Manufacturers welcomed the promotion by donating their latest models to the Commission.

In 1993, houseware-retailing executives ranked bread machines as the best-selling small appliance during the holiday shopping season. According to industry reports, the overall home baking market grew three to five percent annually.

By 1994, bread machines were making a difference in the marketing of wheat. *The Washington Post*

1990s Wheat Awards

Wheat Man of the Year

1990	Dr. Joe Martin	Hays
1991	Del Wiedeman	WaKeeney
1992	Dr. C.W. Deyoe	Manhattan
1993	Dr. Bill Tierney	Manhattan
1994	Lowell Buchet	Manhattan
1995	*Outstanding Service Award*	
	Milton & Doris Giedinghagen	Stafford
	Wheat Couple of the Year	
	Bob & Deloris Paris	Dighton
	Marketing Award	
	Steven Graham	Manhattan
1996	Merrill Nielsen	Sylvan Grove
1998	Dr. Rollie Sears	Manhattan
	Service to Agriculture Award	
	Todd Fuller	Dodge City
	Excellence in Extension Award	
	Dr. Tim Herrman	Manhattan

Wheat Woman of the Year

1990	Charlene Patton	Topeka
1991	Norma Deyoe	Ulysses
1993	Jo Keesling	Chase
1994	Cindy Falk	Onaga
1995	Melanie Eddy	Syracuse
1996	Susan L'Ecuyer	Manhattan
1998	Julie Owens	Manhattan

reported that sale of flour for home baking had increased by 96 percent in the past year alone. Industry estimates reported that almost 5 million bread machines had been sold.

Baking Contest Launched

In 1990, for the first time, the Kansas Wheat Commission, Kansas Wheathearts, Kansas Association of Wheat Growers, and Kansas State Board of Agriculture invited men and women, ages 14 and older, who bake at home to share their best wheat bread recipes in the Celebrate Kansas Wheat baking competition. Regional judging was held in the five KSU Extension regions, where the top three winners received prizes. The first place winners also received travel expenses and overnight accommodations in Manhattan for the state competition. First place winner at the state competition received $500 and the four runners-up received $100 each. The winner was Viola Unruh, from Montezuma, who used the whole wheat bread recipe she had baked weekly for 35 years.

In 1991, the contest was renamed the Kansas Festival of Breads.

In 1994, Steve Korthanke, Robinson, became the first male winner of the contest.

Two sisters, Joyce Taylor, Enterprise, and Ila Beemer, Abilene, won the top prizes in the 1996 Kansas Festival of Breads.

Kansas First Lady Patti Hayden was one of the judges at the first Kansas Wheat Commission baking contest in 1990.

Grains: Harvest the Energy

A special project of the Wheat Foods Council focused on retail sales and education of consumers. A new logo was designed in 1998 to allow shoppers to instantly identify grain foods. Sales of grain products carrying the logo increased by 20 percent over grain products not carrying the logo. A study by the WFC determined that use of the logo, with modest education, increased the grain food category's market share by 7.7 percent.

Spokespersons

In the 1990s, nearly 20 spokespersons presented programs at elementary school classes, high school home economics classes, public library classes, media events, farm tours, the American Royal, county fairs, and the Kansas State Fair.

Their backgrounds were as varied as their audiences, but the "Speak for Wheat" spokespersons shared two things in common: they were educators and they were devoted to the promotion of Kansas wheat. Their common mission was to help increase the demand for wheat and wheat foods at the state level.

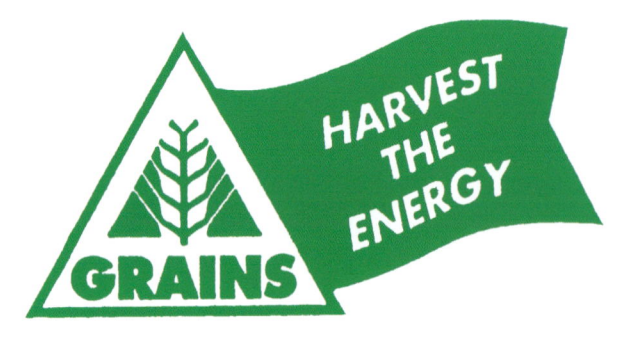

Kansas LEAN

The leading cause of death for Kansans in 1992 was heart disease, and one of the most important risk factors associated with that disease is a diet high in fat. To help counter that statistic, the KWC cooperated with Kansas LEAN (Low-fat Eating for Americans Now).

"The overall goal of Kansas LEAN is to reduce the amount of fat Kansans eat," said Sharon Davis, KWC nutritionist. "It makes sense that low-fat wheat foods and helping consumers balance their high-fat food choices fit into this program." To accomplish that goal, the Wheat Commission developed "Check Your Six," a self-evaluation card that allowed individuals to check the number of servings of grain products they ate each day and defined those servings.

Kansas Secretary of Agriculture Sam Brownback and Governor Mike Hayden stopped by the Kansas Wheat Commission Hard White wheat booth during Ag Day at the Capitol. They are pictured with Lois Schlickau, Haven, Kan., and KWC's Cindy Falk and Sharon Davis.

As chair of the Kansas LEAN Food Professionals Task Force in 1991-92, KWC led this coalition of food professionals in outlining goals to help Kansans reduce the fat in their diets.

For National Nutrition Month in March 1993, KWC Nutritionist Sharon Davis and Home Economist Cindy Falk helped Kansas LEAN teach state legislators how to "budget" — budget fat, that is. At the Fat Bucks Buffet, legislators learned about the importance of managing fat intake in the diet and how key wheat foods are to a low-fat diet.

American Royal

More than 30,000 Kansas citizens, including an estimated 20,000 school children, learned about wheat and wheat products when they visited the World of Agriculture exhibit at the November 1994 American Royal. This was the first of many years the Commission sponsored an exhibit at the event.

New Uses

The KWC funded public research into industrial uses of wheat, including ethanol, since 1969. Through the 1990s this research explored new food and industrial uses of wheat through Kansas State University and led to wheat flour, starch, and gluten utilization in new products.

The KWC worked with Midwest Grain Products in Atchison to develop and commercialize starch-based adhesives, coatings, and films for use in laminated or corrugated boards and packaging materials. In 1995, KWC contracted with MGP and KSU and helped to license and advance biodegradable plastics from starch. In addition, the KWC helped organize a national "Wheat Utilization Summit" exploring new industrial uses for wheat.

Variety Development

During the 1990s two-thirds of the wheat seed planted in Kansas was developed or maintained by Kansas State University. Kansas wheat producers supported about 40% of the KSU wheat breeding program.

In 1994, Kansas State University released 'Jagger,' a Hard Red Winter wheat variety developed for statewide planting. During statewide performance tests, 'Jagger' averaged 52 bushels per acre. It is resistant to stem rust, leaf rust, soil borne mosaic, spindle streak mosaic, tan spot and speckled leaf blotch. That same year, KSU released 'Ike,' a Hard Red Winter wheat variety developed specifically for producers in Western Kansas.

In 1996, the Kansas Agricultural Experiment Station and USDA's Agricultural Research Service cooperatively released '2137,' a Hard Red Winter wheat variety

KSU wheat breeder Rollie Sears developed varieties such as 'Jagger,' which was released in 1994. 'Jagger' became popular across the state because of its high yield, disease resistance, and quality.

Kansas Gold Perspective
by David Frey
KWC staff, 1978-2005
KWC Administrator, 1996-2005

The most impressive fact about the Kansas Wheat Commission is its pivotal support for wheat breeding at Kansas State University. KSU wheat breeding has meant that literally hundreds of millions of people worldwide have been fed with high quality wheat products as the result of investment from Kansas wheat farmers and smart work by the KSU College of Agriculture.

I have fond memories of the years 1978 to 2005 when it was my privilege to work for Kansas farmers. Those years provided opportunities to be involved, on behalf of Kansas wheat producers, with work that makes a real difference in the world.

I write this from Kabul, Afghanistan, a country that became important to the Kansas wheat industry when the Soviets invaded it during Christmastime 1979. You know the story...the U.S. retaliated with an embargo on the Soviet Union, which was essentially an embargo on the sale of 17 million metric tons of U.S. Hard Red Winter wheat (625 million bushels). That wheat had been counted as "sold" but was now forbidden to move to the customer. The event threw U.S. wheat prices into a long term slump and forced U.S. Hard Red Winter wheat to find other world customers. The embargo resulted in direct Soviet demand for Argentinean wheat and thereby created a new Western Hemisphere wheat export competitor.

In those days, the Kansas Wheat Commission began funding the International Grains Program on the KSU campus in addition to strong continuous support of overseas market development through Great Plains Wheat, Inc. and, later, U.S. Wheat Associates, which draw matching funds from USDA's Foreign Agricultural Service.

In an effort to provide alternative wheat choices to customers and alternative crop choices for farmers, the Kansas Wheat Commission initiated support for a new KSU program, specifically for Hard White wheat. Hard White wheat became the first new class of wheat to be grown and marketed in the USA since wheat standards were established.

KSU developed wheat varieties that will long live in the wheat lines of the future. The names of KSU releases are a litany of high quality and high yielding varieties including 'Eagle,' 'Newton,' 'Arkan,' 'Karl,' and 'Jagger' by Kansas breeders Livers, Heyne, Martin and Sears. Wheat of the future will also be affected by the work of KSU's Bikram Gill and Allan Fritz, while the Kansas Wheat Commission has supported all of those programs.

From the hunger and want of Afghanistan, it is easy to see how life giving, real and vital has been the collective investment and work of Kansas wheat producers. Congratulations to Kansas Wheat for fifty years of service to producers, the state of Kansas and anyone who relies on wheat (the most consumed food grain in the world) for their daily bread.

developed for statewide planting. 'Jagger' and '2137' were the leading varieties planted in Kansas fields from 1998 to 2003 and led an increase in statewide average yields.

Other leading varieties in the 1990s were 'Tam 107,' 'Karl'/'Karl92,' '2163' and 'Larned.'

Hard White Wheat

Since the early 1980s KWC had invested in Hard White wheat breeding, and in 1992, KSU released the first-ever U.S. public variety of Hard White wheat, 'Arlin.'

This variety was followed by 'Betty' and 'Heyne,' which were released in 1998, and 'Trego' in 1999.

In addition to funding the research and development of Hard White wheat, KWC helped the American White Wheat Producers Association in its efforts to market this developing class. USDA's newest class of wheat was being recognized for its excellent flour. Hardness testing and grading research offered continued opportunity for producer funding, as did continued research into the grading of Hard White wheat.

Pricing System

The Kansas Wheat Commission worked with Kansas State University to formulate a new and better wheat pricing system. Identity-preserved production and marketing of wheat had the potential to deliver a better price. Unfortunately, the two groups were unable to discover anything truly new and better.

Additionally, KWC worked with a private agricultural consulting firm to research a new pricing system. This system would develop an industry-wide wheat quality program to encourage all segments of the industry to produce quality products demanded by users, domestic and international.

Short Crops Threaten Research, Market Development

1996 was a momentous year in the wheat business. Producers had a brief opportunity to sell $7 wheat and the value of U.S. agricultural exports reached a record high. The U.S. market share of world wheat trade attained the highest level of the 1990s.

Meanwhile, the Kansas wheat crop was officially declared a disaster. Facing two short crops in a row, the Commissioners wrestled with the question of whether to maintain support of wheat research and market development efforts. After surveying producers and holding statewide meetings, the Commission voted to use the authority given it by the 1988 legislature and raise the mill levy to one cent per bushel.

In 1992, KSU released the first-ever U.S. public variety of Hard White wheat, 'Arlin.' This variety was followed by 'Betty' and 'Heyne,' which were released in 1998, and 'Trego' in 1999.

KWC Goes Online

In 1997, the Kansas Wheat Commission entered the information age and started spreading the word about the quality of the state's largest wheat crop ever around the world via the worldwide web and satellite television. At www.kswheat.com, producers, end-users, and others could retrieve information about Kansas wheat 24 hours a day. The Commission and KSU also teamed up to present the "Kansas Wheat Update," a bi-monthly broadcast via satellite on Channel Earth — a farm satellite programming service operated out of Chicago.

Personnel

In 1996, Steven Graham left the Commission to work for Kansas State University. David Frey, a staff member since 1978, was promoted to Administrator. KWC Nutritionist Sharon Patterson Davis left the Commission in 1993 after nine years. Cynthia Falk was hired to replace Davis. Falk had previous experience with the Commission as a spokesperson, part-time Home Economist, resident expert on bread machines, and coordinator of the Kansas Festival of Breads baking contest.

The KWC said goodbye to Susan L'Ecuyer, Communications Specialist for the KWC, Past Chairman of the Wheat Foods Council, and Wheat Woman of the Year for 1996.

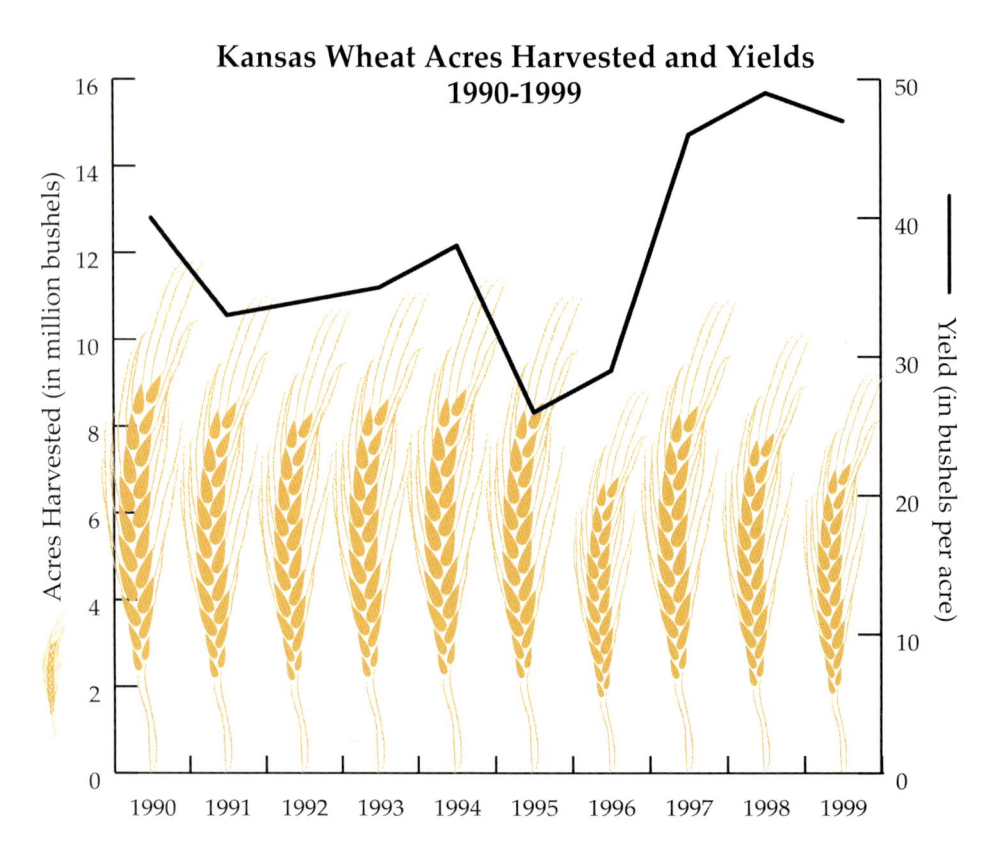

Kansas Wheat Acres Harvested and Yields 1990-1999

VIOLA'S WHEAT BREAD

makes 4 loaves, 16 slices each

VIOLA UNRUH, MONTEZUMA, KANSAS RECEIVED THE CHAMPION PRIZE IN THE FIRST KANSAS FESTIVAL OF BREADS BAKING CONTEST HELD IN 1990. IN ADDITION, VIOLA AND HER RECIPE WERE FEATURED IN AN INTERNATIONAL PUBLICATION, *THE BREAD BOOK*, BY LINDA COLLISTER AND ANTHONY BLAKE.

ingredients
- 6 ½ - 7 cups bread flour
- 2 packages RED STAR® Active Dry Yeast
- ½ cup lukewarm water (110-115°F)
- 2 tablespoons granulated sugar
- 3 cups hot water (120-130°F)
- ⅓ cup brown sugar
- 1 tablespoon salt
- ⅓ cup vegetable shortening
- 3 tablespoons vital wheat gluten
- 2 cups whole wheat flour
- 1 beaten egg

1 Stir and spoon flour into a dry, standard measuring cup. Level off with straight-edged knife.

2 Dissolve yeast in water with granulated sugar. Combine hot water, brown sugar, salt, shortening, vital wheat gluten, and whole wheat flour; mix 2 minutes. Stir in yeast and egg; beat well. Stir in 2 cups bread flour, mix well. Cover, let rest 10 minutes.

3 Stir in enough remaining bread flour to make a moderately soft dough. Knead on a lightly floured surface till smooth and satiny, 10 to 12 minutes.

4 Place in lightly greased bowl, turning to grease surface. Cover, let rise in warm (80°F) place until double. Punch down. Divide in fourths, shape each into a smooth ball. Cover; let rest 10 minutes. Shape into loaves; place in greased 8 ½ x 4 ½ x 2 ½-inch pans.

5 Cover, let rise in warm (90°F) place until double.

6 Bake in preheated 400°F oven 10 minutes; reduce heat to 350°F, bake 25 minutes. Remove from pans; cool on racks.

nutrition information *per serving (one slice): 81 cal, 1 g fat, 3 mg chol, 111 mg sodium, 14 g carbo, 1 g fiber, 2 g pro, 29 mcg folate.*

QUICK SOFT PRETZELS

makes 24 pretzels

A POPULAR HANDS-ON ACTIVITY WITH CHILDREN'S GROUPS IN THE KWC TEST KITCHEN. THE RECIPE SUGGESTS THE FORM, BUT THE BAKER MUST DO THE SHAPING TO CREATE THE PARTICULAR WORK OF ART.

ingredients
- 1 ½ cups lukewarm water (110-115°F)
- 2 packages RED STAR® Active Dry Yeast
- ¼ cup granulated sugar
- 1 ¾ teaspoons salt
- ½ cup vegetable oil
- 5 - 5 ¼ cups all-purpose or bread flour
- 1 egg white
- 1 tablespoon cold water
- Sesame or poppy seeds (optional)

1 Measure water into large bowl. Sprinkle in yeast; stir until dissolved. Add sugar, salt, oil, and 4 cups flour; beat until smooth. Gradually add enough remaining flour to make a soft dough.

2 Knead dough 8 to 10 minutes. Cover dough; let rest 30 minutes. Divide dough into 24 pieces; cover, let rest 5 minutes. Roll each into a uniform 18-inch rope. Shape into a pretzel by making a circle, bringing the ends together, twisting once and then pressing ends onto the bottom curve of the circle.

3 Place on greased or parchment-lined baking sheets. Beat together egg white and cold water; brush pretzels with mixture. If desired, sprinkle on seeds.

4 Bake in preheated 425°F oven 12 to 15 minutes, or until golden. Remove pretzels from baking sheets; cool on wire rack.

nutrition information per serving (one pretzel): 146 cal, 5 g fat, 0 mg chol, 176 mg sodium, 22 g carbo, 1 g fiber, 3 g pro, 54 mcg folate.

SWEET POTATO OR PUMPKIN ROLLS

makes 24 rolls

A GORGEOUS COLORED ROLL THAT IS PERFECT FOR HOLIDAY MEALS.

ingredients
- 1 cup cooked and mashed sweet potatoes or pumpkin
- 3 tablespoons margarine or butter
- 1 package RED STAR® Active Dry Yeast
- 1 ¼ cups lukewarm water (110-115°F)
- 1 egg
- 1 teaspoon salt
- 3 tablespoons granulated sugar
- 5 ¼ - 5 ½ cups bread flour

1 In large mixing bowl, blend lukewarm (110°F) sweet potatoes or pumpkin together with margarine.

2 Dissolve yeast in water; stir into potatoes or pumpkin. Add egg, salt, and sugar; blend. Gradually add 4 cups flour. Stir in enough remaining flour to make a soft, slightly sticky dough.

3 Knead until smooth and elastic, 10 to 12 minutes, being careful not to add extra flour. (The dough will be sticky.) Place dough in a greased bowl; turn to grease top.* Cover; let rise in warm place until double.

4 Punch down dough; cover and let rest 10 minutes. Shape into desired shapes. Cover; let rise in warm place until double.

5 Bake in preheated 400°F oven 15 to 16 minutes, or until golden.

***note**: Dough may be covered and refrigerated at this time for later baking. Punch down whenever double in size. Use within 2 days. To use, keep covered and let dough reach room temperature. Proceed with directions as stated.*

nutrition information *per serving (one roll): 137 cal, 2 g fat, 9 mg chol, 119 mg sodium, 25 g carbo, 1 g fiber, 4 g pro, 55 mcg folate.*

100% WHOLE WHEAT BREAD

makes 2 loaves, 18 slices each

A WONDERFUL BREAD RECIPE USING ALL WHOLE WHEAT FLOUR. A FAVORITE BREAD ENJOYED BY MANY KWC AUDIENCES.

ingredients

- 1 cup lukewarm milk (110-115°F)
- 2 packages RED STAR® Active Dry Yeast
- 1 cup lukewarm water (110-115°F)
- ⅓ cup honey
- 2 beaten eggs
- 5 ¼ - 5 ½ cups whole wheat flour
- 2 tablespoons vital wheat gluten (optional)
- 2 teaspoons salt
- ¼ cup vegetable shortening

nutrition information *per serving (one slice): 90 cal, 2 g fat, 12 mg chol, 138 mg sodium, 16 g carbo, 2 g fiber, 3 g pro, 18 mcg folate.*

1 Scald milk by heating until tiny bubbles form around edge and milk reaches 180°F. Let cool till lukewarm. OR use ⅓ cup dry milk powder and warm water to make 1 cup.

2 In mixing bowl, dissolve yeast in water. Beat in warm milk, honey, eggs, 3 cups flour, and wheat gluten. Beat 3 minutes on medium speed. Cover and allow sponge to rest 30 minutes.

3 Stir in salt and enough remaining flour to form a slightly sticky dough. To avoid adding extra flour in the kneading process, gradually knead in shortening by hand. If using dough hook(s) add shortening. Knead dough by hand or with hook(s) for 12 to 13 minutes or until smooth and elastic.

4 Place dough in an oiled bowl; turn to coat. Cover; let rise in 80°F place until double. Punch down. Cover; let rise again until double.

5 Punch down, divide in half. Cover; let rest 10 minutes while greasing two 9 x 5-inch bread pans. Shape by rolling each half into a 14 x 7-inch rectangle. Starting with shorter side, roll up tightly, pressing dough into roll. Pinch edges and ends to seal. Place in pans, cover with a damp cloth; let rise in a 90°F place until double and indentation remains after touching.

5 Bake in a preheated 400°F oven 10 minutes, then lower the temperature to 375°F and continue to bake 25 to 30 minutes. Tent with foil to prevent over-browning. Remove from pans and cool on wire racks.

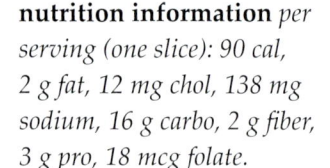

DOUBLE ORANGE SCONES

makes 10 scones

THIS EASY SCONE RECIPE FROM THE KWC APPEARED IN THE NATIONAL SCHOOL FOOD SERVICE MAGAZINE.

ingredients
- 2 cups all-purpose flour
- 3 tablespoons granulated sugar
- 2 ½ teaspoons baking powder
- 2 teaspoons grated orange peel
- ¼ cup cold margarine or butter, diced
- ½ cup drained, chopped mandarin oranges
- ⅓ cup low-fat milk
- 1 beaten egg, or egg substitute
- 1 beaten egg white
- 1 tablespoon granulated sugar

1 Preheat oven to 400°F. Lightly coat cookie sheet with nonstick cooking spray.

2 In a large bowl, combine flour, 3 tablespoons sugar, baking powder, and grated orange peel; mix well. Using a pastry blender, cut in margarine or butter until the mixture resembles coarse meal.

3 Stir in oranges, milk, and egg, just until the dough leaves side of the bowl. Turn dough onto a lightly floured surface and knead lightly 10 times.

4 Place on cookie sheet and flatten dough into an 8-inch circle. Using a knife, cut into 10 wedges; separate slightly. Brush with beaten egg white; sprinkle with 1 tablespoon sugar.

5 Bake 15 to 16 minutes, or until edges are a light brown. Immediately remove from cookie sheet and serve warm.

variation: *To make Cranberry Orange Scones, stir ½ cup chopped, fresh cranberries in step 3.*

to freeze: *Cool baked scones completely; place in freezer bag, pressing out as much air as possible. To reheat, spread frozen scones on cookie sheet and heat for about 5 minutes in a preheated 250°F oven.*

nutrition information *per serving (one scone): 164 cal, 5 g fat, 22 mg chol, 119 mg sodium, 26 g carbo, 1 g fiber, 4 g pro, 43 mcg folate.*

PHOTO COURTESY OF THE HOME BAKING ASSOCIATION

BIERROCKS

makes 6 bierrocks

BIERROCKS, RUSSIAN/GERMAN MEAT-FILLED BREAD DOUGH, MAKE A PERFECT SANDWICH. MAKE THESE SANDWICHES AHEAD OF TIME, FREEZE, THEN WARM IN MICROWAVE FOR A QUICK MEAL.

ingredients

Bread Dough
- 1 package RED STAR® Active Dry Yeast
- 1 cup lukewarm water (110-115°F)
- 2 tablespoons sugar
- 1 teaspoon salt
- 2 tablespoons margarine
- 3 cups all-purpose flour (may be part whole wheat)

Traditional Bierrock Filling
- 1 pound lean ground beef
- 2 cups finely shredded cabbage
- ½ cup finely chopped onion
- ½ teaspoon ground black pepper
- ⅛ teaspoon salt
- Bottled hot pepper sauce (to taste)

Bread Dough

1 For dough, dissolve yeast in water in large mixing bowl. Allow to set 3 to 5 minutes.

2 Stir in sugar, salt, margarine, and enough flour until dough comes together in a ball. Knead dough 6 to 8 minutes, or until smooth and elastic.

3 Let dough rest, covered, 30 minutes. Punch down dough. Cover; let rest 10 minutes. Grease baking sheet with shortening. Lightly grease counter with shortening and roll dough into 12 x 8-inch rectangle. Cut into six, 4-inch squares.

4 Place ½ cup filling in center of each square. Pick up corners of each square and pinch together. Pinch each diagonal seam so square is sealed well.

5 Turn each square seam-side-down on greased baking sheet. Bake in preheated 400°F oven 15 to 18 minutes. Serve warm or freeze and reheat.

Traditional Bierrock Filling

1 Brown ground beef and thoroughly drain. Add remaining ingredients. Cook on low, covered, until vegetables are tender. Cool slightly.

tip: One pound of white or wheat frozen bread dough is a time saver. Defrost dough according to package directions. Another option is to make the dough in the bread machine.

nutrition information *per serving (one bierrock): 425 cal, 12 g fat, 28 mg chol, 535 mg sodium, 55 g carbo, 3 g fiber, 23 g pro, 143 mcg folate.*

BUTTERMILK WHEAT BERRY BREAD

makes 1 (1 ½-pound) loaf, 16 slices

STEVE KORTHANKE, ROBINSON, KANSAS, CREATED THIS 1995 KANSAS "FESTIVAL OF BREADS" CHAMPION RECIPE, USING KANSAS HARD WHITE WHEAT BERRIES.

ingredients

- 1 ½ cups water (80°F)
- 5 tablespoons dried buttermilk
- 3 tablespoons honey
- 3 cups whole wheat flour*
- ¾ cup bread flour
- ½ cup cooked wheat berries
- 2 tablespoons vital wheat gluten
- 1 ½ teaspoons salt
- 1 ½ tablespoons butter
- 1 ½ teaspoons RED STAR® Bread Machine Yeast

*For a milder flavor and golden color, use whole white wheat flour and berries (kernels).

1 Add ingredients to bread machine pan in the order suggested by manufacturer. Recommended cycle: whole wheat cycle (longest setting) and light color setting, if available. Time bake feature may be used.

2 To cook wheat berries (kernels): Place ½ cup clean, uncooked wheat berries in small saucepan; cover with two cups water. Let stand overnight. Simmer, stirring occasionally, 30 to 45 minutes or until berries are tender. Rinse with cold water; drain thoroughly. Place cooled berries in sealable bag and store in the refrigerator. Use as needed. Berries will keep up to one week in the refrigerator.

3 Or, bring berries and water to a boil. Cover, reduce heat and simmer 60 to 90 minutes, stirring occasionally, until water is absorbed and berries are tender.

nutrition information *per serving (one slice): 149 cal, 2 g fat, 5 mg chol, 233 mg sodium, 29 g carbo, 4 g fiber, 5 g pro, 21 mcg folate.*

TRIPLE CHOCOLATE DESSERT BREAD

makes 1 (1 ½-pound) loaf, 16 slices

A TASTY BREAD MACHINE ALTERNATIVE TO A HIGH FAT DESSERT, CREATED BY KANSAS WHEAT COMMISSION SECRETARY JULIE OWENS.

ingredients
- 3 ¼ cups + 2 tablespoons bread flour
- 2 ½ tablespoons nonfat dry milk powder
- 2 ½ tablespoons brown sugar
- 1 ¼ teaspoons salt
- 1 ½ tablespoons butter
- ½ cup chocolate milk powder*
- ½ cup semisweet chocolate morsels
- 2 ½ tablespoons unsweetened baking cocoa
- 1 ½ tablespoons vital wheat gluten
- 2 ¼ teaspoons RED STAR® Bread Machine Yeast
- 1 ¼ cups water (80°F)

1 Add ingredients to bread machine pan in the order suggested by manufacturer.

2 Recommended cycles: Basic/white bread cycle; light color setting OR sweet bread cycle. Timed-bake feature can be used. Note: if machine does not have a light color setting, remove bread 5 minutes before cycle is complete.

3 Check the consistency of the dough after 5 minutes into the kneading cycle. It should be in a moist soft ball. If the dough is too dry, add 1 tablespoon of liquid at a time. If it is too wet, add 1 tablespoon of flour at a time.

4 Allow bread to cool before slicing. If desired, drizzle a confectioners' sugar glaze over the top.

Chocolate milk powder includes products such as Nestle Quick. Do not use a product with NutraSweet. Heat changes the chemical composition of NutraSweet, causing a bitter taste in the final product.

variations: *Use flavored hot cocoa dry mixes, such as raspberry flavor, Dutch chocolate, chocolate Irish cream, chocolate mint, or chocolate almond.*

For the holidays, drizzle with confectioners' sugar icing and decorate with green and red maraschino cherries.

note: *The recipe for a one-pound loaf is available at www.kswheat.com.*

nutrition information *per serving (one slice): 183 cal, 4 g fat, 3 mg chol, 234 mg sodium, 33 g carbo, 2 g fiber, 5 g pro, 75 mcg folate.*

CONFETTI MUFFINS

makes 12 muffins

THESE FLAVORFUL MUFFINS WERE FEATURED ON THE COVER OF THE 1992 KANSAS WHEAT COMMISSION RECIPE BOOK.

ingredients
- 1 ⅓ cups all-purpose flour
- 1 teaspoon baking powder
- ½ teaspoon baking soda
- ¼ teaspoon cayenne pepper
- ⅓ cup yellow cornmeal
- 1 cup low-fat shredded Cheddar cheese
- ⅓ cup chopped green onions
- ½ cup finely chopped red bell pepper
- 2 teaspoons granulated sugar
- 1 beaten egg
- 1 ⅓ cups buttermilk

1 Preheat oven to 425°F. Lightly grease a 12-cup muffin pan.

2 In a large bowl, sift together flour, baking powder, soda, and cayenne pepper. Add the cornmeal, cheese, onions, and red pepper; mix well.

3 In a small bowl, beat together sugar, egg, and buttermilk. Add into dry ingredients all at once, stirring quickly with a fork, just until dry ingredients are moistened. Do not beat.

4 Using an ice cream scoop or spoon, quickly dip batter into muffin cups.

5 Bake 18 minutes, or until the tops of the muffins spring back when touched lightly. Let muffins cool for a few minutes before unmolding by loosening the edges with a knife. Turn out onto a rack and serve warm, or at room temperature.

nutrition information *per serving (one muffin): 123 cal, 2 g fat, 22 mg chol, 214 mg sodium, 19 g carbo, 1 g fiber, 7 g pro, 38 mcg folate.*

THREE GRAIN PILAF

makes 7 cups

AN EASY AND NUTRITIOUS RECIPE USING BULGUR, PARTIALLY COOKED CRACKED WHEAT THAT IS QUICK COOKING. THIS RECIPE HAS BEEN DEMONSTRATED AT NUMEROUS STATE AND NATIONAL PROGRAMS PRESENTED BY THE KANSAS WHEAT COMMISSION.

ingredients
- 1 tablespoon vegetable oil
- 1 cup uncooked bulgur wheat
- ½ cup uncooked long-grain white rice, dry
- ½ cup uncooked pearled barley
- 2 beef or chicken bouillon cubes or 2 tablespoons dry bouillon granules
- 4 cups hot water
- ½ cup coarsely grated carrots
- ½ cup chopped onion
- ½ cup sliced almonds, toasted (optional)

1 Add oil to wok or skillet and heat on medium-high. Add grains and sauté 7 minutes, stirring occasionally.

2 Dissolve bouillon in hot water and stir into grains; add vegetables. Cover; reduce heat and simmer 25 to 30 minutes. Stir occasionally until liquid is absorbed and grains are tender.

3 Remove from heat, let stand 5 minutes and fluff with fork. Garnish with almonds.

note: *Do not substitute instant or brown rice.*

variations: *Season with black pepper or herbs. Add other vegetables such as chopped green pepper, red pepper, celery, peas, or broccoli.*

pearled barley

long-grain white rice

bulgur wheat

nutrition information *per serving (½ cup): 96 cal, 1 g fat, 0 g chol, 18 mg sodium, 19 g carbo, 3 g fiber, 3 g pro, 21 mcg folate.*

BANANA CUPCAKES

makes 14 cupcakes

THESE CUPCAKES TASTES SO GOOD THAT YOU'LL NEVER KNOW THAT HALF THE FAT WAS REPLACED WITH APPLESAUCE BY KATHY WALSTEN, KANSAS WHEAT COMMISSION HOME ECONOMIST.

ingredients
- ¾ cup granulated sugar
- ¼ cup vegetable shortening
- ¼ cup unsweetened applesauce
- 2 beaten eggs
- 1 teaspoon vanilla extract
- 1 ½ cups all-purpose flour
- ½ teaspoon salt
- 1 teaspoon baking powder
- ½ teaspoon baking soda
- 1 tablespoon water
- 1 cup ripe, mashed bananas

1 Preheat oven to 375°F. Coat muffin cups with nonstick cooking spray or line with paper baking cups.

2 In a large mixing bowl, beat sugar, shortening, applesauce, eggs and vanilla until blended.

3 Add flour, salt, baking powder, soda, water, and ripe bananas; beat on medium speed until blended.

4 Fill muffin cups ⅔ full and bake 20 to 25 minutes, or until golden brown.

5 Remove from pans and cool.

variations: *For bananas, substitute 2 cups shredded zucchini and add 1 teaspoon cinnamon.*

Add chopped nuts if desired.

For icing, combine 1 cup confectioners' sugar, 1 - 1 ½ tablespoons milk and 1 teaspoon margarine.

tip: *Over-ripe bananas can be peeled and frozen in a plastic container or freezer bag. Remove from freezer and thaw before using in recipe.*

nutrition information *per serving (one cupcake without icing): 151 cal, 5 g fat, 30 mg chol, 154 mg sodium, 25 g carbo, 1 g fiber, 2 g pro, 27 mcg folate.*

LAYERED ENCHILADA CASSEROLE

makes 12 servings

A TANTALIZING QUICK-TO-FIX CASSEROLE USING ONE OF THE MOST POPULAR WHEAT FOODS-TORTILLAS.

ingredients
- 1 pound extra lean ground beef
- 1 (16-ounce) can fat-free refried beans
- 1 (1 ¼-ounce) package mild taco or chili seasoning mix
- 1 cup water
- 1 (15-ounce) can tomato sauce
- 10 (8-inch) flour tortillas
- 1 cup reduced-fat shredded Cheddar cheese
- Salsa
- Lettuce, shredded

1 Preheat oven to 350°F. Spray a 13 x 9 x 2-inch baking pan with nonstick cooking spray.

2 In a large skillet, brown ground beef and drain well. Stir in beans, seasoning mix, and water. Simmer 5 minutes, stirring occasionally.

3 Pour tomato sauce into a pie pan. Coat both sides of tortillas with sauce.

4 Layer beef mixture and tortillas in baking pan, overlapping tortillas to fit. Sprinkle cheese on top.

5 Bake 20 minutes. If desired, garnish with salsa and lettuce.

tip: Prepare casserole in two 9-inch pans; bake one and freeze one for later use.

variation: Use whole wheat or reduced fat tortillas.

nutrition information *per serving (6.62 oz. serving): 277 cal, 8 g fat, 20 mg chol, 843 mg sodium, 33 g carbo, 4 g fiber, 17 g pro, 57 mcg folate.*

PECAN TWISTS

makes 24 rolls

KWC SPOKESPERSON, CHRISTY WAGNER, MANHATTAN, AND HER WONDERFUL PECAN TWISTS RECIPE WERE FEATURED IN THE APRIL 1994 ISSUE OF MIDWEST LIVING MAGAZINE.

dough

- 2 packages RED STAR® Active Dry Yeast
- ½ cup lukewarm water (110-115°F)
- 1 cup low-fat milk, warmed (110°F)
- 6 tablespoons margarine, softened
- ½ cup granulated sugar
- ½ teaspoon salt
- 2 beaten eggs
- 5 ½ - 6 cups bread flour

filling

- ½ cup packed brown sugar
- ⅓ cup sifted confectioners' sugar
- 1 teaspoon ground cinnamon
- ⅔ cup chopped pecans
- ¼ cup margarine, melted

1 Dissolve yeast in water. In large bowl, combine milk, margarine, sugar, salt, eggs, and yeast. Stir in 3 cups of the flour. Gradually add enough remaining flour to make a soft dough. Knead 10 to 12 minutes by hand or with dough hook. Place dough in a lightly greased bowl; turn to grease top. Cover; let rise in a warm place until double.

2 Punch down dough and divide into four equal pieces. Cover, let rest 10 minutes.

3 For filling, stir together brown sugar, confectioners' sugar, cinnamon, and pecans. Roll two pieces of dough into 12 x 9-inch rectangles. Brush one rectangle with half of the melted margarine; sprinkle with half of the filling. Place second rectangle on top of first. Seal edges. Cut crosswise into 1-inch strips.

4 Twist each strip a few times. Starting with one end, which becomes the center, wrap dough around in a swirling motion, continuing to twist as the dough is wrapped. Tuck end under roll. Place on greased baking sheet. Repeat with remaining dough. Cover; let rise in a warm place until double.

5 Bake in preheated 375°F oven 13 to 15 minutes. If desired, glaze with 1 ½ cups sifted confectioners' sugar, 1 tablespoon melted margarine, 1 teaspoon vanilla, and 2 tablespoons milk.

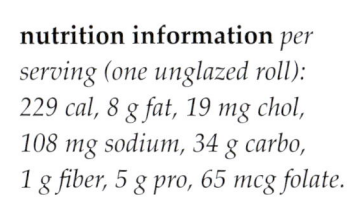

nutrition information *per serving (one unglazed roll): 229 cal, 8 g fat, 19 mg chol, 108 mg sodium, 34 g carbo, 1 g fiber, 5 g pro, 65 mcg folate.*

WALDORF WHEAT SALAD

makes 5 cups, or 10 servings

THIS OLD-TIME FAVORITE SALAD WILL MAKE A DELICIOUS ACCOMPANIMENT TO ANY MEAL.

ingredients
- ¼ cup uncooked wheat kernels
- 1 ¼ cups water
- 1 tablespoon granulated sugar
- ¼ teaspoon ground cinnamon
- 2 tablespoons low-fat mayonnaise
- 1 (6-ounce) container plain or vanilla nonfat yogurt
- ¼ teaspoon vanilla extract
- ½ cup thinly sliced celery
- 2 medium apples, cored, chopped
- ½ cup halved red or green grapes
- ¼ cup chopped English walnuts

1 To cook wheat kernels: place kernels and water in a slow cooker. Cover and cook on LOW overnight or until kernels are tender; drain.

2 In serving bowl, stir together drained wheat kernels, sugar, cinnamon, mayonnaise, yogurt, vanilla, and celery. Cover; chill until ready to serve.

3 Just before serving, stir in apples, grapes, and walnuts.

tip: Visit www.kswheat.com for sources of wheat kernels (berries).

nutrition information *per ½-cup serving:* 81 cal, 3 g fat, 1 mg chol, 40 mg sodium, 12 g carbo, 2 g fiber, 2 g pro, 8 mcg folate.

FAT-FREE CHOCOLATE SQUARES

makes 16 servings

THIS RECIPE WAS DEVELOPED IN 1994 IN THE KWC TEST KITCHEN BY HOME ECONOMIST CINDY FALK TO FILL THE REQUESTS FOR A "NO-FAT" DESSERT.

ingredients
- 1 cup all-purpose flour
- ⅓ cup unsweetened baking cocoa
- ½ teaspoon salt
- 1 teaspoon baking powder
- ¼ teaspoon baking soda
- ¼ teaspoon ground cinnamon
- ½ cup granulated sugar
- ¼ cup brown sugar
- ¼ cup nonfat dry milk powder
- 1 egg white, slightly beaten
- 1 cup unsweetened applesauce
- 1 teaspoon vanilla extract
- Confectioners' sugar (optional)

1 Preheat oven to 350°F. Spray an 8 x 8 x 2-inch baking pan with nonstick cooking spray; set aside.

2 In large bowl, sift together flour, cocoa, salt, baking powder, baking soda, and cinnamon; set aside. In medium bowl, beat the granulated sugar, brown sugar, dry milk powder, egg white, applesauce, and vanilla with a spoon until well combined. Stir wet mixture into dry mixture, mixing just until combined.

3 Spread evenly in prepared pan. Bake 22 to 23 minutes or until toothpick inserted in center comes out clean.

4 Cool on wire rack. If desired, sift on confectioners' sugar. Cut into squares.

nutrition information *per serving (one square):* 83 cal, 0 g fat, 0 mg chol, 121 mg sodium, 19 g carbo, 1 g fiber, 2 g pro, 13 mcg folate.

PHOTO COURTESY OF THE WHEAT FOODS COUNCIL, WWW.WHEATFOODS.ORG

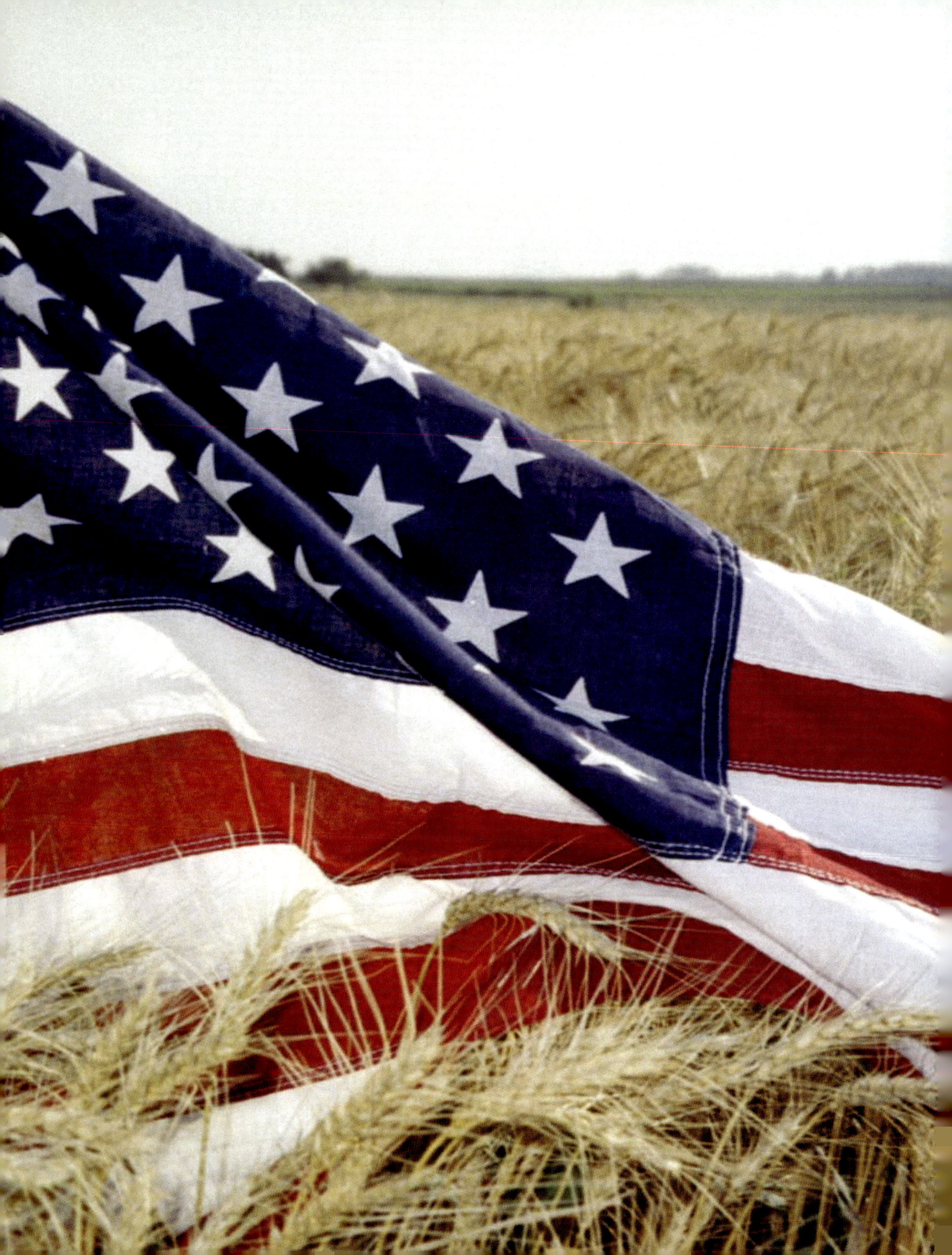

2000s

WHEAT ACRES DECLINE IN THE NEW MILLENNIUM

"We cannot use the red bran, so as soon as you start Hard White winter wheat, I'll be the first customer."
— Dr. Irfan Hashmi, Technical Manager, National Flour Mills Co., Dubai, U.A.E.

The first seven years of the new millennium were filled with ongoing drought and, with that, a need for changes in the Kansas wheat industry.

The first crop of the decade was planted in the past century and harvested in a new century that brought rapid and dramatic changes.

World market competition is changing with foreign buyers of grain having greater discretion for grain choices and concern over quality and milling properties. Our competition in the export business is becoming more determined and intense in their export policies. Our focus has not been on criticism of our foreign competition, but toward intensifying our efforts at quality exports and trade barrier reductions as a means to improve our competitive edge.

The demographics of the U.S. population are also changing dramatically. Today's population is more than two generations away from production agriculture, which means they have a less comprehensive understanding of how wheat grows and is processed into the products they use.

Dietary choices, resulting from lifestyle changes in our society, are stimulating the need for a powerful and informative education plan that teaches all age groups the value of cereal grains for a healthy life.

Photo by Lindsay Moore, 2001 Kansas State Fair entry

Governor Bill Graves signed KSA 2-3001 into law, effective July 1, 2000. The new law restructured the Kansas Wheat Commission and the other commodity commissions. Pictured at the signing are Betty Bunck, Everest; Dean Stoskopf, Hoisington; State Representative Dan Johnson, Hays; and State Senator Steve Morris, Hugoton.

Legislative Restructuring

In 2000, the Kansas Wheat Commission went through a major change in structure as a result of legislative action.

The passage of HB 2674 (K.S.A. 2-3001) by the 2000 Kansas Legislature was a positive step for Kansas wheat producers. For the first time since 1957, all interest earned on funds collected from producers accrued to the grain commodity commissions instead of going to the State General Fund. The restructuring also allowed for more grower involvement because Kansas Wheat Commissioners were elected by Kansas wheat producers, rather than being appointed by the Governor of Kansas. The first elections for Commissioners took place in the spring of 2002.

Additionally, the Commission was no longer required to go through the state budget process, including gubernatorial and legislative pre-approval of all spending. The Kansas Wheat Commission was still an "instrumentality of the state;" however, employees of the Commission were no longer employees of the state of Kansas.

New Logo

KANSAS WHEAT COMMISSION

Kansas grown. Kansas good.

Along with structural changes, in 2001 the Kansas Wheat Commission adopted a new logo. The symbol is anchored around a stylized head of wheat to illustrate the fundamental importance of wheat as a staple food for the consumer, and as an economic cornerstone to Kansas growers and residents. The sunburst radiates outward to represent the life giving power of wheat as a food, and its far-reaching economic significance in America and around the world.

Its goal was to raise the level of pride Kansas wheat producers have for what they produce, and in return, show the world that Kansas wheat producers "are giving the world our best."

Grain Science Complex

Education on the international level changed with the new Grain Science and Industry facilities and classrooms at Kansas State

University. These new facilities demonstrate to buyers and traders a strong commitment to promoting Kansas-grown grain.

The first building to be completed in the five-building complex was the International Grains Program Conference Center, which was supported with a five-year commitment from the KWC. The classroom and grain grading lab are equipped for simultaneous translation of up to three languages and offer audio, visual and multimedia equipment for presentations.

International Grains Program

The KSU International Grains Program was designed to educate foreign business leaders and government officials about U.S. grains and oil seeds. Its mission is to promote and assist market development efforts for U.S. commodities, including wheat.

IGP achieves its mission through technical training and assistance programs. These programs are targeted at international flour and feed millers, international grain buyers, overseas government officials, and other public and private sector parties involved in grain procurement and/or use. IGP activities also extend beyond short courses to working with trade teams and visitors and facilitating overseas technical assistance.

Drought Forum

Producers were able to voice their concerns about the drought conditions across the Great Plains region during a producer forum in 2002. Ross Davidson, Administrator of the Risk Management Agency of USDA, traveled through Kansas and Colorado to assess the drought and its impact on producers. He also participated in an aerial tour of Western Kansas.

Harvest Salute to Kansas Wheat Producers

During harvest of 2002, KWC launched its first Harvest Salute to Kansas Wheat Producers. The purpose of the campaign was to honor the contributions of Kansas wheat producers during the harvest season. Kansas farm families have built a global reputation for high

Current and past commissioners posed for a photo in front of a plaque at the new International Grains Program facility. The plaque stated that the building was dedicated to Kansas wheat producers.

You've given the world your best.

Harvest Salute to Kansas Wheat Producers

KANSAS WHEAT | KANSAS CITY BOARD OF TRADE | DeBruce Grain

quality wheat, which is vital to our state's economy, our way of life and our ability to contribute to the nations of the world. The campaign was designed to recognize those efforts, and the worldwide contributions of Kansas wheat producers. The campaign was facilitated through Kansas elevators, which promoted it in their areas, displayed posters carrying the campaign's theme, and handed out promotional items to producers as they brought in their wheat. Much of the cost of this campaign was underwritten by corporate sponsors. The annual campaign continued through the 2000s.

In conjunction with the campaign, Governor Bill Graves issued a formal proclamation declaring June as Kansas Wheat Producers Appreciation Month.

U.S. Wheat Associates

U.S. Wheat Associates, the industry's market development organization, represents wheat growers from 18 states, working in over 120 countries. USW is headquartered in Washington, D.C., with 15 overseas offices and a West Coast office in Portland, Ore. Kansas Wheat Commission has traditionally been the largest state contributor to USW. For each $1 producers invest in USW, the Foreign Agricultural Service of the USDA contributes between $2 and $3 to USW.

In 2005, Lane County, Kan. wheat producer Ron Suppes was elected to serve as an officer of USW. It had been nearly 10 years since Kansas last had an officer on the USW board. Suppes became Chairman of USW in 2007.

U.S. Wheat Exports 2000-2006

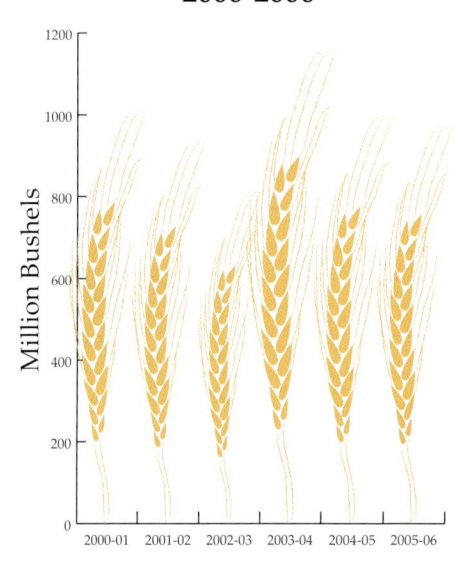

Top Markets for U.S. Wheat 2000s

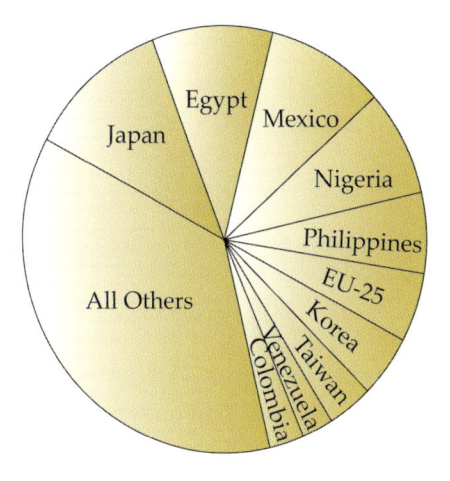

Trade Teams

Many trade teams traveled to the United States to learn about the quality of U.S. wheat and about the U.S. wheat marketing system. The majority of the teams that come to the U.S. make a stop in Manhattan during their trip. The KWC has an excellent location because it is near Kansas State University, American Institute of Baking, and USDA's Grain Marketing and Production Research Center. Many international visitors fly into Kansas City, where they visit the Kansas City Board of Trade, Federal Grain Inspection Service Technical Center, and large grain companies. While in Manhattan, they tour KSU's Wheat Quality Lab, International Grains Program, and Department of Grain Science and Industry.

Teams including representatives from Brazil, Turkey, Zambia, United Arab Emirates, Lebanon, Jordan, Egypt, Algeria, Nigeria, Republic of Georgia, Kenya, China, Korea, Japan, Vietnam, Libya, Peru, Sri Lanka, Yemen, South Africa, Mexico, Colombia, and the Middle East visited Kansas in the 2000s.

A number of these trade team members expressed interest in Hard White wheat. They also inquired about how long it would be before there was enough production for it to be an exportable commodity.

Cuba purchases HRW wheat

After a 40-year hiatus, Kansas wheat finally made its way into Cuba, with pleasing results. In a momentous occasion for the American wheat farmer, the first commercial shipload of U.S. wheat in four decades left for Cuba in January 2002. This shipment was the first "installment" of 2.6 million bushels of Hard Red Winter wheat purchased by Cuban officials in the wake of Hurricane Michelle.

The Hard Red Winter wheat from Kansas, Texas, and Oklahoma was loaded aboard the *M.V.H. Ismael Kaptanoglu* at the Port of Galveston, Texas and started the four-day journey to Havana, Cuba.

The United States was previously unable to trade with Cuba

Representatives of U.S. Wheat Associates traveled to Cuba to meet with Cuban President Fidel Castro. Pictured with Castro are USW President Alan Tracy and KWC Commissioner Mike Brown.

In 2006, the KWC hosted a Nigerian flour miller recognition event in Manhattan, Kan. The flour mill executives from eight milling companies in Nigeria are pictured with the Kansas Wheat staff at the event, which was held at the International Grains Program conference center.

In 2004, Iraq bought nearly nine million bushels of U.S. Hard Red Winter wheat. These were the first wheat purchases Iraq had made from the U.S. since 1998. In 2005, the Kansas Wheat Commission hosted a dinner meeting for the first Iraqi buying delegation in many years.

because of the embargo established in October 1960. Diplomatic relations broke the following January. U.S. trade legislation was passed in 2000, which allowed for exemption of food and medicine from sanctions. However, other features of the bill included a tightening of the travel ban of U.S. citizens allowed to travel to Cuba and the placement of restrictions on both the federal government and U.S. banks from financing the sales of U.S. wheat to Cuba.

Elie Posner, a wheat-milling expert and U.S. Wheat Associates consultant, traveled to Cuba to provide a review of the mill equipment and advise the operators how the particular mill should be adjusted to best utilize the U.S. Hard Red Winter wheat.

Nigeria becomes #1 buyer

Since an import ban on wheat was removed in 1992, Nigeria became a top market for U.S. wheat and specifically, Hard Red Winter wheat. USW established an office in Lagos, Nigeria, in 2000. Trade teams from Nigeria traveled to the U.S. and to Kansas year after year.

In 2006, the KWC hosted a Nigerian flour miller recognition event in Manhattan, Kan. A prestigious group of flour mill executives from eight milling companies in Nigeria attended the event and received special recognition and appreciation for their continued purchases of U.S. Hard Red Winter wheat. Nigeria purchased nearly 100 million bushels of U.S. wheat in 2005.

WETEC

The Wheat Export Trade Education Committee worked since the mid-1980s to make sure that U.S. wheat trade was treated fairly in the World Trade Organization. The WTO is the international organization dealing with the global rules of trade between nations. Its main function is to ensure that trade flows as smoothly, predictably and freely as possible. This function of WETEC was handed over to USW and the National Association of Wheat Growers in 2006, when WETEC voted to disband.

Wheat Foods Council

Investing in the future, the KWC continues membership the Wheat Foods Council. The WFC is an industry-wide partnership to increase grain food consumption through nutrition education and promotion programs. KWC's Nutrition Educator Cindy Falk served on the executive board during the 2000s, serving as Chairperson in 2003.

Fad Diets

Post September 11, 2001, "comfort food," casual home entertaining, connection to home, and simplicity were the hottest food trends in 2002. The WFC launched "Grains: the Feel-good Food" program to respond to this trend.

Unfortunately, while consumers were seeking to feel good about what they ate, the media stopped them in their tracks with a constant barrage of misinformation and confusion about carbohydrates. The WFC shifted gears quickly and responded to controversial issues by publishing media alerts, fact sheets, and letters. Priorities were guarding the image of grain foods and refocusing target audiences on the benefits of eating grain foods.

Bread Bytes

Bread Bytes, the new bimonthly column written by KWC Nutrition Educator Cindy Falk appeared in Kansas newspapers. It was also picked up by papers out-of-state and in Canada. Topics included whole grains, wheat flour information, nutritional benefits of wheat foods, bread machines, home baking, and Kansas flour mills.

Kansas Festival of Breads

The Kansas Festival of Breads baking contest was held every other year. In the 2000 contest, eight finalists competed at Kansas State University and sponsors included the Kansas Wheathearts, Kansas Department of Commerce and Housing's Agriculture Product Development Division, and the Kansas Wheat Commission. Publicity generated from the contest appeared in many Kansas publications. In addition, *The Tennessean* and *The Idaho Statesman* newspapers

Key media had the opportunity to learn how grain foods add more energy to their day during an action-packed "Grains: Harvest the Energy" Industry Tour. Tour stops in the Kansas City area were to a wheat farm, wheat field art unveiling, ADM Milling, Interstate Bakeries, American Institute of Baking, and the Kansas City Board of Trade.

The 2006 Kansas Festival of Breads baking contest was held at Pottorf Hall, where nearly 300 breads were judged and winners were chosen in each of four categories — youth, adult, seniors, and professionals.

published articles about the baking contest.

In 2002, the contest was modified. Participants baked their products at home, delivered them to their county extension office or other pickup location. Drivers traveled around the state to pick up breads and delivered them all to Manhattan, where they were judged on taste, quality, appearance, originality, ease of preparation, and practicality. There were four categories — youth, adult, seniors and, for the first time, professionals.

MyPyramid

The 2000 U.S. Dietary Guidelines for Americans separated the grain recommendation from the fruit and vegetable guideline. The guideline recommended to consumers to "Build a healthy base — Choose a variety of grains daily, especially whole grains." This separate recommendation emphasized the important role grain foods play in the diet. Consumers were recommended to enjoy six to 11 daily servings of grains, with at least three coming from whole grains.

In 2005, a new MyPyramid was released, taking the place of the Food Guide Pyramid. The new MyPyramid guidelines were included in the 2005 KWC recipe book, which was distributed to exhibit visitors and collectors across the country.

The new image stresses the value of various foods; grains—particularly whole grains—are still a valued and important step toward healthier living. Despite the low-carb craze of the early 2000s, the six color bands on the new MyPyramid image represent the importance of eating a variety of carbohydrate-rich foods to achieve good health. This verifies "fad diets" that recommend cutting out one type of food are not an option for healthy living.

Best of Breads in Kansas

The Best of Breads in Kansas directory was unveiled in 2002. Since Kansas is number one in wheat production and milling, it is a great opportunity to promote the quality of breads that are made from Kansas wheat. The brochure was available at the Kansas Travel Information centers around the state, at the establishments featured in the booklet, and on the KWC web site.

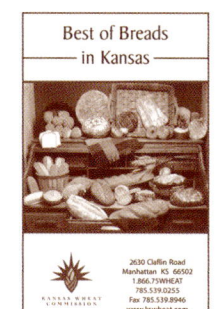

The first Best of Breads in Kansas Award was presented to WheatFields Bakery and Café, Lawrence, Kan., in 2004. Bagatelle Bakery, Wichita, was presented with the award in 2005, followed by Capers Café and Bakery, Salina, in 2006. The goals of this award were to recognize extraordinary bakeries in the Wheat State, instill an appreciation for high quality baked products, and increase the volume of bread consumed.

Flour Power 5-K

The KWC and KSU's Health and Nutrition Society sponsored the first annual Flour Power 5-K Run/Walk in 2005 to highlight research by Dr. Mark Haub. Dr. Haub's research studied the effects of heart rate, perceived exertion and amount of work on cyclists, triathletes, and track athletes on both grain-based diets and low-carbohydrate diets. During the same high-intensity exercise, the exercise felt less difficult and heart rates were lower on the grain-based diet. The grain-based diet allowed the athletes to train at a higher workload than the low-carbohydrate diet.

Wheat Foods Council President Marcia Scheideman discussed the Council's role in promoting grain foods and the health benefits of grains. The race was held again in 2006 under the name, "Run Your Buns Off."

At the Flour Power 5-K Run/Walk in 2005, Dr. Mark Haub presented research which demonstrated athletes need complex carbohydrates for energy and to fuel working muscles.

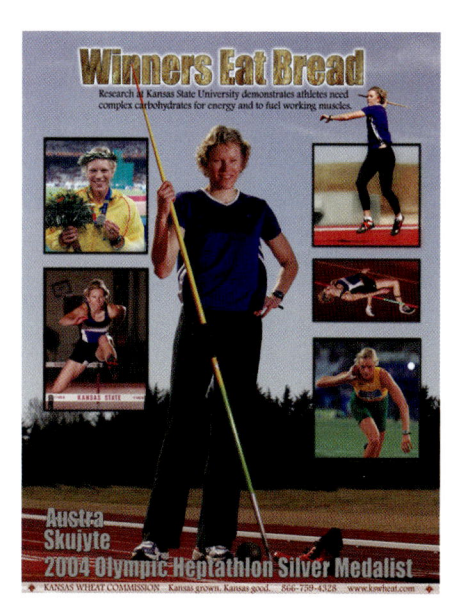

Austra Skujyte, 2004 Heptathlon Silver Medalist, appeared on a poster, which she autographed at the Flour Power race. Skujyte, who set the world record in the women's decathlon, worked with the KWC to promote grain-based foods as an essential part of a successful athlete's diet.

Kansas Wheat spokesperson Betty Kandt, Manhattan, presented programs on grains.

Spokespersons gathered in front of pallets of flour at the Stafford County Flour Mill, where they toured during a training session.

Spokespersons

More than 20 spokespersons helped the KWC reach all areas of the state. They provided programs at farm shows; preschool, elementary, and secondary classrooms; health fairs; county extension meetings; care homes; public libraries; 4-H events; health organization meetings; senior citizen meetings; and wheat plot tours. These spokespersons reached more than 150,000 people a year.

Bake and Take Day

Home baking and community spirit were essential for the annual Bake and Take Day, held annually on the fourth Saturday of March. Prizes were given to participants who wrote in to tell about their Bake and Take Day activities.

Kansas Wheat Feeds Hurricane Victims

Twenty thousand cereal bars left Kansas in January 2006 to feed victims of Hurricanes Katrina and Rita. Kansas Wheat sponsored cereal bar development research at KSU, who worked with Harvest Lark Company, Chapman, Kan., to provide the manufacturing and distribution of the cereal bars.

Fields of Gold: Wheat Lessons for Growing Kids

A new preschool packet was developed by the KWC and Sharon Davis, consultant. More than 10,000 preschool packets were distributed to educators. Materials included ready-to-go, hands-on wheat and wheat food lessons with related take-home sheets for parents, a poster, and a recipe book donated by General Mills.

KFAC

The Kansas Foundation for Agriculture in the Classroom developed "Connecting Kansas Kids, Crops and Critters," an agricultural school assembly program, for presentation to Kansas school children.

2001 marked the beginning of a collaborative effort to develop an elementary packet which featured

Kansas' top five crops — wheat, corn, grain sorghum, soybeans, and sunflowers. This effort became a reality in 2002. KWC worked with KFAC and a number of other groups to develop an educator's guide and student magazine targeted to third grade students.

Research

Kansas State University hired Allan Fritz as their Manhattan wheat breeder in 2000. KWC research goals are to increase yields, improve production techniques, boost nutritional content and protect the world's food supply from disease and pests. The return on investment for wheat research is significant. It was estimated that for every dollar invested in wheat research at KSU, there is a $12 return on investment to the Kansas wheat producer.

Some topics of research included no-till wheat production, continued Hard Red Winter and Hard White wheat breeding, development of Clearfield wheat, pest resistance, mapping the wheat genome, cancer suppression by wheat products, and dual-purpose wheats.

Biotechnology

In Kansas and other areas of the Great Plains, the full yield potential of wheat is not reached in any given year due to a variety of stresses which include leaf rust, scab, and take-all, as well as extremes in temperature and rainfall. Through genetic engineering, researchers at KSU are looking for ways to confer resistance to these fungal diseases. Another project at KSU was introducing genes from maize into wheat and testing the effectiveness of these genes toward the control of leaf rust, stem rust, and stripe rust.

Hard White Wheat

Producers in Kansas and other states rallied for the Hard White Wheat Incentive Program in the 2002 Farm Bill. This new class of wheat provided an opportunity for market growth in the competitive export markets.

In this decade we may see a dynamic change from Hard Red Winter wheat to Hard White wheat which may increase the U.S. world market share.

Domestic demand for HW picked up as companies started introducing whole white wheat products. New bread products hit the shelves as a result of the new dietary guidelines released in 2005, which stated "make half your grains whole."

Wheat Genome Sequencing

In 2005, KSU and KWC began the effort to sequence the wheat genome. Eversole Associates is working to position wheat as the next major crop species for sequencing by securing funding from various international and domestic sources. Without a sequenced wheat genome, the wheat industry will not have the scientific foundation necessary to drive the discoveries that will fuel growth and sustain profitability in wheat production and marketing.

Spinosad

Spinosad was developed as an alternative pesticide for the management of stored-wheat insects. In 2005, the EPA issued a registration for spinosad as a stored grain and seed protectant on commodities, including wheat. KWC supported this research since 1999, which was lead by Dr. Bhadriraju Subramanyam at Kansas State University.

Value-Added

A massive amount of solid-plastic wastes are produced from grocery bags, trash bags, fast food serving and eating utensils, and flowerpots. Research at KSU found ways to create a biodegradable plastic from the starches found in wheat. This research enhanced the utilization of wheat as an industrial raw material.

In April 2005, Jerry McReynolds, President of the Kansas Association of Wheat Growers, and Tom Morton, Chairman of the Kansas Wheat Commission, signed a Cooperative Agreement between the two Kansas wheat organizations.

Speaking with One Voice

Jerry McReynolds, President of the Kansas Association of Wheat Growers, and Tom Morton, Chairman of the Kansas Wheat Commission, signed a Cooperative Agreement between the two wheat organizations, with an effective date of July 1, 2005. This agreement was the beginning of a new era for the two groups.

Under the Cooperative Agreement, the KWC and KAWG share one staff and one office, but they still remain two separate organizations.

In December of 2005, the groups adopted a joint strategic plan, "Kansas Wheat: Profitability through Innovation," and the vision statement, "Leaders in the adoption of profitable innovations for wheat."

Personnel

Administrator David Frey left the Commission in 2005, after serving Kansas wheat producers for nearly 28 years. KWC Assistant Administrator Dusti Fritz was appointed to serve as Interim Administrator during a nationwide search for the Chief Executive Officer of both Kansas wheat groups. In August 2005, Fritz was hired as the first female executive for both Kansas wheat organizations.

Production

A priority for the KWC through the 2000s was outreach to Kansas producers through producer meetings and print and other media. Targeted meetings centered around a specific topics, such as Hard White wheat, biotechnology, wheat marketing, and cellulosic ethanol, drew crowds of producers. In addition to these meetings, KWC attended farm shows, field days, the state fair, and a number of other venues.

The early years of the decade resulted in Kansas producers planting around 10 million acres, which was less than plantings of nearly 12 million acres during the 1990s. Years of drought affected the western portions of the state, which dramatically affected their economies and communities. Production techniques have adapted to new technologies and the increasing need to conserve natural resources including soil, water, and air. The leading varieties were 'Jagger,' 'Jagalene,' '2137,' and 'Overley.'

TORTILLAS IN A BAG

makes 6 (8-inch) tortillas

A POPULAR WHEAT FOOD THAT CHILDREN LOVE TO MAKE AND EAT.

ingredients
- 1 ½ cups all-purpose flour
- 1 teaspoon baking powder
- ½ teaspoon salt
- 2 tablespoons vegetable shortening
- ½ cup hot water

1 In a large self-locking plastic bag, combine flour, baking powder, and salt. Close bag and shake to mix. Add shortening and work into flour until fine particles form. Add the hot water and knead the dough in the bag until it forms a ball.

2 Remove dough from bag and place on a lightly floured work surface; knead 15 strokes. Divide into six equal pieces; shape into balls. Cover; let rest 15 minutes.

3 On a lightly floured surface, roll each piece as thin as possible. Roll from the center out, turning several times to form an 8-inch circle.

4 Heat an ungreased griddle or skillet over medium heat. Cook until the surface begins to bubble and the under side is speckled golden-brown, about 15 to 20 seconds. Cook other side. Stack tortillas under a cloth as they are done and serve warm.

variations: *Use ½ cup corn meal and 1 cup all-purpose flour, or use ¾ cup whole wheat flour and ¾ cup all-purpose flour.*

nutrition information *per serving (one tortilla): 152 cal, 5 g fat, 0 mg chol, 234 mg sodium, 24 g carbo, 1 g fiber, 3 g pro, 48 mcg folate.*

HOLIDAY CRUNCH

A FAVORITE TREAT THAT USES VITAMIN-ENRICHED, HIGH FIBER CEREAL

makes 24 servings

PHOTO COURTESY OF THE WHEAT FOODS COUNCIL, WWW.WHEATFOODS.ORG

ingredients
- 3 cups Wheat Chex® or Rice Chex® cereal
- 1 ½ cups MultiGrain Cheerios® cereal
- 1 cup pretzel sticks
- 1 cup cashews
- 1 cup M&M's® candy, plain
- 8 squares (13 ounces) vanilla or butterscotch almond bark

1 Line a 15 x 10 x 1-inch baking pan with waxed paper. In a large bowl, combine Wheat Chex® cereal, Cheerios®, pretzels, cashews, and M&M's®.

2 In a heatproof bowl, microwave the almond bark 2 to 3 minutes. Stir occasionally until melted. Remove carefully, using pot holders.

3 Pour melted almond bark over the dry ingredients and stir gently just until coated.

4 Immediately pour onto prepared baking sheet. Spread evenly. Refrigerate 30 minutes or until firm. Remove waxed paper. Break into bite-size pieces and store in an airtight container.

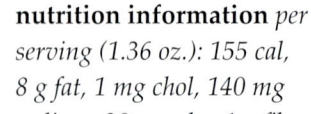

nutrition information *per serving (1.36 oz.): 155 cal, 8 g fat, 1 mg chol, 140 mg sodium, 20 g carbo, 1 g fiber, 3 g pro, 31 mcg folate.*

WHOLE WHITE WHEAT ITALIAN FOCACCIA (FO-KA-CHA)

makes 2 focaccia (16 servings each)

A 2002 KANSAS FESTIVAL OF BREADS WINNING RECIPE MADE BY NAOMI JOHNSON, GREAT BEND, KAN.

ingredients

sponge
- 2 cups whole wheat flour*
- 1 package RED STAR® Active Dry Yeast
- 1 teaspoon sugar
- 1 ½ teaspoons garlic powder
- 1 tablespoon dried Italian seasoning
- 2 cups lukewarm water (110-115°F)

dough
- 2 teaspoons salt
- 1 tablespoon olive oil
- 2 tablespoons dried grated Parmesan Cheese
- 1 cup whole wheat flour
- 1 ½ - 2 cups bread flour
- Cornmeal

toppings (optional)
- Olive oil, Parmesan or Romano Cheese, Kosher salt, Italian seasoning, fresh herbs

Contestant used whole white wheat flour in recipe. Log on to www.kswheat.com for sources of whole white wheat flour.

nutrition information *per serving (one serving): 67 cal, 1 g fat, 0 mg chol, 154 mg sodium, 13 g carbo, 2 g fiber, 3 g pro, 13 mcg folate.*

1 For sponge, combine in bowl, whole wheat flour, yeast, sugar, garlic powder, Italian seasoning, and water. Mix 2 minutes. Cover with plastic wrap; let rest 20 minutes.

2 Stir in salt, olive oil, and cheese. Add whole wheat flour; mix 2 minutes. Gradually add enough of the bread flour to form a soft dough. Knead dough 5 to 8 minutes. Place in lightly greased bowl. Cover; let rise until double.

3 Divide dough into two pieces. Gently pull or stretch each piece of dough into a circle or rectangle ¾-inch thick. Place on greased baking sheets or pizza pans that have been dusted with cornmeal. Cover, let rise 20 to 25 minutes.

4 Dimple dough with fingertips every ½ inch. Brush with oil; sprinkle on cheese and, if desired, Kosher salt. Let rest 5 minutes.

5 Bake in preheated 400°F oven 15 to 20 minutes, or until golden. During last several minutes of baking, sprinkle with Italian seasoning or fresh herbs. Best served fresh.

SUGARLESS APPLE CAKE

makes 24 servings

THIS RECIPE WAS DEVELOPED IN THE KWC TEST KITCHEN FOR THOSE REQUESTING SUGAR-FREE RECIPES.

ingredients
- 3 cups finely chopped unpeeled apples
- 1 cup raisins, moistened and drained
- ½ cup chopped pecans, optional
- 2 cups all-purpose flour
- 1 cup whole wheat flour
- 1 ½ teaspoons baking soda
- 1 ½ teaspoons ground cinnamon
- ½ cup vegetable oil
- 4 beaten eggs
- ¾ cup, thawed, unsweetened frozen apple juice concentrate

1 Preheat oven to 350°F. Coat a 15 x 10 x 1-inch jelly-roll pan with nonstick cooking spray. In medium bowl, combine chopped apples, raisins, and pecans; set aside.

2 In large bowl, mix by hand the all-purpose flour, whole wheat flour, soda, and cinnamon. Stir in oil, eggs, and apple juice concentrate. Mix 1 minute. Stir in apple mixture, mixing 30 hand strokes or until thoroughly combined.

3 Spread in pan and bake 23 to 25 minutes, or until toothpick comes out clean. Cool on wire rack.

nutrition information *per serving (one piece of cake): 150 cal, 6 g fat, 35 mg chol, 93 mg sodium, 23 g carbo, 2 g fiber, 3 g pro, 21 mcg folate.*

ITALIAN CHEESE BRAID

makes 1 large braid, 24 slices

YOUTH DIVISION CHAMPION IN THE 2004 KANSAS FESTIVAL OF BREADS WAS JASON SMELSER, OSKALOOSA, KANSAS. HE ENTERED THIS WINNING RECIPE.

ingredients
- ¾ cup lukewarm water (110-115°F)
- 1 ¾ teaspoons RED STAR® Active Dry Yeast
- 2 tablespoons granulated sugar
- 1 beaten egg
- 3 - 3 ¼ cups bread flour
- ½ cup low-fat small curd cottage cheese
- ½ cup grated dried three cheeses*
- 1 tablespoon butter
- 1 teaspoon dried Italian seasoning
- ½ teaspoon dried basil leaves
- ½ teaspoon garlic powder
- 1 teaspoon dried minced onion
- 1 ½ teaspoons salt

topping
- 1 beaten egg
- 1 - 2 tablespoons dried grated Parmesan cheese

*Parmesan, Romano and Asiago Cheeses or Grated Parmesan Romano Cheese

nutrition information *per serving (one slice): 82 cal, 2 g fat, 23 mg chol, 216 mg sodium, 12 g carbo, .5 g fiber, 4 g pro, 29 mcg folate.*

1 In mixer bowl, combine water, yeast, and sugar. Add egg, 1 cup flour, cottage cheese, dried cheeses, and butter; beat 2 minutes. Combine seasonings and add to mixture. Gradually add enough of the remaining flour to make a soft dough.

2 Knead dough 10 to 12 minutes, or until soft and elastic. Place dough in a greased bowl; turn to grease top. Cover with a warm, damp cloth. Let rise until double.

3 Punch dough down. Divide into thirds and shape into balls; cover. Let rest 10 minutes. Roll each piece into a 20-inch rope. Braid loosely and pinch ends of ropes together and tuck the sealed portion under the braid. Place on greased baking sheet. Spray loaf lightly with water; cover with plastic wrap. Let rise until double. Brush braid with beaten egg; sprinkle with Parmesan cheese.

4 Bake in preheated 350°F oven 28 to 30 minutes, turning baking sheet several times. Cover with foil last 10 minutes to prevent over-browning. Bake until golden and done. Remove from pan and cool on rack.

WHEAT MUFFINS

makes 12 muffins

THE LARGE-QUANTITY WHEAT MUFFIN RECIPE AND PHOTO APPEARED IN A FLOUR POWER ARTICLE IN THE JUNE/JULY 2005 SCHOOL FOOD SERVICE AND NUTRITION MAGAZINE.

ingredients
- ½ cup margarine or butter
- ½ cup granulated sugar
- ½ cup light brown sugar
- 1 teaspoon baking soda
- 1 beaten egg
- ¼ teaspoon vanilla extract
- 1 cup low-fat milk
- 2 cups whole wheat flour

nutrition information *per serving (one muffin): 203 cal, 8 g fat, 19 mg chol, 196 mg sodium, 31 g carbo, 3 g fiber, 4 g pro, 3 mcg folate.*

1 Preheat oven to 400°F. Have ingredients at room temperature.

2 Line muffin pan with paper baking cups or coat muffin cup with nonstick cooking spray.

3 In a large mixing bowl, beat margarine or butter with an electric mixer on medium to high speed for 30 to 40 seconds. Add the granulated sugar, brown sugar, and baking soda; beat mixture until combined.

4 Add egg and vanilla. Stir in milk and gradually add the whole wheat flour. Mix the ingredients together so dry ingredients are barely moistened. Over mixing will make the muffins tough with tunnels.

5 Fill muffin cups ⅔ full and bake 15 to 17 minutes, or until lightly browned.

6 Remove from pan and transfer muffins to a wire rack to cool.

PHOTO COURTESY OF THE WHEAT FOODS COUNCIL, WWW.WHEATFOODS.ORG

Poultry Recipes

Delicious Frozen Chicken Dinner

(Ready in about: 50 minutes | **Servings:** 2)

Ingredients:
- 2 frozen chicken breasts (8 - 10 ounces each)
- 2 tbsp. olive oil, divided.
- 1 small onion, peeled, diced
- 3/4 cup chicken stock
- 1 bag (12-ounces) green beans, trimmed
- 1 tsp. black pepper, divided.
- 1/4 cup fresh parsley, chopped.
- 1 cup wild rice blend
- 3 tsp. kosher salt, divided.
- 1 tbsp. Moroccan seasoning "Ras el Hanout"
- 1/4 cup honey mustard sauce

Instructions:
1. Select SEAR/SAUTÉ and set to HIGH. Allow to preheat for 5 minutes
2. After 5 minutes, add 1 tbsp. oil and onion. Cook, stirring occasionally, for 3 minutes, until onions are fragrant. Add wild rice, 2 tsp. salt, and Moroccan seasoning. Cook, stirring frequently, until the rice is coated with oil and very shiny. Add chicken stock and stir to incorporate
3. Place frozen chicken breasts on reversible rack, making sure rack is in the higher position. Place rack inside pot over rice mixture
4. Assemble pressure lid, making sure the PRESSURE RELEASE valve is in the SEAL position. Select PRESSURE and set to HIGH. Set time to 22 minutes. Select START/STOP to begin
5. While chicken and rice are cooking, toss green beans in a bowl with the remaining oil, salt, and pepper
6. When pressure cooking is complete, allow pressure to naturally release for 10 minutes. After 10 minutes, quick release any remaining pressure by turning the PRESSURE RELEASE valve to the VENT position. Carefully remove lid when unit has finished releasing pressure
7. Lift reversible rack out of the pot. Stir parsley into rice, then add green beans directly on top of the rice
8. Brush chicken breasts on all sides with honey mustard sauce, then return the reversible rack to the pot over rice and green beans. Close crisping lid. Select BROIL and set time to 10 minutes. Select START/STOP to begin.
9. Cooking is complete when internal temperature reaches 165°F. Serve chicken with green beans and rice

Turkey Meatballs in Tomato Sauce

(Ready in about: 15 minutes | **Servings:** 4)

Ingredients:
- 1 lb. ground turkey
- 1 large egg, at room temperature and beaten in a small bowl
- 1 (28-ounce) can whole tomatoes, drained and roughly chopped. (about 3 ½ cups)
- 1 medium yellow onion, chopped.
- 2 medium celery stalks, thinly sliced
- 1/2 cup plain dried breadcrumbs
- 1/4 cup finely grated Parmesan cheese (about 1/2-ounce)
- 2 tbsp. unsalted butter
- 1/2 cup chicken broth

- 1 tbsp. packed fresh oregano leaves, minced
- 1/4 tsp. grated nutmeg
- 1/4 cup heavy cream
- 1/2 tsp. dried oregano
- 1/2 tsp. dried rosemary
- 1/2 tsp. ground black pepper
- 1/2 tsp. salt

Instructions:
1. Mix the ground turkey, egg, breadcrumbs, cheese, oregano, rosemary, pepper and 1/4 tsp. salt in a large bowl until well combined. Form the mixture into 12 balls
2. Melt the butter in the Ninja Foodi Multi-cooker turned to the sauté function. Add the onion and celery; cook, often stirring, until the onion turns translucent, about 3 minutes
3. Stir in the tomatoes, broth, oregano and the remaining 1/4 tsp. salt. Drop the meatballs into the sauce.
4. High pressure for 10 minutes. Lock the lid on the Ninja Foodi Multi-cooker and then cook for 10 minutes.
5. To get 10 minutes' cook time, press *Pressure* button and use the Time Adjustment button to adjust the cook time to 10 minutes
6. Pressure Release. Use the quick release method to drop the pot's pressure to normal
7. Finish the dish. Unlock and open the cooker. Turn the Ninja Foodi Multi-cooker to its sauté function.
8. Stir in the cream and nutmeg; simmer, stirring all the while, for 1 minute to reduce the cream a little and blend the flavors

Sweet Chipotle Chicken Wings

(Ready in about: 25 minutes | **Servings:** 2)

Ingredients:
- 3 tbsp. Mexican hot sauce (such as Valentina brand)
- 1 tsp. minced canned chipotle in adobo sauce
- 1 cup water, for steaming
- 2 tbsp. honey

Instructions:
1. If using whole wings, cut off the tips and discard. Cut the wings at the joint into two pieces each the *drumette and the flat
2. Add the water and insert the steamer basket or trivet. Place the wings on the steamer insert
3. High pressure for 10 minutes. Close the lid and the pressure valve and then cook for 10 minutes.
4. To get 10 minutes' cook time, press *Pressure* button and the time selector
5. Pressure Release. Use the quick release method. Finish the dish. While the wings are cooking, make the sauce. In a large bowl, whisk together the hot sauce, honey and minced chipotle
6. Close crisping lid. Select *Air Crisp*, set temperature to 390°F and set time to 10 minutes. Select START/STOP to begin. Serve!

Herbed Whole Roasted Chicken

(Ready in about: 50 minutes | **Servings:** 4)

Ingredients:
- 1 whole uncooked chicken (4 ½ - 5 lb.)
- 1 tbsp. whole black peppercorns
- 2 tbsp. plus 2 tsp. kosher salt, divided.
- 1/4 cup hot water
- 1/4 cup honey
- Juice of 2 lemons (1/4 cup lemon juice)
- 5 sprigs fresh thyme
- 5 cloves garlic, peeled, smashed
- 1 tbsp. canola oil
- 2 tsp. ground black pepper

Instructions:
1. Rinse chicken and tie legs together with cooking twine
2. In a small bowl, mix together lemon juice, hot water, honey, and 2 tbsp. salt. Pour mixture into the pot. Place whole peppercorns, thyme, and garlic in the pot
3. Place chicken into the Cook & Crisp basket and place basket in pot. Assemble pressure lid, making sure the pressure release valve is in the SEAL position. Select PRESSURE and set to HIGH. Set time to 22 minutes. Select START/STOP to begin
4. When pressure cooking is complete, allow pressure to naturally release for 5 minutes. After 5 minutes, quick release remaining pressure by moving the pressure release valve to the VENT position. Carefully remove lid when unit has finished releasing pressure
5. Brush chicken with canola oil or spray with cooking spray. Season with salt and pepper
6. Close crisping lid. Select AIR CRISP, set temperature to 400°F, and set time to 8 minutes. Select START/STOP to begin. Cook until desired level of crispness is reached, adding up to 10 additional minutes
7. Cooking is complete when internal temperature reaches 165°F. Remove chicken from basket using 2 large serving forks. Let rest for 5 to 10 minutes before serving

Enchilada Chicken Breasts

(Ready in about: 30 minutes | **Servings:** 4)

Ingredients:
- 4 (6 to 8-ounce) boneless skinless chicken breasts
- 1/2 cup light-colored beer, preferably a Pilsner or an IPA
- 1 (8-ounce) can tomato sauce (1 cup)
- 1 tsp. packed dark brown sugar
- 1 tsp. ground cumin
- 1 tsp. smoked paprika
- 1/2 tsp. onion powder
- 1/4 tsp. garlic powder
- 2 tbsp. olive oil
- 2 tbsp. chili powder
- 2 tbsp. fresh lime juice
- 1/2 tsp. salt
- 1/2 tsp. ground black pepper

Instructions:
1. Mix the brown sugar, cumin, smoked paprika, salt, pepper, onion powder and garlic powder in a medium bowl. Massage the spice rub onto the chicken breasts
2. Heat the oil in the Ninja Foodi Multi-cooker using the *Sauté* function. Set the breasts in the cooker and brown well, turning once, about 6 minutes
3. Mix the tomato sauce, beer, chili powder and lime juice in the bowl the spices were in; pour the sauce over the breasts.
4. High pressure for 15 minutes. Close the lid and Cook for 15 minutes
5. To get 15 minutes' cook time, press the *Pressure* Button and adjust the time

6. Pressure Release. Use the quick release method to bring the pot's pressure back to normal
7. Close crisping lid. Select *Air Crisp*, set temperature to 390°F and set time to 9 minutes. Check after 6 minutes, cooking for an additional 3 minutes if dish needs more browning. Serve the chicken with the sauce ladled on top

Turkey Breast

(**Ready in about:** 1 hour 10 minutes | **Servings:** 4)

Ingredients:
- 1 frozen turkey breast with frozen gravy packet
- 1 whole onion

Instructions:
1. Place frozen turkey breast, rozen gravy packet and whole onion in the Ninja Foodi Multi-cooker
2. High pressure for 30 minutes. Lock the lid on the Ninja Foodi Multi-cooker and then cook for 30 minutes.
3. To get 30 minutes' cook time, press *Pressure* button and use the Time Adjustment button to adjust the cook time to 30 minutes
4. Pressure Release. Use natural release method
5. Remove lid, turn turkey breast over
6. High pressure for 30 minutes. Replace lid on the Ninja Foodi Multi-cooker and then cook for 30 minutes.
7. To get 30 minutes' cook time, press *Pressure* button
8. and use the Time Adjustment button to adjust the cook time to 30 minutes
9. Pressure Release. Use natural release method, again.
10. Finish the dish. Close crisping lid. Select *Air Crisp*, set temperature to 360°F and set time to 10 minutes. Check after 5 minutes, cooking for an additional 5 minutes if dish needs more browning
11. Remove mesh. Remove turkey and slice. Places slices and turkey gravy into serving dish

Instant Penne with Chicken

(**Ready in about:** 10 minutes | **Servings:** 4)

Ingredients:
- 1/2 lb. penne or similar pasta shape
- 3 (4-ounce) boneless, skinless chicken thighs
- Parmigiano Reggiano or similar cheese, for garnish
- 3 garlic cloves, minced or pressed (about 1 tbsp.)
- 1 small green bell pepper, seeded and cut into 1-inch chunks (about 1 ½ cups)
- 1 ½ cups Quick Marinara Sauce or plain tomato sauce
- 1/2 tsp. dried Italian herbs, divided. (or 1/4 tsp. dried oregano and 1/4 tsp. dried basil)
- 3 cups arugula or baby spinach
- 2 tbsp. minced sun dried tomatoes (optional)
- 1 tbsp. all purpose flour
- 1 tsp. kosher salt, divided.
- 1/8 tsp. granulated garlic or garlic powder
- 1/8 tsp. freshly ground black pepper
- 1 tbsp. olive oil
- 1 cup thinly sliced onion
- 1/2 cup dry white or red wine
- 1 3/4 cups water

Instructions:
1. In a small bowl or jar with a shaker top, mix the flour, 1/2 tsp. of kosher salt the granulated garlic, 1/4 tsp. of Italian herbs and the pepper. Sprinkle the flour mixture over both sides of the chicken thighs, coating as evenly as possible
2. Set Ninja Foodi Multi-cooker to *Sauté*, heat the olive oil until it shimmers and flows like water. Add the chicken thighs and cook for 5 minutes or until golden brown
3. Turn the thighs over and cook the other side for 5 minutes more or until that side is also golden brown. Remove the thighs to a rack or cutting board and cool for 3 minutes
4. With the Ninja Foodi Multi-cooker on *Sauté* add the onion, green bell pepper and garlic. Cook for about 3 minutes, stirring until the onions just start to brown
5. Pour in the wine and scrape the bottom of the pan to release the browned bits, cooking until the wine is almost completely evaporated
6. Add the Quick Marinara Sauce the remaining 1/2 tsp. of kosher salt the sun dried tomatoes (if using) the remaining 1/4 tsp. of Italian herbs the water the chicken and the penne
7. High pressure for 5 minutes. Lock the lid on the Ninja Foodi Multi-cooker and then cook for 5 minutes.
8. To get 5 minutes' cook time, press *Pressure* button and use the Time Adjustment button to adjust the cook time to 5 minutes
9. Pressure Release. Use the quick release method
10. Finish the dish. Unlock and remove the lid. The penne should be almost done and the sauce will be a little thin
11. Add the arugula and stir. With the Ninja Foodi Multi-cooker set to *Sauté*, cook for 3 to 4 minutes or until the pasta is done to your liking the arugula is wilted and the sauce has thickened. Serve topped with grated Parmigiano Reggiano

Delicious Chicken Pot Pie Recipe

(Ready in about: 35 minutes | Servings: 6)

Ingredients:
- 2 lb. uncooked boneless skinless chicken breasts, cut in 1-inch cubes
- 1/2 stick (1/4 cup) unsalted butter
- 1/2 large onion, peeled, diced
- 1 large carrot, peeled, diced
- 2 cloves garlic, peeled, minced
- 1 stalk celery, diced
- 1/2 cup frozen peas
- 1 ½ tsp. fresh thyme, minced
- 2 tsp. kosher salt
- 1/2 tsp. black pepper
- 1/2 cup heavy cream
- 1 cup chicken broth
- 1 tbsp. fresh Italian parsley, minced
- 1/4 cup all-purpose flour

Instructions:
1. Select SEAR/SAUTÉ and set to MD:HI. Select START/STOP to begin. Allow to preheat for 5 minutes. After 5 minutes, add butter to pot. Once it melts, add onion, carrot, and garlic, and SAUTÉ until softened, about 3 minutes
2. Add chicken and broth to the pot. Assemble pressure lid, making sure the PRESSURE RELEASE valve is in the SEAL position. Select PRESSURE and set to HIGH. Set time to 5 minutes. Select START/STOP to begin
3. When pressure cooking is complete, quick release the pressure by moving the PRESSURE RELEASE valve to the VENT position. Carefully remove lid when unit has finished releasing pressure

4. Select SEAR/SAUTÉ and set to MD:HI. Select START/STOP to begin. Add remaining ingredients to pot, except pie crust. Stir until sauce thickens and bubbles, about 3 minutes
5. Lay pie crust evenly on top of the filling mixture, folding over edges if necessary. Make a small cut in center of pie crust so that steam can escape during baking. Close the crisping lid. Select BROIL and set time to 10 minutes. Select START/STOP to begin
6. When cooking is complete, remove pot from unit and place on a heat-resistant surface. Let rest 10 to 15 minutes before serving

Chicken Breasts with White Wine

(Ready in about: 25 minutes | **Servings:** 4)

Ingredients:
- 4 (12-ounce) bone in, skin on chicken breasts
- 1 (4-inch) fresh rosemary sprig
- 1/2 cup fresh orange juice
- 1/2 cup dry but light white wine, such as Sauvignon Blanc
- 1/2 tbsp. potato starch or cornstarch
- 1 tbsp. honey
- 3 tbsp. unsalted butter
- 1/2 tsp. salt
- 1/2 tsp. ground black pepper

Instructions:
1. Melt the butter in a Ninja Foodi Multi-cooker, turned to the sauté function. Season the chicken with the salt and pepper, then add two breasts skin side down to the cooker
2. Brown well, turning once, about 5 minutes; transfer to a large bowl. Brown the remaining breasts and leave them in the cooker
3. Return the first two breasts to the cooker, arranging them so that all are skin up but overlapping only as necessary, thinner parts over thick. Pour the orange juice and wine over the chicken. Tuck in the rosemary and drizzle everything with honey
4. High pressure for 18 minutes. Lock the lid on the Ninja Foodi Multi-cooker and then cook for 18 minutes.
5. To get 18 minutes' cook time, press *Pressure* button and use the Time Adjustment button to adjust the cook time to 18 minutes
6. Pressure Release. Use the quick release method to bring the pot's pressure back to normal.
7. Finish the dish. Unlock and open the pot. Discard the rosemary sprig. Use kitchen tongs to transfer the chicken breasts to individual serving plates or a serving platter
8. Dissolve the potato starch or cornstarch with 1/2 tbsp. water in a small bowl. Turn the Ninja Foodi to its sauté function; bring the sauce to a simmer
9. Add this slurry and cook, stirring all the time, until thickened, about 20 seconds. Ladle the sauce over the chicken to serve

Aromatic Turkey Breast

(Ready in about: 1 hour 20 minutes | **Servings:** 4)

Ingredients:
- 6.5 lb. bone in, skin on turkey breast
- 1 (14 oz.) can turkey or chicken broth
- 1 large onion, quartered
- 1 stock celery, cut in large pieces
- 1 sprig thyme
- 3 tbsp. cornstarch
- 3 tbsp. cold water
- Salt and pepper, to taste

Instructions:
1. Season turkey breast liberally with salt and pepper. Put trivet in the bottom. Add chicken broth, onion, celery and thyme. Add the turkey to the cooking pot breast side up
2. High pressure for 45 minutes. Lock the lid on the Ninja Foodi Multi-cooker and then cook for 45 minutes.
3. To get 45 minutes' cook time, press *Pressure* button and use the adjust button to adjust the cook time to 45 minutes
4. Pressure Release. Use a natural pressure release for 10 minutes, then do a quick pressure release
5. Check if the turkey is done. If it isn't, lock the lid in place and cook it for a few more minutes
6. Finish the dish. Close crisping lid. Select *Air Crisp*, set temperature to 360°F and set time to 10 minutes. Check after 5 minutes, cooking for an additional 5 minutes if dish needs more browning. Carefully remove turkey and place on large plate. Cover with foil
7. Strain and skim the fat off the broth. Whisk together cornstarch and cold water; add to broth in cooking pot. Select Sauté and stir until broth thickens
8. Add salt and pepper to taste. Slice the turkey and serve immediately

Olive and Lemon Ligurian Chicken

(Ready in about: 35 minutes | **Servings:** 6 to 8)

Ingredients:
- 3.5-ounce (100g) Black Gourmet Salt-Cured Olives (Taggiesche, French or Kalamata)
- 3 sprigs of Fresh Rosemary (two for chopping, one for garnish)
- 1 whole chicken, cut into parts or package of bone in chicken pieces, skin removed (or not) 1/2 cup (125ml) dry white wine
- 2 garlic cloves, chopped.
- 2 sprigs of Fresh Sage
- 1/2 bunch of Parsley Leaves and stems
- 3 lemons, juiced (about a 3/4 cup or 180ml)
- 4 tbsp. extra virgin olive oil
- 1 tsp. sea salt
- 1/4 tsp. pepper
- 1 fresh lemon, for garnish (optional)

Instructions:
1. Prepare the marinade by finely chopping together the garlic, rosemary, sage and parsley. Place them in a container and add the lemon juice, olive oil, salt and pepper. Mix well and set aside
2. Remove the skin from the chicken (save it for a chicken stock)
3. In the preheated Ninja Foodi Multi-cooker, with the lid off, add a swirl of olive oil and brown the chicken pieces on all sides for about 5 minutes
4. De-glaze cooker with the white wine until it has almost all evaporated (about 3 minutes)

5. Add the chicken pieces back in this time being careful with the order. Put all dark meat (wings, legs, thighs) first and then the chicken breasts on top so that they do not touch the bottom of the Ninja Foodi Multi-cooker.
6. Pour the remaining marinade on top. Don't worry if this does not seem like enough liquid the chicken will also release its juices into the cooker, too
7. High pressure for 10 minutes. Lock the lid on the Ninja Foodi Multi-cooker and then cook for 10 minutes.
8. To get 10 minutes' cook time, press *Pressure* button and adjust the time
9. Pressure Release. When time is up, open the cooker by releasing the pressure using the Quick Release Method
10. Finish the dish. Close crisping lid. Select *Air Crisp*, set temperature to 390°F and set time to 10 minutes. Check after 5 minutes, cooking for an additional 5 minutes if dish needs more browning
11. Take the chicken pieces out of the cooker and place on a serving platter tightly covered with foil
12. Reduce the cooking liquid in the Ninja Foodi Multi-cooker, if necessary, with the lid off to 1/4 of its amount or until it becomes thick and syrupy
13. Put all of the chicken pieces back into the Ninja Foodi Multi-cooker to warm up. Mix and spoon the thick glaze onto the chicken pieces and simmer it in the glaze for a few minutes before serving
14. Sprinkle with fresh rosemary, olives and lemon slices. When serving, caution your guests that the olives still have their pits!

Yummy Spicy Turkey Chili

(**Ready in about:** 55 minutes | **Servings:** 4)

Ingredients:
- 1 lb. ground turkey
- 1/4 cup your favorite hot sauce
- 1 (15-ounce) can fire roasted diced tomatoes
- 1 (15-ounce) can kidney beans, including their liquid
- 1 medium yellow onion, diced
- 2 green bell peppers, seeded and diced
- 2 fresh cayenne peppers, chopped. (seeds included)
- 4 cloves garlic, chopped.
- 1 cup grated Monterey Jack cheese
- 1 tbsp. olive oil
- 1 tsp. ground cumin
- 1/2 tsp. dried oregano leaves
- 1/4 cup chopped cilantro

Instructions:
1. Set the Ninja Foodi Multi-cooker to its *Sauté* setting and add the oil. Add the onions, peppers and garlic and sauté until the onions soften and begin to brown, about 10 minutes. Add the cumin and oregano and sauté two more minutes, until aromatic
2. Add the ground turkey, breaking it up with a spoon or spatula. Sauté until opaque and cooked through, about 5 minutes
3. Add the hot sauce, canned tomatoes and kidney beans and stir to combine
4. High pressure for 45 minutes. Lock the lid on the Ninja Foodi Multi-cooker and then cook for 45 minutes.
5. To get 45 minutes' cook time, press *pressure* button and use the adjust button to adjust the cook time to 45 minutes.
6. Pressure Release. Use natural release method
7. Finish the dish. Top with grated cheese and cilantro and serve with rice or cornbread, if desired

Turkey Gluten Free Gravy

(Ready in about: 55 minutes | **Servings:** 6)

Ingredients:
- 1 (4 - 5 lb.) bone in, skin on turkey breast
- 2 tbsp. ghee or butter (use coconut oil for AIP)
- 1 medium onion, cut into medium dice
- 1 large carrot, cut into medium dice
- 1 celery rib, cut into medium dice
- 1 garlic clove, peeled and smashed
- 1 ½ cups bone broth (preferably from chicken or turkey bones)
- Black pepper (omit for AIP)
- 2 tsp. dried sage
- 1/4 cup dry white wine
- 1 bay leaf
- 1 tbsp. tapioca starch (optional)
- Salt to taste

Instructions:
1. Set the *Sauté* function. Pat turkey breast dry and generously season with salt and pepper. Melt cooking fat in the Ninja Foodi Multi-cooker
2. Brown turkey breast, skin side down, about 5 minutes and transfer to a plate, leaving fat in the pot
3. Add onion, carrot and celery to pot and cook until softened, about 5 minutes. Stir in garlic and sage and cook until fragrant, about 30 seconds
4. Pour in wine and cook until slightly reduced about 3 minutes. Stir in broth and bay leaf. Using a wooden spoon, scrape up all browned bits stuck on the bottom of pot.
5. Place turkey skin side up in the pot with any accumulated juices
6. High pressure for 35 minutes. Lock the lid on the Ninja Foodi Multi-cooker and then cook for 35 minutes.
7. To get 35 minutes' cook time, press *Pressure* button and use the Time Adjustment button to adjust the cook time to 35
8. Pressure Release. Use quick release method and carefully remove lid
9. Finish the dish. Close crisping lid. Select *Air Crisp*, set temperature to 375°F and set time to 10 minutes. Check after 5 minutes, cooking for an additional 5 minutes if dish needs more browning.
10. Transfer turkey breast to carving board or plate and tent loosely with foil, allowing it to rest while you prepare the gravy
11. Use an immersion blender or carefully transfer cooking liquid and vegetables to blender and puree until smooth. Return to heat and cook until thickened and reduced to about 2 cups. Adjust seasoning to taste. Slice turkey breast and serve with hot gravy. Enjoy!

Crispy Chicken Thighs with Carrots and Rice Pilaf

(Ready in about: 25 minutes | **Servings:** 4)

Ingredients:
- 4 uncooked boneless skin-on chicken thighs
- 1 box (6-ounces) rice pilaf
- 2 tbsp. honey, warmed
- 1/2 tsp. smoked paprika
- 1 3/4 cups water
- 1 tbsp. butter
- 4 carrots, peeled, cut in half, lengthwise
- 2 tsp. kosher salt, divided.
- 1 tbsp. extra-virgin olive oil
- 2 tsp. poultry spice
- 1/2 tsp. ground cumin

Instructions:
1. Place rice pilaf, water, and butter into pot; stir to incorporate
2. Place reversible rack in the pot, making sure rack is in the higher position. Place carrots in center of rack. Arrange chicken thighs, skin side up, around the carrots. Assemble pressure lid, making sure the PRESSURE RELEASE valve is in the SEAL position. Select PRESSURE and set to HIGH. Set time to 4 minutes. Select START/STOP to begin
3. While chicken and rice are cooking, stir together warm honey, smoked paprika, cumin, and 1 tsp. salt. Set aside
4. When pressure cooking is complete, quick release the pressure by moving the PRESSURE RELEASE valve to the VENT position. Carefully remove lid when unit has finished releasing pressure
5. Brush carrots with seasoned honey. Brush chicken with olive oil, then season evenly with poultry spice and remaining salt
6. Close crisping lid. Select BROIL and set time to 10 minutes. Select START/STOP to begin. When cooking is complete, serve chicken with carrots and rice

Green Chicken Curry

(**Ready in about:** 25 minutes | **Servings:** 6 to 8)

Ingredients:
- 3 lb. boneless skinless chicken thighs, cut into 1/2-inch by 2 inch lengths
- 12-ounces green beans, trimmed and cut into 2 inch pieces
- Cream from the top of a (13.5-ounce) can coconut milk
- 1 tsp. Diamond Crystal kosher salt or 3/4 tsp. fine sea salt
- The rest of the (13.5-ounce) can coconut milk
- 4 tbsp. green curry paste (a whole 4-ounces can)
- 1 tbsp. fish sauce (plus more to taste)
- 1 tbsp. soy sauce (plus more to taste)
- 1 tbsp. brown sugar (plus more to taste)
- 1 tbsp. vegetable oil
- 1 medium onion, peeled and sliced thin
- 3 cloves garlic, crushed
- 1/2- inch piece of ginger, peeled and crushed
- 1 cup chicken stock or water
- Juice from 1 lime
- Minced basil (preferably Thai basil)
- Minced cilantro
- Jasmine rice
- Lime wedges

Instructions:
1. Heat the vegetable oil in the Ninja Foodi Multi-cooker until shimmering, use Sauté mode. Stir in the onion, garlic and ginger and Sauté until the onion starts to soften, about 3 minutes
2. Fry the curry paste: Scoop the cream from the top of the can of coconut milk and add it to the pot, then stir in the curry paste. Cook, often stirring, until the curry paste darkens, about 5 minutes
3. Sprinkle the chicken with the kosher salt. Add the chicken to the pot and stir to coat with curry paste. Stir in the rest of the can of coconut milk, chicken stock, fish sauce, soy sauce and brown sugar
4. High pressure for 10 minutes. Lock the lid on the Ninja Foodi Multi-cooker and then cook for 10 minutes.
5. To get 10 minutes' cook time, press *Pressure* button and use the Time Adjustment button to adjust the cook time to 10 minutes

6. Pressure Release. Use the quick release method to bring the pot's pressure back to normal
7. Finish the dish. Close crisping lid. Select *Air Crisp*, set temperature to 390°F and set time to 15 minutes. Check after 10 minutes, cooking for an additional 5 minutes if dish needs more browning
8. Finish the curry: Remove the lid from the Ninja Foodi Multi-cooker, then set Sauté mode. Stir in the lime juice and the green beans and simmer the curry until the green beans are crisp tender, about 4 minutes
9. Taste the curry for seasoning, adding more soy sauce (to add salt) or brown sugar (to add sweet) as needed. Ladle the curry into bowls, sprinkle with minced cilantro and basil and serve with Jasmine rice

Sweet Soy Chicken Wings

(**Ready in about:** 40 minutes | **Servings:** 2 to 4)

Ingredients:
- 1 ½ lb. chicken wings
- Chicken Wing Marinade
- 1/2 large shallot or 1 small shallot, roughly minced
- 4 cloves garlic, roughly minced
- 2 tbsp. light soy sauce
- 1 tbsp. ginger, sliced
- 1 tbsp. honey
- 1 tbsp. dark soy sauce
- 1 tbsp. Shaoxing wine
- 1 to 2-star anise
- 1/2 cup warm water
- 1 tbsp. peanut oil
- 1 ½ tbsp. cornstarch
- 1 tsp. sugar
- 1/4 tsp. salt

Instructions:
1. Marinate the chicken wings with the Chicken Wing Marinade for 20 minutes
2. Heat the Ninja Foodi Multi-cooker using the *Sauté* function
3. Add 1 tbsp. of peanut oil into the pot. Add the marinated chicken wings into the pot. Then, brown the chicken wings for roughly 30 seconds on each side. Flip a few times as you brown them as the soy sauce and sugar can be burnt easily. Remove and set aside
4. Add the minced shallot, star anise and sliced ginger, then stir for roughly a minute. Add the minced garlic and stir until fragrant (roughly 30 seconds)
5. Mix 1 tbsp. of honey with 1/2 cup of warm water, then add it into the pot and deglaze the bottom of the pot with a wooden spoon
6. Place all the chicken wings with all the meat juice and the leftover chicken wing marinade into the pot.
7. High pressure for 5 minutes. Lock the lid on the Ninja Foodi Multi-cooker and then cook for 5 minutes.
8. To get 5 minutes' cook time, press *Pressure* button and use the Time Adjustment button to adjust the cook time to 5 minutes
9. Pressure Release. Let the pressure to come down naturally for at least 10 minutes, then quick release any pressure left in the pot
10. Finish the dish. Close crisping lid. Select *Air Crisp*, set temperature to 390°F and set time to 10 minutes. Check after 10 minutes, cooking for an additional 5 minutes if dish needs more browning
11. Open the lid carefully and taste one of the honey soy chicken wings and the honey soy sauce. Season with more salt or honey if desired

12. Remove all the chicken wings from the pot and set aside. Turn the Ninja Foodi Multi-cooker to its sauté function. Mix 1 ½ tbsp. of cornstarch with 1 tbsp. of cold running tap water. Keep mixing and add it into the honey soy sauce one third at a time until desired thickness
13. Turn off the heat and add the chicken wings back into the pot. Coat well with the honey soy sauce and serve immediately!

Stuffed Chicken Recipe

(**Ready in about:** 30 minutes | **Servings:** 4)

Ingredients:
- 4 Chicken Breasts, skinless
- 1 cup Baby Spinach, frozen
- 1/2 cup crumbled Feta Cheese
- 2 tbsp. Olive Oil
- 2 tsp dried Parsley
- 1/2 tsp dried Oregano
- 1/2 tsp Garlic Powder
- Salt and Black Pepper to taste
- 1 cup Water

Instructions:
1. Wrap the chicken in plastic and put on a cutting board. Use a rolling pin to pound flat to a quarter inch thickness. Remove the plastic wrap.
2. In a bowl, mix spinach, salt, and feta cheese and scoop the mixture onto the chicken breasts. Wrap the chicken to secure the spinach filling in it.
3. Use toothpicks to secure the wrap firmly from opening. Gently season the chicken pieces with oregano, parsley, garlic powder, and pepper.
4. Select Sear/Sauté mode on Foodi Ninja. Heat the oil, add the chicken, and sear to golden brown on each side. Work in 2 batches.
5. Remove the chicken onto a plate and set aside. Pour the water into the pot and use a spoon to scrape the bottom of the pot to let loose any chicken pieces or seasoning that is stuck to the bottom of the pot. Fit the reversible rack into the pot with care as the pot will still be hot.
6. Transfer the chicken onto the rack. Seal the lid and select Pressure mode on High pressure for 10 minutes. Press Start/Stop.
7. Once the timer has ended, do a quick pressure release. Close the crisping lid and cook on Bake/Roast mode for 5 minutes at 370 F.
8. Plate the chicken and serve with a side of sautéed asparagus, and some slices of tomatoes.

Awesome Turkey Sloppy Joes

(**Ready in about:** 35 minutes | **Servings:** 2)

Ingredients:
- 1 large or 2 small turkey thighs (1 ½ lb. total), skin removed
- 1/4 small red or green bell pepper, chopped. (about 2 tbsps.)
- 1 tbsp. cider or wine vinegar, plus additional as needed
- 2 tsp. ancho or New Mexico chili powder
- 1 tsp. Dijon mustard
- 1/2 tsp. Worcestershire sauce
- 1 tbsp. olive oil
- 1/4 cup chopped onion
- 1 garlic clove, minced or pressed
- Kosher salt
- 2/3 cup tomato sauce
- 1/4 cup beer or water
- 1 tbsp. packed brown sugar
- 2 hamburger buns

Instructions:
1. Set the Ninja Foodi Multi-cooker to *Sauté*, heat the olive oil until it shimmers and flows like water. Add the onion, bell pepper and garlic and sprinkle with a pinch or two of kosher salt. Cook for about 5 minutes, stirring, until the onions just begin to brown
2. Add the tomato sauce, beer, cider vinegar, brown sugar, chili powder, mustard and Worcestershire sauce. Bring to a simmer. Stir to make sure the brown sugar is dissolved. Place the turkey thigh in the cooker
3. High pressure for 30 minutes. Lock the lid on the Ninja Foodi Multi-cooker and then cook for 30 minutes
4. To get 30 minutes' cook time, press *Pressure* button and use the Time Adjustment button to adjust the cook time to 30 minutes
5. Pressure Release. Use the natural release
6. Unlock and remove the lid; transfer the turkey to a plate or cutting board to cool.
7. Finish the dish. Set the Ninja Foodi Multi-cooker to *Sauté* and simmer the sauce for about 5 minutes or until it's the consistency of a thick tomato sauce
8. Skim any visible fat from the surface and discard. Taste and adjust the seasoning. Serve on the hamburger buns

One Pot Chicken and Rice

(**Ready in about:** 20 minutes | **Servings:** 4)

Ingredients:
- 6 dried shiitake mushrooms, marinated
- 2 rice measuring cups (360 ml) Jasmine rice, rinse
- 6 to 8 chicken drumsticks, marinated
- Green onions for garnish
- 1 tbsp. ginger, shredded
- 1 tsp. Salt
- 1 ½ cup (375 ml) water

Marinade:
- 1 tbsp. light soy sauce
- 1 tsp. dark soy sauce
- 1 tbsp. ginger, shredded
- 1 tsp. five spice powder
- 1/2 tsp. sugar
- 1/2 tsp. cornstarch
- A dash of white pepper powder
- 1 tsp. Shaoxing rice wine

Instructions:
1. Place the dried shiitake mushrooms in a small bowl. Rehydrate them with cold water for 20 minutes.
2. Chop the drumsticks into 2 pieces. Then, marinate the chicken and mushrooms in the marinade sauce for 20 minutes
3. Rinse rice under cold water by gently scrubbing the rice with your fingertips in a circling motion. Pour out the milky water and continue to rinse until the water is clear. Then, drain the water
4. Add the rice, 1 tsp. of salt and marinated chicken and mushrooms and 1 ½ cup of water in the Ninja Foodi Multi-cooker
5. High pressure for 10 minutes. Lock the lid on the Ninja Foodi Multi-cooker and then cook for 10 minutes.
6. To get 10 minutes' cook time, press *Pressure* button and adjust the time
7. Pressure Release. Let the pressure to come down naturally for at least 15 minutes, then quick release any pressure left in the pot. Serve immediately

Texas Trail Chili

(Ready in about: 20 minutes | **Servings:** 8)

Ingredients:
- 1 ½ lb. ground beef, turkey or chicken
- 2 Cups favorite Bloody Mary mix (spicy preferred)
- 4 tbsp. (or more if you like) favorite chili powder, divided.
- 2 Cans (14-ounces each) kidney beans, drained and rinsed well
- 2 Cans (14-ounces each) diced tomatoes with green chilies (or 28-ounce can diced tomatoes with juice)
- 2 tbsp. canola oil
- 1 large onion, peeled, chopped.
- 1 ½-Cups Water
- Corn chips
- Shredded cheese
- Sliced green onions
- Sour cream

Instructions:
1. In the Ninja Foodi Multi-cooker pot, heat the oil. Use *Sauté* Function. Add the onion and Sauté about 8 minutes until it becomes lightly golden brown. Add the meat and cook until it browns, breaking it up as it cooks
2. When meat is done, remove turkey thighs to a cutting board and cover loosely with foil
3. Stir in the Bloody Mary mix and heat, stirring and scraping up any browned bits on the bottom of the pan.
4. Add the tomatoes, beans and 2 tbsp. of the chili powder. Stir well. Bring to just a boil; add the water
5. High pressure for 5 minutes. Lock the lid on the Ninja Foodi Multi-cooker and then cook for 5 minutes
6. To get 5 minutes' cook time, press *Pressure* button and use the Time Adjustment button to adjust the cook time to 5 minutes
7. Pressure Release. Use the Quick Release method
8. Finish the dish. Just before serving stir in tbsp. of the chili powder then let it stand 5 minutes.
9. Ladle into bowls and garnish as desired

Delicious Chicken and Coconut Curry

(Ready in about: 35 minutes | **Servings:** 4)

Ingredients:
- 4 Chicken Breasts
- 2 cup Green Beans, cut in half
- 2 Red Bell Pepper, seeded and cut in 2-inch sliced
- 2 Yellow Bell Pepper, seeded and cut in 2-inch slices
- 1/2 cup Chicken Broth
- 2 cups Coconut Milk
- 4 tbsp. Red Curry Paste
- 4 tbsp. Sugar
- 2 tbsp. Lime Juice
- Salt and Black Pepper to taste

Instructions:
1. Add the chicken, red curry paste, salt, pepper, coconut milk, broth and sugar, in the Ninja Foodi inner pot
2. Close the pressure lid, secure the pressure valve, and select Pressure mode on High for 15 minutes. Press Start/Stop
3. Once the timer has ended, do a quick pressure release, and open the lid.

4. Remove the chicken onto a cutting board and close the crisping lid. Select Broil mode. Add the bell peppers, green beans, and lime juice.
5. Stir the sauce with a spoon and cook for 4 minutes
6. Slice the chicken with a knife, pour the sauce and vegetables over and serve warm

Chicken with Mushrooms and Artichoke Hearts

(**Ready in about:** 18 minutes | **Servings:** 6)

Ingredients:
- 2 (8-ounce) or 4 (4-ounce) bone in, skin on chicken thighs
- 4-ounces' white button or cremini mushrooms, trimmed and quartered
- 1 tbsp. olive oil
- 1/2 cup frozen artichoke hearts, thawed
- 1/3 cup low sodium chicken broth
- 1/4 cup sliced onion
- 1/2 cup dry white wine
- 1 bay leaf
- 1/4 tsp. dried thyme
- Freshly ground black pepper
- 1/2 tsp. kosher salt

Instructions:
1. Using 1/2 tsp. of kosher salt, sprinkle the chicken thighs on both sides
2. In the Ninja Foodi Multi-cooker set to *Sauté*, heat the olive oil until it shimmers and flows like water. Add the chicken thighs, skin sidedown and cook, undisturbed, for about 6 minutes or until the skin is dark golden brown and most of the fat under the skin has rendered
3. Turn the thighs to the other side and cook for about 3 minutes more or until that side is light golden brown. Remove the thighs
4. Carefully pour off almost all the fat, leaving just enough (about 1 tbsp.) to cover the bottom of the Ninja Foodi Multi-cooker with a thick coat. Add the onion and mushrooms and cook for about 5 minutes or until softened. Add the white wine and cook for 3 to 5 minutes or until reduced by half
5. Add the bay leaf, thyme, artichokes and chicken broth and bring to a simmer. Return the chicken to the pot, skin side up
6. High pressure for 12 minutes. Lock the lid on the Ninja Foodi Multi-cooker and then cook for 12 minutes.
7. To get 12 minutes' cook time, press *Pressure* button and use the Time Adjustment button to adjust the cook time to 12 minutes
8. Pressure Release. After cooking, use the natural method to release pressure
9. Finish the dish. Unlock and remove the lid. Remove the chicken thighs from the pan and set aside. Remove the bay leaf
10. Strain the sauce into a fat separator and let it rest until the fat rises to the surface. If you don't have a fat separator, let the sauce sit for a few minutes; then spoon or blot off any excess fat from the top and discard.
11. Pour the defatted sauce back into the cooker and add the chicken thighs and the solids from the sauce. If you prefer a thicker sauce, turn the Ninja Foodi Multi-cooker to the *Sauté* function and simmer the sauce for several minutes until it's reduced to the consistency you like
12. Adjust the seasoning, adding more salt if necessary and several grinds of pepper and serve

Pork Recipes

Pork Loin and Apples

(Ready in about: 43 minutes | **Servings:** 8)

Ingredients:
- 1 (3 lb.) boneless pork loin roast
- 1 large red onion, halved and thinly sliced
- 2 medium tart green apples, such as Granny Smith, peeled, cored and thinly sliced
- 1/2 cup moderately sweet white wine, such as Riesling
- 2 tbsp. unsalted butter
- 1/4 cup chicken broth
- 4 fresh thyme sprigs
- 2 bay leaves
- 1/2 tsp. salt
- 1/2 tsp. ground black pepper

Instructions:
1. Melt the butter in the Ninja Foodi Multi-cooker, set on the *Sauté* function. Add the pork loin and brown it on all sides, turning occasionally, about 8 minutes in all. Transfer to a large plate
2. Add the onion to the pot; cook, often stirring, until softened, about 3 minutes. Stir in the apple, thyme and bay leaves. Pour in the wine and scrape up any browned bits on the bottom of the pot
3. Pour in the broth; stir in the salt and pepper. Nestle the pork loin into this apple mixture; pour any juices from the plate into the pot
4. High pressure for 30 minutes. Lock the lid on the Ninja Foodi Multi-cooker and then cook for 30 minutes.
5. To get 30 minutes' cook time, press *Pressure* button and adjust the time
6. Pressure Release. Use the quick release method to bring the pot's pressure to normal
7. Finish the dish. Close crisping lid and select Broil, set time to 7 minutes.
8. Transfer the pork to a cutting board; let stand for 5 minutes while you dish the sauce into serving bowls or onto a serving platter. Slice the loin into 1/2-inch-thick rounds and lay these over the sauce

Amazing Pork Chops with Applesauce

(Ready in about: 30 minutes | **Servings:** 4)

Ingredients:
- 2 to 4 pork loin chops (we used center cut, bone-on)
- 2 gala apples, thinly sliced
- 1 tsp. cinnamon powder
- 1 tbsp. honey
- 1/2 cup unsalted homemade chicken stock or water
- 1 tbsp. grapeseed oil or olive oil
- 1 small onion, sliced
- 3 cloves garlic, roughly minced
- 2 tbsp. light soy sauce
- 1 tbsp. butter
- Kosher salt and ground black pepper to taste
- 2 pieces whole cloves (optional)
- 1 ½ tbsp. cornstarch mixed with 2 tbsp. water (optional)

Instructions:
1. Make a few small cut around the sides of the pork chops so they will stay flat and brown evenly
2. Season the pork chops with a generous amount of kosher salt and ground black pepper
3. Heat up your Ninja Foodi Multi-cooker. Add grapeseed oil into the pot. Add the seasoned pork chops into the pot, then let it brown for roughly 2 – 3 minutes on each side. Remove and set aside
4. Add the sliced onions and stir. Add a pinch of kosher salt and ground black pepper to season if you like. Cook the onions for roughly 1 minute until softened. Then, add garlic and stir for 30 seconds until fragrance
5. Add in the thinly sliced gala apples, whole cloves (optional) and cinnamon powder, then give it a quick stir. Add the honey and partially deglaze the bottom of the pot with a wooden spoon
6. Add chicken stock and light soy sauce, then fully deglaze the bottom of the pot with a wooden spoon. Taste the seasoning and add more salt and pepper if desired.
7. Place the pork chops back with all the meat juice into the pot
8. High pressure for 10 minutes. Lock the lid on the Ninja Foodi Multi-cooker and then cook for 10 minutes.
9. To get 10 minutes' cook time, press *Pressure* button and use the Time Adjustment button to adjust the cook time to 10 minutes
10. Pressure Release. Let it fully natural release (roughly 10 minutes). Open the lid carefully
11. Finish the dish. Close crisping lid. Select *Air Crisp*, set temperature to 375°F and set time to 10 minutes. Check after 10 minutes, cooking for an additional 5 minutes if dish needs more browning
12. Remove the pork chops and set aside. Turn the Multi-cooker to the Sauté setting. Remove the cloves and taste the seasoning one more time
13. Add more salt and pepper if desired. Add butter and stir until it has fully dissolved into the sauce
14. Mix the cornstarch with water and mix it into the applesauce one third at a time until desired thickness
15. Drizzle the applesauce over the pork chops and serve immediately with side dishes!

Peppers and Pork Stew

(Ready in about: 18 minutes | **Servings:** 4)

Ingredients:

- 1 large yellow or white onion, chopped.
- 1 large green bell pepper, stemmed, cored and cut into 1/4-inch-thick strips
- 1 lb. boneless center-cut pork loin chops, cut into 1/4-inch-thick strips
- 1 large red bell pepper, stemmed, cored and cut into 1/4-inch-thick strips
- 1 (14-ounce) can diced tomatoes, drained (about 1 3/4 cups)
- 2 tsp. minced, seeded fresh jalapeño chile
- 2 tsp. dried oregano
- 2 tbsp. olive oil
- 2 tsp. minced garlic
- 2 ½ cups canned hominy drained and rinsed
- 1 cup chicken broth

Instructions:
1. Heat the oil in a Ninja Foodi Multi-cooker, turned to the Sauté function. Add the onion and both bell peppers; cook, often stirring, until the onion softens, about 4 minutes
2. Add the garlic, jalapeño and oregano; stir well until aromatic, less than 20 seconds. Add the hominy, tomatoes, broth and pork; stir over the heat for 1 minute
3. High pressure for 12 minutes. Lock the lid on the Ninja Foodi Multi-cooker and then cook for 12 minutes.
4. To get 12 minutes' cook time, press *Pressure* button and use the Time Adjustment button to adjust the cook time to 12 minutes
5. Pressure Release. Use the quick release method to bring the pot's pressure back to normal. Unlock and open the cooker. Stir well before serving

Delicious Pulled Pork Sandwiches

(Ready in about: 60 minutes | **Servings:** 8)

Ingredients:
- 2 ½ – 3 lb. uncooked boneless pork shoulder, cut in 1-inch cubes
- 1 can (6-ounces) tomato paste
- 2 tbsp. barbecue seasoning
- 1 cup apple cider vinegar
- 1 tbsp. garlic powder
- 2 tsp. kosher salt
- Coleslaw and Potato rolls for servings

Instructions:
1. Add pork, spices, and vinegar to the pot. Assemble pressure lid, making sure the pressure release valve is in the SEAL position. Select PRESSURE and set to HIGH. Set time to 35 minutes. Select START/STOP to begin
2. When pressure cooking is complete, quick release the pressure by turning the pressure release valve to VENT position. Carefully remove lid when unit has finished releasing pressure
3. Select SEAR/SAUTÉ and set to MEDIUM-HIGH. Select START/STOP to begin
4. Add tomato paste and stir to incorporate. Allow pork to simmer for 10 minutes, or until the liquid has reduced by half, as shown above, stirring occasionally with a wooden spoon or silicone tongs to shred the pork.
5. Serve pulled pork on potato rolls topped with coleslaw

Honey Mustard Pork Tenderloin Recipe

(Ready in about: 30 minutes | **Servings:** 4)

Ingredients:
- 2 lb Pork Tenderloin
- 1 tbsp. Worcestershire Sauce
- 1/2 tbsp. Cornstarch
- 1/2 cup Chicken Broth
- 1/4 cup Balsamic Vinegar
- 1 clove Garlic, minced
- 2 tbsp. Olive Oil
- 1/4 cup Honey
- 1 tsp. Sage Powder
- 1 tbsp. Dijon Mustard
- 4 tbsp. Water
- Salt and Black Pepper to taste

Instructions:
1. Put the pork on a clean flat surface and pat dry using paper towels. Season with salt and pepper. Select Sear/Sauté mode
2. Heat the oil and brown the pork on both sides, for about 4 minutes in total. Remove the pork onto a plate and set aside

3. Add in honey, chicken broth, balsamic vinegar, garlic, Worcestershire sauce, mustard, and sage. Stir the ingredients and return the pork to the pot
4. Close the lid, secure the pressure valve, and select Pressure mode on High for 15 minutes. Once the timer has ended, do a quick pressure release. Remove the pork with tongs onto a plate and wrap it in aluminum foil
5. Next, mix the cornstarch with water and pour it into the pot. Select Sear/Sauté mode, stir the mixture and cook until it thickens. Then, turn the pot off after the desired thickness is achieved
6. Unwrap the pork and use a knife to slice it with 3 to 4-inch thickness. Arrange the slices on a serving platter and spoon the sauce all over it. Serve with a syrupy sautéed Brussels sprouts and red onion chunks

Pork Shoulder Chops With Carrots

(Ready in about: 52 minutes | **Servings:** 4 to 6)

Ingredients:
- 3 lb. bone in pork shoulder chops, each 1/2 to 3/4 inch thick
- 6 medium carrots
- 1/3 cup maple syrup
- 1/3 cup chicken broth
- 3 medium garlic cloves
- 1 tbsp. bacon fat
- 1/3 cup soy sauce
- 1/2 tsp. ground black pepper

Instructions:
1. Melt the bacon fat in a Ninja Foodi Multi-cooker, turned to the browning function. Add about half the chops and brown well, turning once, about 5 minutes. Transfer these to a large bowl and brown the remaining chops
2. Stir the carrots and garlic into the pot; cook for 1 minute, constantly stirring. Pour in the soy sauce, maple syrup and broth, stirring to dissolve the maple syrup and to get up any browned bits on the bottom of the pot. Stir in the pepper. Return the shoulder chops and their juices to the pot. Stir to coat them in the sauce
3. High pressure for 40 minutes. Lock the lid on the Ninja Foodi Multi-cooker and then cook for 40 minutes
4. To get 40 minutes' cook time, press *Pressure* button and use the Time Adjustment button to adjust the cook time to 40 minutes
5. Pressure Release. Let the pressure to come down naturally for at least 14 to 16 minutes, then quick release any pressure left in the pot
6. Finish the dish. Close crisping lid and select Broil, set time to 7 minutes.
7. Transfer the chops, carrots and garlic cloves to a large serving bowl. Skim the fat off the sauce and ladle it over the servings

Tasty Crispy Pork Carnitas

(Ready in about: 1 hour 12 minutes | **Servings:** 10)

Ingredients:
- 2 ½-lb. trimmed, boneless pork shoulder blade roast
- 3/4 cup reduced-sodium chicken broth
- 2 - 3 chipotle peppers in adobo sauce (to taste)
- 1/2 tsp. sazon
- 1/4 tsp. dry oregano
- 1/4 tsp. dry adobo seasoning
- 1/2 tsp. garlic powder
- 2 bay leaves
- 6 cloves garlic, cut into sliver
- 1 ½ tsp. cumin
- 2 tsp. kosher salt
- black pepper, to taste

Instructions:
1. Season pork with salt and pepper. Bring the cooker to high pressure by pressing the Sauté button and brown pork on all sides on high heat for about 5 minutes. Remove from heat and allow to cool
2. Using a sharp knife, insert blade into pork about 1-inch deep and insert the garlic slivers, you'll want to do this all over. Season pork with cumin, sazon, oregano, adobo and garlic powder all over
3. Pour chicken broth, add chipotle peppers and stir, add bay leaves and place pork in the Ninja Foodi Multi-cooker
4. High pressure for 50 minutes. Lock the lid on the Ninja Foodi Multi-cooker and then cook for 50 minutes.
5. To get 50 minutes' cook time, press *Pressure* button and use the Time Adjustment button to adjust the cook time to 50 minutes
6. Pressure Release. Use natural release method. Close crisping lid and select Broil, set time to 7 minutes. Serve and Enjoy!

Pork Tenderloin Braised Apples

(Ready in about: 50 minutes | **Servings:** 4)

Ingredients:
- 1/2 cup Diamond Crystal kosher salt or 1/4 cup fine table salt
- 1/4 cup granulated sugar

For The Pork and Apples
- 1 (1 lb.) pork tenderloin, trimmed of silver skin and halved crosswise
- 1 medium Granny Smith apple or another tart apple, peeled and cut into 1/4-inch slices
- Kosher salt, for salting and seasoning
- 2 tbsp. unsalted butter
- 2 cups very hot tap water
- 2 cups ice water
- For The Brine (optional)
- 1 cup thinly sliced onion
- 3/4 cup apple juice, cider or hard cider
- 1/2 cup low sodium chicken broth
- 2 tbsp. heavy (whipping) cream
- 1 tsp. Dijon mustard, plus additional as needed

Instructions:

To make the brine (if using)
1. In a large stainless steel or glass bowl, dissolve the salt and sugar in hot water; then stir in the ice water. Submerge the pork in the brine and refrigerate for 2 to 3 hours. Drain and pat dry.

To make the pork and apples

2. If you choose not to brine the pork, sprinkle it liberally with kosher salt. Set to *Sauté/browning* heat the butter just until it stops foaming
3. Add the pork halves, browning on all sides, about 4 minutes' total. Transfer to a plate or rack and set aside.
4. Add the onion slices to the cooker and cook, stirring, for 2 to 3 minutes or until they just start to brown. Add the apple slices and cook for 1 minute. Add the apple juice and scrape the browned bits from the bottom of the pot
5. Bring to a simmer and cook for 2 to 3 minutes or until the juice has reduced by about one-third. Add the chicken broth and return the pork tenderloin to the cooker, placing the pieces on top of the apples and onions
6. High pressure for 45 minutes. Lock the lid on the Ninja Foodi Multi-cooker and then cook for 45 minutes.
7. To get 45 minutes' cook time, press *pressure* button and use the adjust button to adjust the cook time to 45 minutes
8. Pressure Release. Use the quick release method
9. Finish the dish. Close crisping lid. Discard the bay leaves. Select *Air Crisp*, set temperature to 375°F and set time to 10 minutes. Check after 5 minutes, cooking for an additional 5 minutes if dish needs more browning.
10. Transfer the pork to a plate or rack and tent it with aluminum foil while you finish the sauce
11. Turn the Ninja Foodi Multi-cooker to *Sauté*, simmer for about 6 minutes or until the liquid is reduced by about half. Stir in the heavy cream and mustard and taste, adding kosher salt or more mustard as needed.
12. Slice the pork into 3/4-inch pieces and place on a serving platter. Spoon the apples, onions and sauce over the pork and serve

Ninja Pulled Pork

(Ready in about: 1 hour 33 minutes | **Servings:** 10)

Ingredients:

- 1 (4- to 4½ lb.) bone in skinless pork shoulder, preferably pork butt
- Up to 1 ½ cups light-colored beer, preferably a pale ale or amber lager
- 1/2 tsp. garlic powder
- 1/2 tsp. ground cloves
- 1/2 tsp. ground cinnamon
- 2 tbsp. smoked paprika
- 2 tbsp. packed dark brown sugar
- 1 tbsp. ground cumin
- 1/2 tbsp. dry mustard
- 1 tsp. ground coriander
- 1 tsp. dried thyme
- 1 tsp. onion powder
- 1 tsp. salt
- 2 tsp. ground black pepper

Instructions:

1. Mix the smoked paprika, brown sugar, cumin, pepper, mustard, coriander, thyme, onion powder, salt, garlic powder, cloves and cinnamon in a small bowl. Massage the mixture all over the pork
2. Set the pork in the Ninja Foodi Multi-cooker. Pour 1cup beer into the electric cooker without knocking the spices off the meat
3. High pressure for 80 minutes. Lock the lid on the Ninja Foodi Multi-cooker and then cook for 80 minutes.
4. To get 80 minutes' cook time, press *Pressure* button and use the Time Adjustment button to adjust the cook time to 80 minutes

5. Pressure Release. Let its pressure fall to normal naturally, 25 to 35 minutes
6. Finish the dish. Close crisping lid and select Broil, set time to 7 minutes
7. Transfer the meat to a large cutting board. Let stand for 5 minutes. Use a spoon to skim as much fat off the sauce in the pot as possible
8. Set the *Sauté* function. Bring the sauce to a simmer, stirring occasionally; continue boiling the sauce, often stirring, until reduced by half, 7 to 10 minutes
9. Use two forks to shred the meat off the bones; discard the bones and any attached cartilage. Pull any large chunks of meat apart with the forks and stir the meat back into the simmering sauce to reheat. Serve and Enjoy!

Pork Roast with Spicy Peanut Sauce

(**Ready in about:** 30 minutes | **Servings:** 6)

Ingredients:

- 3 lb Pork Roast
- 1 large Red Bell Pepper, seeded and sliced
- 1 cup Hot Water
- 1 large White Onion, sliced
- 1 tbsp. Lime Juice
- 1 tbsp. Garlic Powder
- 1 tsp. Ginger Puree
- 1/2 cup Soy Sauce
- 1 tbsp. Plain Vinegar
- 1/2 cup Peanut Butter
- Salt and Pepper to taste
- 2 Chilies, deseeded, chopped.
- Chopped Peanuts, Chopped Green Onions, Lime Wedges to garnish

Instructions:

1. Add the soy sauce, vinegar, peanut butter, lime juice, garlic powder, chilies, and ginger puree, to a bowl. Whisk together and even
2. Add a few pinches of salt and pepper, and mix it. Open the Ninja Foodi lid, and place the pork in the inner pot. Pour the hot water and peanut butter mixture over it
3. Close the lid, secure the pressure valve, and select Pressure mode on High pressure for 15 minutes. Press Start/Stop to start cooking. Once the timer has stopped, do a quick pressure release
4. Use two forks to shred it, inside the pot, and close the crisping lid. Cook on Broil mode for 4 - 5 minutes, until the sauce thickens
5. On a bed of cooked rice, spoon the meat with some sauce and garnish it with the chopped peanuts, green onions, and the lemon wedges

Simple Spare Ribs with Wine

(**Ready in about:** 30 minutes | **Servings:** 4)

Ingredients:

- 1 lb. pork spare ribs, cut into pieces
- 1 tbsp. corn starch
- 1 tbsp. oil

Black Bean Marinade:

- 3 cloves garlic, minced
- 1 tsp. sesame oil
- 1 tsp. sugar
- 1 tbsp. Shaoxing wine
- 1 – 2 tsp. water
- Green onions as garnish
- 1 tsp. fish sauce (optional)

- 1 tbsp. ginger, grated
- 1 tbsp. black bean sauce
- 1 tbsp. light soy sauce
- A pinch of white pepper

Instructions:
1. Marinate the pork spare ribs with Black Bean Marinade in an oven-safe bowl. Then, sit it in the fridge for 25 minutes
2. First, mix 1 tbsp. of oil into the marinated spare ribs. Then, add 1 tbsp. of cornstarch and mix well. Finally, add 1 – 2 tsp. of water into the spare ribs and mix well
3. Add 1 cup of water into the Ninja Foodi Multi-cooker. Place steam rack in the Ninja Foodi Multi-cooker. Then, put the bowl of spare ribs on the rack
4. High pressure for 15 minutes. Lock the lid on the Ninja Foodi Multi-cooker and then cook for 15 minutes.
5. To get 15 minutes' cook time, press *Pressure* Button and then adjust the time
6. Pressure Release. Let the pressure to come down naturally for at least 15 minutes, then quick release any pressure left in the pot
7. Finish the dish. Close crisping lid. Select *Air Crisp*, set temperature to 375°F and set time to 10 minutes. Check after 5 minutes, cooking for an additional 5 minutes if dish needs more browning
8. Taste and add one tsp. of fish sauce and green onions as garnish if you like. Serve immediately

Delicious Pork Carnitas in Lettuce Cups

(Ready in about: 30 minutes | **Servings:** 6)

Ingredients:
- 3 lb Pork Shoulder
- 1 small head Butter Lettuce, leaves removed, washed and dried
- 2 tbsp. Olive Oil
- 1 tsp. Cumin Powder
- 1 tsp. Garlic Powder
- 1 tsp. White Pepper
- 2 tsp. dried Oregano
- 1/2 tsp. Cayenne Pepper
- 1/2 tsp. Coriander Powder
- 1 tsp. Red Pepper Flakes
- 2 Limes, cut in wedges
- 2 Carrots, grated
- 1 ½ cup Water
- 1 Onion, chopped.
- Salt to taste

Instructions:
1. In a bowl, add onion, cayenne, coriander, garlic, cumin, white pepper, dried oregano, red pepper flakes, and salt. Mix them well with a spoon
2. Drizzle over the pork and rub to coat. Then, wrap the meat in plastic wrap and refrigerate overnight
3. On the next day, open the Ninja Foodi lid, and select Sear/Sauté mode. Pour 2 tbsp. of olive oil in the pot and while heating, take the pork out from the fridge, remove the wraps and place it in the pot
4. Brown it on both sides for 6 minutes and then pour the water. Close the lid, secure the pressure valve, and select Pressure mode on High pressure for 15 minutes. Press Start/Stop to start cooking
5. Once the timer has stopped, do a quick pressure release. Use two forks to shred the pork, inside the pot. Close the crisping lid, and select Bake/Roast mode. Set for 10 minutes at 350°F
6. When ready, turn off the heat and begin assembling
7. Arrange double layers of lettuce leaves on a flat surface, make a bed of grated carrots in them, and spoon the pulled pork on them.
8. Drizzle a sauce of choice (I used mustardy sauce) over them, and serve with lime wedges for freshness.

Pulled Pork with Crispy Biscuits

(Ready in about: 1 hour 10 minutes | **Servings:** 8)

Ingredients:

- 2 ½ –3 lb. uncooked boneless pork shoulder, fat trimmed, cut in 2-inch cubes
- 3 tbsp. barbecue seasoning
- 2 tsp. kosher salt
- 1 cup apple cider vinegar
- 1 tbsp. garlic powder
- 1 can (6-ounces) tomato paste
- 1 tube (16.3-ounces) refrigerated biscuit dough

Instructions:

1. Place pork, spices, and vinegar in the pot. Assemble pressure lid, making sure the PRESSURE RELEASE valve is in the SEAL position. Select PRESSURE and set to HIGH. Set time to 35 minutes. Select START/STOP to begin.
2. When pressure cooking is complete, quick release the pressure by moving the PRESSURE RELEASE valve to the VENT position. Carefully remove lid when unit has finished releasing pressure
3. Select SEAR/SAUTÉ and set to MD:HI. Select START/STOP to begin. Add tomato paste and stir to incorporate. Allow pork to simmer for 10 minutes, or until the liquid has reduced by half. Stir occasionally, using a wooden spoon or silicone tongs to shred the pork
4. Tear each uncooked biscuit so that it is in two halves, like a hamburger bun. Place biscuit halves evenly across the surface of the pork
5. Close crisping lid. Select BAKE/ROAST, set temperature to 350°F, and set time to 10 minutes. Check after 8 minutes, cooking for an additional 2 minutes if biscuits need more browning. When cooking is complete, serve immediately

Pork Chops with Mushroom Gravy

(Ready in about: 35 minutes | **Servings:** 4)

Ingredients:

- 4 Pork Chops
- 8-ounce Cremini Mushrooms, sliced
- 1 small Onion, chopped.
- 1 tsp. Garlic Powder
- 1 (10 oz) can Mushroom Soup
- 1 cup Beef Broth
- 1 sprig Fresh Thyme
- 1 tbsp. Olive Oil
- 3 cloves Garlic, minced
- Salt and Pepper, to taste
- Chopped Parsley to garnish

Instructions:

1. Select Sear/Sauté mode. Add oil, mushrooms, garlic, and onion. Sauté them, stirring occasionally with a spoon, until nice and translucent, for 3 minutes
2. Season the pork chops with salt, garlic powder, and pepper, and add them to the pot followed by the thyme and broth. Seal the lid and select Pressure mode on High pressure for 10 minutes. Press Start/Stop to start cooking
3. Once the timer has ended, do a natural pressure release for about 10 minutes, then a quick pressure release to let the remaining steam out
4. Close the crisping lid and cook on Broil mode for 5 minutes. When ready, add the mushroom soup. Stir it until the mixture thickens a little bit. Dish the pork and gravy into a serving bowl and garnish with parsley.
5. Serve with a side of creamy sweet potato mash

Pork Loin with Vegetable Sauce

(Ready in about: 35 minutes | **Servings:** 4)

Ingredients:
- 2 lb Pork Loin Roast
- 1 tbsp. Cornstarch
- 3 Carrots, chopped.
- 1 cup Chicken Broth
- 2 tbsp. Worcestershire Sauce
- 1 medium Onion, diced
- 2 tbsp. Butter
- 3 stalks Celery, chopped.
- 2 tsp. dried Basil
- 2 tsp. dried Thyme
- 3 cloves Garlic, minced
- 1 tsp. Yellow Mustard
- 1/4 cup Water
- 1/2 tbsp. Sugar
- Salt and Pepper, to taste

Instructions:
1. Select Sear/Sauté mode, and heat oil. Season the pork with salt and pepper. Sear the pork to golden brown on both sides. Takes about 4 minutes
2. Then, add the garlic and onions, and cook them until soft, for about 4 minutes
3. Top with the celery, carrots, chicken broth, Worcestershire sauce, mustard, thyme, basil, and sugar.
4. Close the lid, secure the pressure valve, and select Pressure mode on High pressure for 15 minutes. Press Start/Stop to start cooking
5. Once the timer is off, do a quick pressure release. Next, add the cornstarch to the water, in a bowl, and mix with a spoon, until nice and smooth
6. Add it to the pot, close the crisping lid, and cook on Broil mode, for 3 - 5 minutes, until the sauce becomes a slurry with a bit of thickness, and the pork is nice and tender
7. Adjust the seasoning, and ladle to a serving platter. Serve with a side of steamed almond garlicky rapini mix.

Tasty Ranch Pork Chops

(Ready in about: 25 minutes | **Servings:** 4)

Ingredients:
- 4 Pork Loin Chops
- 1/2 cup Chicken Broth
- 1 (15 oz) can Mushroom Soup Cream
- 1-ounce Ranch Dressing and Seasoning Mix
- Chopped Parsley to garnish

Instructions:
1. Add pork, mushroom soup cream, ranch dressing and seasoning mix, and chicken broth, inside the inner pot of your Ninja Foodi
2. Close the lid, secure the pressure valve, and select Pressure mode on High pressure for 10 minutes. Press Start/Stop
3. Once the timer has ended, do a natural pressure release for 10 minutes, then a quick pressure release to let the remaining steam out
4. Close the crisping lid and cook for 5 minutes on Broil mode, until tender. Serve with well-seasoned sautéed cremini mushrooms, and the sauce

Delicious Braised Pork Neck Bones

(**Ready in about:** 40 minutes | **Servings:** 6)

Ingredients:
- 3 lb Pork Neck Bones
- 4 tbsp. Olive Oil
- 1 White Onion, sliced
- 1/2 cup Red Wine
- 2 cloves Garlic, smashed
- 1 tbsp. Tomato Paste
- 1 tsp. dried Thyme
- 1 cup Beef Broth
- Salt and Black Pepper to taste

Instructions:
1. Open the lid and select Sear/Sauté mode. Warm the olive oil
2. Meanwhile season the pork neck bones with salt and pepper. After, place them in the oil to brown on all sides. Work in batches
3. Each batch should cook in about 5 minutes. Then, remove them onto a plate.
4. Add the onion and season with salt to taste. Stir with a spoon and cook the onions until soft, for a few minutes. Then, add garlic, thyme, pepper, and tomato paste. Cook them for 2 minutes, constant stirring to prevent the tomato paste from burning
5. Next, pour the red wine into the pot to deglaze the bottom. Add the pork neck bones back to the pot and pour the beef broth over it
6. Close the lid, secure the pressure valve, and select Pressure mode on High pressure for 10 minutes. Press Start/Stop to start cooking
7. Once the timer has ended, let the pot sit for 10 minutes before doing a quick pressure release. Close the crisping lid and cook on Broil mode for 5 minutes, until nice and tender.
8. Dish the pork neck into a serving bowl and serve with the red wine sauce spooned over and a right amount of broccoli mash

BBQ Pork with Ginger Coconut and Sweet Potatoes

(Ready in about: 35 minutes | **Servings:** 4)

Ingredients:

- 4 frozen uncooked boneless pork chops (8-ounces each)
- 3 sweet potatoes, peeled, cut in 1-inch cubes
- 1/2 cup unsweetened coconut milk
- 1 tsp. Chinese five spice powder
- 1/2 stick (1/4 cup) butter
- 1 tbsp. fresh ginger, peeled, minced
- 1/4 cup hoisin sauce
- 1/3 cup honey
- 1 ½ tbsp. soy sauce
- 1 tsp. kosher salt
- 1/2 tsp. white pepper

Instructions:

1. Place potatoes and coconut milk into the pot. Place reversible rack inside pot over potatoes, making sure rack is in the higher position
2. Place pork chops on rack. Assemble pressure lid, making sure the PRESSURE RELEASE valve is in the SEAL position. Select PRESSURE and set to HIGH. Set time to 4 minutes. Select START/STOP to begin.
3. While pork chops and potatoes are cooking, whisk together hoisin sauce, honey, soy sauce, and Chinese five spice powder
4. When pressure cooking is complete, quick release the pressure by moving the PRESSURE RELEASE valve to the VENT position. Carefully remove lid when unit has finished releasing pressure
5. Remove rack with pork from pot. Mash sweet potatoes with butter, ginger, and salt, using a mashing utensil that won't scratch the nonstick surface of the pot
6. Place rack with pork back in pot and brush top of pork generously with 1/2 of sauce mixture.
7. Close crisping lid. Select BROIL and set time to 15 minutes. Select START/STOP to begin. After 5 minutes, open lid, flip pork chops, then brush them with remaining sauce
8. Close lid to resume cooking. Check after 10 minutes and remove if desired doneness is achieved. If not, cook up to 5 more minutes, checking frequently. When cooking is complete, remove pork from rack and allow to rest for 5 minutes before serving with mashed potatoes

Beef & Lamb Recipes

BBQ Pulled Beef Sandwiches

(Ready in about: 1 hour | **Servings:** 2 to 4)

Ingredients:
- 2 lb. Beef of choice
- 4 cups finely shredded Cabbage (the secret ingredient and you'll never know it's in there.)
- 2 cups Water
- 1/2 cup of your favorite BBQ Sauce
- 1 cup Ketchup
- 1/3 cup Worcestershire Sauce
- 1 tbsp. mustard
- 1 tbsp. Horse Radish

Instructions:
1. Add and stir in ingredients to your Ninja Foodi Multi-cooker
2. High pressure for 35 minutes. Lock the lid on the Ninja Foodi Multi-cooker and then cook for 35 minutes.
3. To get 35 minutes' cook time, press *Pressure* button and adjust the time
4. Pressure Release. Use natural release method. Finish the dish. Remove the lid from the Ninja Foodi Multi-cooker. Close crisping lid. Select *Air Crisp*, set temperature to 390°F and set time to 15 minutes.
5. Check after 10 minutes, cooking for an additional 5 minutes if dish needs more browning
6. Set the beef aside. Set the Ninja Foodi Multi-cooker to a *Sauté* mode, Sauté the sauce until it reaches the desired consistency. Serve and Enjoy

Easy Short Ribs and Root Vegetables

(Ready in about: 1 hour 15 minutes | **Servings:** 6)

Ingredients:
- 6 uncooked bone-in beef short ribs (about 3 lb.), trimmed of excess fat and silver skin
- 2 tsp. kosher salt, divided.
- 3 carrots, peeled, cut in 1-inch pieces
- 3 parsnips, peeled, cut in 1-inch pieces
- 2 tsp. black pepper, divided.
- 3 cloves garlic, peeled, minced
- 1 onion, peeled, chopped.
- 1/4 cup Marsala wine
- 1/4 cup beef broth
- 2 tbsp. brown sugar
- 2 tbsp. fresh thyme, minced, divided.
- 2 tbsp. olive oil, divided.
- 1 cup pearl onions
- 1/4 cup fresh parsley, minced

Instructions:
1. Season short ribs on all sides with 1 tsp. salt and 1 tsp. pepper. Select SEAR/SAUTÉ and set to HIGH. Select START/STOP to begin. Heat 1 tbsp. oil in the pot for 3 minutes
2. After 3 minutes, add short ribs to pot and cook until browned on all sides, about 10 minutes
3. Add onion, wine, broth, brown sugar, garlic, 1 tbsp. thyme, 1/2 tsp. salt, and 1/2 tsp. pepper to pot. Assemble pressure lid, making sure the PRESSURE RELEASE valve is in the SEAL position. Select PRESSURE and set to HIGH. Set time to 40 minutes. Select START/STOP to begin
4. Toss carrots, parsnips, and pearl onions with remaining oil, thyme, salt, and pepper
5. When pressure cooking is complete, quick release the pressure by moving the PRESSURE RELEASE valve to the VENT position. Carefully remove lid when unit has finished releasing pressure

6. Place the reversible rack inside pot over ribs, making sure rack is in the higher position. Place vegetable mixture on rack. Close crisping lid. Select BAKE/ROAST, set temperature to 350°F, and set time to 15 minutes. Select START/STOP to begin
7. Once vegetables are tender and roasted, transfer them and the ribs to a serving tray and tent loosely with aluminum foil to keep warm
8. Select SEAR/SAUTÉ and set to HIGH. Bring liquid in pot to simmer for 5 minutes. Transfer to bowl and let sit for 2 minutes, then spoon off top layer of fat. Stir in parsley. When cooking is complete, serve sauce with vegetables and ribs

Braised Short Ribs

(**Ready in about:** 1 hour 5 minutes | **Servings:** 4 to 6)

Ingredients:
- 4 lb. beef short ribs, about 3 inches thick, cut into 3 rib portions
- 1/4-cup rice wine (or dry sherry)
- 1/4-cup pear juice (or apple juice)
- 2 green onions cut into 1-inch lengths
- 3 cloves garlic, smashed
- 3 quarter-sized slices of ginger
- 1 tsp. vegetable oil
- 1/2-cup water
- 1/2-cup soy sauce
- 2 tsp. sesame oil
- Minced green onions
- Gochujang sauce

Instructions:
1. Heat the vegetable oil in the Ninja Foodi Multi-cooker using the *Sauté* function, until the oil is shimmering. Add the green onion, garlic and ginger and sauté for 1 minute or until you can smell the garlic
2. Add the short ribs, water, soy sauce, rice wine, pear juice and sesame oil. Stir until the ribs are completely coated
3. High pressure for 45 minutes. Lock the lid on the Ninja Foodi Multi-cooker and then cook for 45 minutes.
4. To get 45 minutes' cook time, press *Meat/Chicken* button and use the "ADJUST" button to adjust the cook time to 45 minutes
5. Pressure Release. Let the pressure to come down naturally for at least 15 minutes, then quick release any pressure left in the pot
6. Finish the dish. Close crisping lid. Select "BROIL" and set time to 8 minutes. Check after 5 minutes, cooking for an additional 3 minutes if dish needs more browning
7. Remove the short ribs from the pot with a slotted spoon. Serve the ribs with the degreased sauce

Easy Sausage and Peppers

(**Ready in about:** 25 minutes | **Servings:** 5 to 6)

Ingredients:
- 2 ½ lb. sweet Italian sausages in their casings
- 1 medium red onion, halved and thinly sliced
- 2 medium garlic cloves, slivered
- 1 cup red (sweet) vermouth
- 4 large red bell peppers, stemmed, seeded and cut into strips
- 2 tbsp. olive oil
- 2 tbsp. balsamic vinegar
- 1/4 tsp. grated nutmeg

Instructions:
1. Heat the oil in a Ninja Foodi Multi-cooker, turned to the sauté function. Prick the sausages with a fork, add them to the pot and brown on all sides, about 6 minutes. Transfer to a large bowl
2. Add the peppers and onion; cook, stirring almost constantly, just until the pepper strips glisten, about 2 minutes
3. Add the garlic, cook a few seconds and then stir in the vermouth, vinegar and nutmeg. Nestle the sausages into the mixture
4. High pressure for 10 minutes. Lock the lid on the Ninja Foodi Multi-cooker and Cook for 10 minutes.
5. To get 10 minutes' cook time, press the *Pressure* button and adjust the time
6. Pressure Release. Use the quick release method to bring the pot's pressure back to normal
7. Remove the lid from the Ninja Foodi Multi-cooker. Close crisping lid. Select *Air Crisp*, set temperature to 390°F and set time to 10 minutes
8. Check after 8 minutes, cooking for an additional 2 minutes if dish needs more browning. Stir well before serving

BBQ Baby Back Ribs

(**Ready in about:** 52 minutes | **Servings:** 4)

Ingredients:
- 1 (4 lb.) rack baby back ribs, cut into 2 or 3 sections to fit in the cooker
- 1/4 cup canned tomato paste
- 2 tbsp. cider vinegar
- 1 tbsp. sweet paprika
- 1/2 tbsp. coriander seeds
- 1/2 tbsp. fennel seeds
- 1 tsp. onion powder
- 1 tsp. dried thyme
- 1/2 tsp. ground allspice
- 1/4 tsp. celery seeds
- 1/2 tsp. salt
- 1/2 tsp. ground black pepper

Instructions:
1. Whisk the tomato paste, vinegar, paprika, coriander and fennel seeds, onion powder, thyme, allspice, salt, pepper and celery seeds with 3/4 cup water in an electric Multi-cooker until the tomato paste dissolves.
2. Add the ribs; toss to coat thoroughly and evenly in the sauce
3. High pressure for 32 minutes. Lock the lid on the Ninja Foodi Multi-cooker and then cook for 32 minutes.
4. To get 32 minutes' cook time, press *Pressure* button and use the Time Adjustment button to adjust the cook time to 32 minutes
5. Pressure Release. Let the pressure to come down naturally for at least 15 minutes, then quick release any pressure left in the pot
6. Finish the dish. Remove the lid from the Ninja Foodi Multi-cooker. Close crisping lid. Select *Air Crisp*, set temperature to 400°F and set time to 15 minutes. Check after 10 minutes, cooking for an additional 5 minutes if dish needs more browning
7. Transfer the rib rack sections to a large rimmed baking sheet. Set the electric one to its browning function. Bring the sauce to a simmer. Cook, stirring occasionally, until the sauce has thickened, 3 to 5 minutes.
8. Position the oven rack 4 to 6 inches from the broiler; heat the broiler. Brush a light coating of the sauce onto the ribs, then broil until glazed and hot, 6 to 8 minutes, turning once
9. Slice the racks between the bones to make individual ribs. Serve with the extra sauce on the side

Classic Brisket with Veggies

(**Ready in about:** 1 hour 20 minutes | **Servings:** 4 to 6)

Ingredients:
- 2 lb. or larger regular brisket, rinsed and patted dry
- 2 ½ cup homemade beef broth or make from Knorr Beef Base
- 2 tbsp. olive oil
- 5 or 6 red potatoes
- 2 cup large chunks carrots
- 3 tbsp. Worcestershire Sauce
- 4 bay leaves
- Granulated garlic
- Knorr Demi-Glace sauce
- 1/2 cup dehydrated onion
- 2 stalks celery in 1 chunks
- Fresh ground black pepper
- 3 tbsp. heaping chopped garlic
- 1 large yellow onion
- 5 or 6 red potatoes

Instructions:
1. Put the Ninja Foodi Multi-cooker on the sauté setting. Put in 1 tbsp. (more if needed) of the oil and caramelize the onions. Once golden, remove from pot, put in a bowl and set aside. But keep the Ninja Foodi Multi-cooker on the *Sauté* setting
2. Rub the freshly ground pepper on both sides of the brisket. Do the same with the granulated garlic. Add 1 tbsp. olive oil (or more) and only lightly sear the brisket on all sides
3. Add back the onions, garlic, Worcestershire sauce, bay leaves, dehydrated onion and beef broth
4. High pressure for 50 minutes. Close the lid and the pressure valve and then cook for 50 minutes.
5. To get 50 minutes' cook time, press *Pressure* button and use the Time Adjustment button to adjust the cook time to 50 minutes
6. While the meat is cooking, peel and cut up all the veggies. When the meat is done, use the quick pressure release feature and then remove the lid. Add all of the veggies, replace the lid and cook at high pressure for to 10 minutes
7. To get 10 minutes' cook time, press *Steam* button
8. Pressure Release. When the time is up, turn the pot off, use the quick release again and remove the lid.
9. Finish the dish. Close crisping lid. Select ""BROIL"" and set time to 8 minutes. Check after 5 minutes, cooking for an additional 3 minutes if dish needs more browning
10. Use a platter to remove the veggies and meat. Use the *Sauté* setting and bring the broth to a boil, then add the Knorr Demi-Glace mixing with a Wisk
11. Adjust seasonings as needed. Serve with Cole Slaw or other salad, homemade rolls or Italian garlic bread. Be sure to remove the bay leaves before serving. Serve and Enjoy

Beef Stuffed Peppers

(Ready in about: 40 minutes | **Servings:** 6)

Ingredients:
- 1 lb. uncooked ground beef
- 1 tbsp. garlic powder
- 4 large bell peppers, seeds and stems removed, tops chopped.
- 1 tsp. black pepper
- 3 tbsp. paprika
- 1 ½ tsp. ground cumin
- 1 cup brown rice
- 1 cup chicken stock
- 1/4 cup dry white wine
- 1 cup whole cashews, chopped.
- 1 tbsp. ground cinnamon
- 1/2 tsp. ground cloves
- 1 ½ tbsp. kosher salt, divided.
- 1 small onion, peeled, finely chopped.
- 1/2 cup fresh parsley, chopped.

Instructions:
1. In a small mixing bowl, stir together the garlic powder, black pepper, cinnamon, cloves, 1 ½ tsp. salt, paprika, and cumin; set aside
2. Add beef, onion, rice, stock, wine, and 2 tbsp. spice mix to the pot, breaking apart meat. Assemble pressure lid, making sure the PRESSURE RELEASE valve is in the SEAL position. Select PRESSURE and set to HIGH. Set time to 15 minutes. Select START/STOP to begin
3. When pressure cooking is complete, naturally release the pressure for 10 minutes, then quick release any remaining pressure by moving the PRESSURE RELEASE valve to the VENT position. Carefully remove lid when unit has finished releasing pressure
4. Stir meat mixture, then add chopped pepper tops, cashews, fresh parsley, and remaining salt. Using a rubber or wooden spoon, stuff mixture into the 4 bell peppers
5. Place stuffed peppers in the pot. Close crisping lid. Select BAKE/ROAST, set temperature to 360°F, and set time to 15 minutes. Select START/STOP to begin. When cooking is complete, serve immediately

Delightful Lamb Shanks with Pancetta

(Ready in about: 1 hour 15 minutes | **Servings:** 4)

Ingredients:
- 1 (28-ounce) can diced tomatoes, drained (about 3 ½ cups)
- 4 (12-ounce) lamb shanks
- 1 (6-ounce) pancetta chunk, chopped.
- 2 cups dry, light white wine, such as Sauvignon Blanc
- 1-ounce dried mushrooms, preferably porcini, crumbled
- 2 tbsp. olive oil
- 1 small yellow onion, chopped.
- 3 tbsp. packed celery leaves, minced
- 2 tbsp. minced chives
- 2 tbsp. all-purpose flour
- 1/2 tsp. ground black pepper

Instructions:
1. Heat the oil in the Ninja Foodi Multi-cooker, turned to the *Sauté* function. Add the pancetta and brown well, about 6 minutes, stirring often. Use a slotted spoon to transfer the pancetta to a large bowl
2. Add two of the shanks to the cooker; brown on all sides, turning occasionally, about 8 minutes. Transfer them to the bowl and repeat with the remaining shanks

3. Add the onion to the pot; cook, often stirring, until softened, about 4 minutes. Stir in the tomatoes, dried mushroom crumbles, celery leaves and chives. Cook until bubbling, about minutes, stirring often
4. Whisk the wine, flour and pepper in a medium bowl until the flour dissolves; stir this mixture into the sauce in the pot. Cook until thickened and bubbling, about 1 minute
5. Return the shanks, pancetta and their juices to the cooker
6. High pressure for 60 minutes. Close the lid and the pressure valve and then cook for 60 minutes
7. To get 60 minutes' cook time, press *Pressure* button and use the Time Adjustment button to adjust the cook time to 60 minutes
8. Turn off the Ninja Foodi Multi-cooker or unplug it, so it doesn't jump to its keep-warm setting
9. Pressure Release. Let its pressure return to normal naturally, 20 to 30 minutes
10. Finish the dish. Remove the lid from the Ninja Foodi Multi-cooker. Close crisping lid. Select *Air Crisp*, set temperature to 375°F and set time to 18 minutes. Check after 10 minutes, cooking for an additional 8 minutes if dish needs more browning
11. Transfer a shank to each serving bowl. Skim any surface fat from the sauce with a flatware spoon. Ladle the sauce and vegetables over the lamb shanks

Lamb with Enchilada Sauce

(**Ready in about:** 1 hour 10 minutes | **Servings:** 3 to 4)

Ingredients:
- 3 lamb shoulder
- 1 (19-ounces can) Old El Paso Enchilada sauce
- 1 Spanish onion
- Cilantro, chopped without the stems
- Corn tortillas (3 to 4 per person)
- 3 garlic cloves, minced
- 2 tbsp. oil
- Salt to taste
- Limes cut into 8ths
- Chipotle-style rice
- Black beans or refried beans

Instructions:
1. Marinate lamb overnight in Old El Paso Enchilada sauce (mild, medium or hot)
2. Turn on the Ninja Foodi Multi-cooker to *Sauté* mode. Add oil. Put in the onions and cook until soft, add garlic and cook for 1 minute
3. Add the lamb and marinade wait until boil
4. High pressure for 45 minutes. Lock the lid on the Ninja Foodi Multi-cooker and then cook for 45 minutes.
5. To get 45 minutes' cook time, press *Pressure* button and use the adjust button to adjust the cook time to 45 minutes
6. Pressure Release. Let the pressure to come down naturally for at least 15 minutes, then quick release any pressure left in the pot
7. Finish the dish. Remove the lid from the Ninja Foodi Multi-cooker. Close crisping lid. Select *Air Crisp*, set temperature to 375°F and set time to 15 minutes. Check after 10 minutes, cooking for an additional 5 minutes if dish needs more browning
8. Cut the limes, heat the beans put the hot rice into a serving bowl
9. Set the Lamb aside. Ladle a generous amount of sauce over it
10. Heat up 3 to 4 corn tortillas. Put the lamb mixture onto a soft warm corn tortilla, sprinkle on cilantro, then squeeze with lime juice. Serve and Enjoy!

Beef Chili & Cornbread Casserole

(Ready in about: 60 minutes | **Servings:** 8)

Ingredients:

- 2 lb. uncooked ground beef
- 3 cans (14-ounces each) kidney beans, rinsed, drained
- 1 can (28-ounces) crushed tomatoes
- 1 cup beef stock
- 1 large white onion, peeled, diced
- 1 green bell pepper, diced
- 1 jalapeño pepper, diced, seeds removed
- 4 cloves garlic, peeled, minced
- 2 tbsp. kosher salt
- 1 tbsp. ground black pepper
- 2 tbsp. ground cumin
- 1 tbsp. onion powder
- 1 tbsp. garlic powder
- 2 cups Cheddar Corn Bread batter, uncooked (see recipe page 61)
- 1 cup shredded Mexican cheese blend
- Sour cream, for serving

Instructions:

1. Place beef, beans, tomatoes, and stock into the pot, breaking apart meat. Assemble pressure lid, making sure the PRESSURE RELEASE valve is in the SEAL position. Select PRESSURE and set to HIGH. Set time to 15 minutes. Select START/STOP to begin
2. When pressure cooking is complete, quick release the pressure by moving the PRESSURE RELEASE valve to the VENT position. Carefully remove lid when unit has finished releasing pressure
3. Select SEAR/SAUTÉ. Set temperature to MD, Select START/STOP. Add onion, green bell pepper, jalapeño pepper, garlic, and spices; stir to incorporate. Bring to a simmer and cook for 5 minutes, stirring occasionally.
4. Dollop corn bread batter evenly over the top of the chili. Close crisping lid. Select BAKE/ROAST, set temperature to 360°F, and set time to 26 minutes. Select START/STOP to begin
5. After 15 minutes, open lid and insert a wooden toothpick into the center of the corn bread. If corn bread is not done, close lid to resume cooking for another 8 minutes.
6. When corn bread is done, sprinkle it with cheese and close lid to resume cooking for 3 minutes, or until cheese is melted. When cooking is complete, top with sour cream and serve

Special Lamb Shanks Provençal

(Ready in about: 1 hour 10 minutes | **Servings:** 5 to 6)

Ingredients:

- 2 large (12-ounce) lamb shanks
- 2 medium plum tomatoes, coarsely chopped. or 1/2 cup diced canned tomatoes, drained
- 1/2 cup dry white wine or dry white vermouth
- 1 cup Chicken Stock or low sodium broth
- Freshly ground black pepper
- 1 tbsp. olive oil
- 1 cup sliced onion
- 2 garlic cloves, finely minced
- 1 bay leaf
- 1/3 cup pitted Kalamata olives
- 2 tbsp. coarsely chopped fresh parsley
- 1 tsp. kosher salt, plus additional for seasoning
- 1 lemon, sliced very thin

Instructions:
1. Sprinkle the lamb shanks with 1 tsp. of kosher salt and several grinds of pepper. The longer ahead of the cooking time you can do this the better
2. Cover and let sit for 20 minutes to 2 hours at room temperature or refrigerate for up to 24 hours
3. Heat the vegetable oil in the Ninja Foodi Multi-cooker using the *Sauté* function, until the oil is shimmering and flows like water. Add the lamb shanks and brown on all sides, about 6 minutes' total
4. Remove them to a plate. Add the onion and garlic and sprinkle with a pinch or two of kosher salt. Cook, stirring, for about 3 minutes or until the onions just begin to brown. Add the tomatoes and cook until most of their liquid evaporates
5. Add the white wine and stir, scraping up the browned bits from the bottom of the cooker
6. Cook for 2 to 3 minutes or until the wine reduces by about half; then add the Chicken Stock and bay leaf. Return the lamb shanks to the cooker and place the lemon slices over them.
7. High pressure for 40 minutes. Lock the lid on the Ninja Foodi Multi-cooker and then cook for 40 minutes.
8. To get 40 minutes' cook time, press *Pressure* button and adjust the time
9. Pressure Release. After cooking, use the natural method to release pressure
10. Finish the dish. Remove the lid from the Ninja Foodi Multi-cooker. Close crisping lid. Select *Air Crisp*, set temperature to 375°F and set time to 18 minutes. Check after 10 minutes, cooking for an additional 8 minutes if dish needs more browning
11. Transfer the lamb to a cutting board or plate and tent it with aluminum foil. Strain the sauce into a fat separator and let it rest until the fat rises to the surface
12. If you don't have a fat separator, let the sauce sit for a few minutes, then spoon or blot off any excess fat from the top and discard
13. Pour the defatted sauce back into the cooker along with the strained vegetables. If you want a thicker sauce, simmer the liquid for about 5 minutes or until it reaches the desired consistency
14. Stir in the olives and parsley. Place the shanks in shallow bowls, pour the sauce and vegetables over the lamb and serve
15. Lamb shanks benefit from salting in advance, which makes them much more flavorful and helps them brown beautifully. If you have the time, salt them up to 24 hours in advance. Place them on a tray and refrigerate, covered loosely with foil

Lamb and Eggplant Casserole

(**Ready in about:** 18 minutes | **Servings:** 4)

Ingredients:
- 1 ½ lb. lean ground lamb
- 1 (small eggplant) (about 3/4 lb.), stemmed and diced
- 8-ounces dried spiral-shaped pasta, such as rotini
- 1 tbsp. minced garlic
- 2 tbsp. olive oil
- 1 medium red onion, chopped.
- 1/2 cup canned tomato paste
- 3/4 cup dry red wine, such as Syrah
- 2 ¼ cups chicken broth
- 1/2 tbsp. dried oregano
- 1/2 tsp. dried dill
- 1 tsp. ground cinnamon
- 1/2 tsp. salt
- 1/2 tsp. ground black pepper

Instructions:
1. Heat the oil in the Ninja Foodi Multi-cooker turned to the *Sauté* function. Add the onion and cook, often stirring, until softened, about 4 minutes. Add the garlic and cook until aromatic, less than 1 minute
2. Crumble in the ground lamb; cook, stirring occasionally until it has lost its raw color, about 5 minutes. Add the eggplant and cook for 1 minute, often stirring, to soften a bit. Pour in the red wine and scrape up any browned bits in the pot as it comes to a simmer
3. Stir in the broth, tomato paste, cinnamon, oregano, dill, salt and pepper until everything is coated in the tomato sauce. Stir in the pasta until coated
4. High pressure for 8 minutes. Lock the lid on the Ninja Foodi Multi-cooker and then cook for 8 minutes.
5. To get 8 minutes' cook time, press *Pressure* button and use the Time Adjustment button to adjust the cook time to 8 minutes
6. Pressure Release. Use the quick release method
7. Remove the lid from the Ninja Foodi Multi-cooker. Close crisping lid. Select "BROIL" and set time to 5 minutes. Cooking for an additional 4 minutes if dish needs more browning. Unlock and open the pot. Stir well before serving

Mouthwatering Beef Stew

(**Ready in about:** 25 minutes | **Servings:** 4)

Ingredients:
- 1 ½ lb. lean ground beef (about 93% lean)
- 1 large sweet potato (about 1 lb.), peeled and shredded through the large holes of a box grater
- 1 tbsp. olive oil
- 1 large yellow onion, chopped.
- 1 tsp. ground cinnamon
- 1 tsp. ground cumin
- 1/2 tsp. dried sage
- 1/2 tsp. dried oregano
- 2 ½ cups beef broth
- 2 tbsp. yellow cornmeal
- 2 tbsp. honey
- 1/2 tsp. salt
- 1/2 tsp. ground black pepper

Instructions:
1. Heat the oil in the Ninja Foodi Multi-cooker turned to the Sauté function. Crumble in the ground beef; cook, stirring occasionally, until it loses its raw color and browns a bit, about 5 minutes
2. Add the onion; cook, often stirring, until softened, about 3 minutes.
3. Stir in the sweet potato, cinnamon, cumin, sage, oregano, salt and pepper
4. Cook for 1 minute, stirring constantly. Stir in the cornmeal and honey; cook for 1 minute, often stirring, to dissolve the cornmeal. Stir in the broth
5. High pressure for 5 minutes. Lock the lid on the Ninja Foodi Multi-cooker and then cook for 5 minutes.
6. To get 5 minutes' cook time, press *Pressure* button and use the Time Adjustment button to adjust the cook time to 5 minutes
7. Pressure Release. Use the quick release method to drop the pot's pressure to normal.
8. Finish the dish. Remove the lid from the Ninja Foodi Multi-cooker. Close crisping lid. Select *Air Crisp*, set temperature to 390°F and set time to 20 minutes
9. Check after 15 minutes, cooking for an additional 15 minutes if dish needs more browning. Stir well and set aside, loosely covered, for 5 minutes before serving.

Tex-Mex Meatloaf Recipe

(Ready in about: 45 minutes | **Servings:** 8)

Ingredients:

- 1 lb. uncooked ground beef
- 1 tbsp. garlic powder
- 2 tsp. ground cumin
- 2 tsp. chili powder
- 1 tsp. cayenne pepper
- 1 egg
- 1 bell pepper, diced
- 2 tsp. kosher salt
- 1/4 cup fresh cilantro leaves
- 1/4 barbecue sauce, divided.
- 1/2 jalapeño pepper, seeds removed, minced
- 1 small onion, peeled, diced
- 3 corn tortillas, roughly chopped.
- 1 cup water
- 1 cup corn chips, crushed

Instructions:

1. Stir together beef, egg, bell pepper, jalapeño pepper, onion, tortillas, spices, cilantro, and tbsp. barbecue sauce in a large mixing bowl
2. Place meat mixture in the 8 ½-inch loaf pan and cover tightly with aluminum foil
3. Pour water into pot. Place the loaf pan on the reversible rack, making sure rack is in the lower position. Place rack with pan in pot. Assemble the pressure lid, making sure the PRESSURE RELEASE valve is in the SEAL position.
4. Select PRESSURE and set to HIGH. Set time to 15 minutes. Select START/STOP to begin
5. When pressure cooking is complete, quick release the pressure by moving the PRESSURE RELEASE valve to the VENT position. Carefully remove lid when unit has finished releasing pressure
6. Carefully remove foil from loaf pan and close crisping lid. Select BAKE/ROAST, set temperature to 360°F, and set time to 15 minutes. Select START/STOP to begin
7. While the meatloaf is cooking, stir together the crushed corn chips and 2 tbsp. barbecue sauce in a bowl.
8. After 7 minutes, open lid and top meatloaf with the corn chip mixture. Close lid to resume cooking. When cooking is complete, remove meatloaf from pot and allow to cool for 10 minutes before serving

Delicious Lamb Casserole

(Ready in about: 1 hour 5 minutes | **Servings:** 6 to 8)

Ingredients:

- 1-lb. rack of lamb
- 1 lb. of baby potatoes
- 2 carrots
- 1 large onion
- 2 stalks of celery
- 2 medium size tomatoes
- 1 to 2 tsp. of salt depending on the salt content of the chicken stock
- 2 cups of chicken stock
- 2 tsp. of Paprika
- 2 tbsp. of ketchup
- 2 tsp. of cumin powder
- 3 tbsp. of sherry or red wine
- A splash of beer if you have one in hand
- 3 to 4 large cloves of garlic
- A pinch of dried rosemary
- A pinch of dried oregano leaves

Instructions:

1. Dice the tomatoes, onion and garlic, cut potatoes and carrots, cut the rack of lamb into two halves. Put all the ingredients, in the Ninja Foodi Multi-cooker
2. High pressure for 35 minutes. Lock the lid on the Ninja Foodi Multi-cooker and then cook for 35 minutes.
3. To get 35 minutes' cook time, press *Pressure* button and adjust the time
4. Pressure Release. Use Natural-Release Method for 10 minutes and then Quick Release
5. Remove the lid from the Ninja Foodi Multi-cooker. Close crisping lid. Select *Air Crisp*, set temperature to 400°F and set time to 15 minutes
6. Check after 10 minutes, cooking for an additional 5 minutes if dish needs more browning. Serve and Enjoy!

Pot Roast

(**Ready in about:** 1 hour 50 minutes | **Servings:** 4 to 6)

Ingredients:
- 1 (3- to 3½ lb.) boneless beef chuck roast
- 1 ½ lb. small white or yellow potatoes
- 1/2-ounce dried mushrooms, preferably porcini
- 1 tbsp. olive oil
- 1 large yellow onion, chopped.
- 2 tsp. minced garlic
- 1 ½ cups beef broth
- 3 tbsp. tomato paste
- 1 (4-inch) rosemary sprig
- 1 tsp. salt
- 1/2 tsp. ground black pepper

Instructions:
1. Heat the oil in the Ninja Foodi Multi-cooker. Turn on the Multi-cooker to the Sauté setting then wait for it to boil.
2. Season the roast with the salt and pepper; brown it on both sides, turning once, about 10 minutes. Transfer the meat to a large bowl
3. Add the onion; cook, often stirring, until translucent, about 4 minutes. Add the garlic; cook, stirring constantly, until aromatic, about 30 seconds. Pour 1 ¼ cup broth in the Ninja Foodi Multi-cooker
4. Add the tomato paste and stir well until dissolved. Tuck the rosemary into the sauce and crumble in the mushrooms. Nestle the meat into the sauce, adding any juices in the bowl
5. High pressure for 60 minutes. Close the lid and the pressure valve and then cook for 60 minutes.
6. To get 60 minutes' cook time, press *Pressure* button and use the Time Adjustment button to adjust the cook time to 60 minutes
7. Pressure Release. Use the quick release method
8. Unlock and open the cooker; sprinkle the potatoes around the meat
9. High pressure for 30 minutes. Close the lid and the pressure valve again and cook for 30 minutes.
10. To get 30 minutes' cook time, press *Pressure* button.
11. Pressure Release. Use the natural release method 20 to 30 minutes
12. Finish the dish. Close crisping lid. Select "BROIL" and set time to 8 minutes. Check after 5 minutes, cooking for an additional 3 minutes if dish needs more browning
13. Transfer the roast to a cutting board; set aside for 5 minutes. Discard the rosemary sprig.
14. Slice the meat into 2-inch irregular chunks and serve these in bowls with the vegetables, mushrooms and broth. Serve

Sausage and Chard Pasta Sauce

(Ready in about: 18 minutes | **Servings:** 5 to 6)

Ingredients:
- 1-lb. mild Italian pork sausage meat, any casings removed
- 3 small hot chiles, such as cherry peppers or Anaheim chiles, stemmed, seeded and chopped.
- 1 medium red onion, chopped.
- 1/2 cup dry red wine, such as Syrah
- 1/2 cup canned tomato paste
- 1/4 cup chicken broth
- 4 cups stemmed and chopped Swiss chard
- 2 tbsp. olive oil
- 1 tbsp. minced garlic
- 1 tbsp. dried basil
- 2 tsp. dried oregano

Instructions:
1. Heat the oil in a Ninja Foodi Multi-cooker, turned to the sauté function.
2. Add the onion and cook, often stirring, until softened, about 4 minutes. Add the chiles and garlic; cook until aromatic, stirring all the while, about 1 minute
3. Crumble in the sausage meat, breaking up any clumps with a wooden spoon.
4. Stir until it loses its raw color. Stir in the wine, tomato paste, broth, basil and oregano until the tomato paste dissolves. Add the chard and stir well
5. High pressure for 6 minutes. Lock the lid onto the cooker, set the machine's timer to cook at high pressure for 6 minutes
6. To get 6 minutes' cook time, press the *Pressure* button and use the Time Adjustment button to adjust the cook time to 6 minutes
7. Pressure Release. Use the quick release method to drop the pressure back to normal.
8. Finish the dish. Remove the lid from the Ninja Foodi Multi-cooker. Close crisping lid. Select "BROIL" and set time to 5 minutes
9. Check after 4 minutes, cooking for an additional 4 minutes if dish needs more browning. Stir well before serving

Red Beef Curry

(Ready in about: 1 hour 10 minutes | **Servings:** 6 to 8)

Ingredients:
- 8-ounce can bamboo shoots, drained
- 2 lb. flat iron steak (or chuck blade steak), cut into 2 inches by 1/2-inch strips
- 1 medium onion, peeled and sliced into 1/2-inch wedges
- 1 red bell pepper, cored, stemmed and sliced into 1/2-inch strips
- Cream from the top of a (13.5-ounce) can coconut milk
- 1 tbsp. vegetable oil
- 3 cloves garlic, crushed
- 1/2-inch piece of ginger, peeled and crushed
- 4 tbsp. red curry paste (a whole 4-ounces can)
- 1 tbsp. fish sauce (plus more to taste)
- 1 tbsp. soy sauce (plus more to taste)
- 1/2 cup chicken stock or water
- Juice of 1 lime
- Minced cilantro
- Minced basil (preferably Thai basil)
- Lime wedges
- Jasmine rice
- 1 tsp. Diamond Crystal kosher salt or 2 tsp. fine sea salt

Instructions:
1. Heat the vegetable oil in the Ninja Foodi Multi-cooker using the *Sauté* function, until the oil is shimmering. Stir in the onion, red bell pepper, garlic and ginger and sauté until the onion starts to soften about 3 minutes.
2. Fry the curry paste: Scoop the cream from the top of the can of coconut milk and add it to the pot, then stir in the curry paste. Cook, often stirring, until the curry paste darkens, about 5 minutes
3. Sprinkle the beef with the kosher salt. Add the beef to the pot and stir to coat with curry paste. Stir in the rest of the can of coconut milk, bamboo shoots, chicken stock, fish sauce and soy sauce
4. High pressure for 12 minutes. Lock the lid on the Ninja Foodi Multi-cooker and then cook for 12 minutes
5. To get 12 minutes' cook time, press *Pressure* button and adjust the cook time.
6. Pressure Release. Let the pressure to come down naturally for at least 20 minutes, then quick release any pressure left in the pot
7. Finish the dish. Remove the lid from the Ninja Foodi Multi-cooker. Close crisping lid. Select "BROIL" and set time to 8 minutes. Check after 5 minutes, cooking for an additional 3 minutes if dish needs more browning
8. Stir in the lime juice and then taste the curry for seasoning, adding more fish sauce or brown sugar as needed.
9. Ladle the curry into bowls, sprinkle with minced cilantro and basil and serve with Jasmine rice. Serve and Enjoy!

Beef Ribs

(**Ready in about:** 1 hour 20 minutes | **Servings:** 4 to 6)

Ingredients:
- 4 lb. beef ribs (about 8), ask the butcher to saw or chop them in half
- 1/4 cup rice vinegar (or white balsamic vinegar)
- 1 knob fresh ginger, peeled and finely chopped.
- 2/3 cup salt-free (homemade) beef stock
- 2 cloves garlic, peeled and smashed
- 1 pinch red pepper flakes
- 1/3 cup raw sugar
- 1 tbsp. sesame oil
- 2/3 cup soy sauce
- 1 to 2 tbsp. water
- 2 tbsp. cornstarch

Instructions:
1. Turn on the Ninja Foodi Multi-cooker to *Sauté* mode. Add sesame oil garlic, ginger and red pepper flakes and sauté for a minute
2. Then, de-glaze with vinegar, mix-in the sugar, soy sauce and beef stock - mix well
3. Add the ribs to the Ninja Foodi Multi-cooker coating them with the mixture
4. High pressure for 60 minutes. Close and lock the lid of the Ninja Foodi Multi-cooker, cook at high pressure for 60 minutes
5. To get 60 minutes' cook time, press *Pressure* button and use the Time Adjustment button to adjust the cook time to 60 minutes.
6. Pressure Release. Use the Natural release method (20 minutes)

7. Finish the dish. Remove the lid from the Ninja Foodi Multi-cooker. Close crisping lid. Select "BROIL" and set time to 10 minutes. Check after 6 minutes, cooking for an additional 4 minutes if dish needs more browning
8. Make a slurry with the cornstarch and water and then mix into the rib cooking liquid in the Ninja Foodi Multi-cooker. *Sauté* the mixture until it reaches the desired consistency. Serve and Enjoy!

Beef Stew

(Ready in about: 1 hour 25 minutes | **Servings:** 4 to 6)

Ingredients:
- 2 lb. beef stew meat
- 5 scrubbed medium-sized potatoes chopped.
- 2 packets McCormick Stew Seasoning (or stew seasoning of your choice for 2 lb. meat)
- 1 cup raw green beans
- 1 cup carrots chopped.
- 1 onion chopped
- 4 stalks celery
- 4 cups water

Instructions:
1. Add the beef Stew meet, McCormick Stew Seasoning Packets and the water to the Ninja Foodi Multi-cooker
2. High pressure for 45 minutes. Lock the lid on the Ninja Foodi Multi-cooker and then cook for 45 minutes
3. To get 45 minutes' cook time, press *Pressure* button and use the adjust button to adjust the cook time to 45 minutes
4. Pressure Release. Release the pressure using Natural Release
5. Remove the lid and stir.
6. Add vegetables below the maximum fill line, put the lid back on.
7. High pressure for 15 minutes. Lock the lid on the Ninja Foodi Multi-cooker and cook for 15 minutes
8. To get 15 minutes' cook time, press *Pressure* button and then adjust the time
9. Pressure Release. Use Natural Release Method. Serve and enjoy

Fish & Seafood Recipes

Special Fish Filets

(Ready in about: 15 minutes | **Servings:** 2)

Ingredients:
- 4 White Fish fillets (any white fish)
- 1 lb. Cherry Tomatoes; halved
- 1 cup Black salt-cured Olives (French, Taggiesche or Kalamata)
- 1 bunch of fresh Thyme Olive Oil
- 1 clove of garlic; pressed
- 2 tbsp. Pickled Capers
- Salt and pepper to taste

Instructions:
1. Prepare the base of the Ninja Foodi Multi-cooker with 1½ to 2 cups of water and trivet or steamer basket.
2. Line the bottom of the heat-proof bowl with cherry tomato halves (to keep the fish filet from sticking), add Thyme (reserve a few sprigs for garnish)
3. Place the fish fillets over the cherry tomatoes, sprinkle with remaining tomatoes, crushed garlic, a dash of olive oil and a pinch of salt
4. Insert the dish in the Ninja Foodi Multi-cooker - if your heat proof dish does not have handles construct them by making a long aluminum sling
5. High pressure for 5 minutes. Lock the lid on the Ninja Foodi Multi-cooker and then cook for 5 minutes.
6. To get 5 minutes' cook time, press *Pressure* button and then adjust the time
7. Pressure Release. Perform a quick release to release the cooker's pressure
8. Finish the dish. Close crisping lid and select Broil, set time to 7 minutes
9. Distribute fish into individual plates, top with cherry tomatoes and sprinkle with olives, capers, fresh Thyme, a crackle of pepper and a little swirl of fresh olive oil

Chili Garlic Black Mussels Recipe

(Ready in about: 45 minutes | **Servings:** 4)

Ingredients:
- 1 ½ lb Black Mussels, cleaned and de-bearded
- 3 tbsp. Olive Oil
- 1 White Onion, chopped finely
- 10 Tomatoes, skin removed and chopped.
- 3 large Chilies, seeded and chopped.
- 1 cup Dry White Wine
- 3 cups Vegetable Broth
- 1/3 cup fresh Basil Leaves
- 3 cloves Garlic, peeled and crushed
- 4 tbsp. Tomato Paste
- 1 cup fresh Parsley Leaves

Instructions:
1. Heat the olive oil on Sear/Sauté mode, and stir-fry the onion, until soft. Add the chilies and garlic, and cook for 2 minutes, stirring frequently
2. Stir in the tomatoes and tomato paste, and cook for 2 more minutes. Then, pour in the wine and vegetable broth. Let simmer for 5 minutes
3. Add the mussels, close the lid, secure the pressure valve, and press Steam mode on High pressure for 3 minutes. Press Start/Stop to start cooking

4. Once the timer has ended, do a natural pressure release for 15 minutes, then a quick pressure release, and open the lid
5. Remove and discard any unopened mussels. Then, add half of the basil and parsley, and stir. Close the crisping lid and cook on Broil mode for 5 minutes
6. Dish the mussels with sauce in serving bowls and garnish it with the remaining basil and parsley. Serve with a side of crusted bread

Special Farro with Fennel and Smoked Trout

(Ready in about: 22 minutes | **Servings:** 4)

Ingredients:
- 1 cup semi perlato farro
- 12-ounces smoked trout; skinned and chopped.
- 1 large fennel bulb; trimmed and shaved into thin strips
- 1/4 cup regular or low fat sour cream
- 1/2 cup regular or low fat mayonnaise
- 3 tbsp. lemon juice
- 1 tsp. sugar
- 2 tbsp. Dijon mustard
- 1 tsp. ground black pepper

Instructions:
1. Pour the farro into the Ninja Foodi Multi-cooker; pour in enough water that the grains are submerged by 2 inches
2. High pressure for 17 minutes. Lock the lid on the Ninja Foodi Multi-cooker and then cook for 17 minutes.
3. To get 17 minutes' cook time, press *Pressure* button and use the Time Adjustment button to adjust the cook time to 17 minutes
4. Pressure Release. Use the quick release method to drop the pot's pressure to normal
5. Finish the dish. Unlock and open the cooker. Place the fennel strips in a colander set in the sink and drain the farro into the colander over the fennel. Toss well, then let cool for 30 minutes in the colander
6. Whisk the mayonnaise, sour cream, lemon juice, mustard, sugar and pepper in a large serving bowl until creamy. Add the farro, fennel and smoked trout; toss gently to coat well

Delightful Tuna Noodle

(Ready in about: 24 minutes | **Servings:** 2)

Ingredients:
- 8-ounces of dry wide egg noodles (uncooked)
- 1 can (14-ounces) diced tomatoes with basil; garlic and oregano(undrained) or any kind you have on hand.
- 1 jar (7.5 oz.) marinated artichoke hearts; drained with saving the liquid, then chop it up
- 1 tbsp. of Oil
- 1/2 cup of chopped red onion
- 1 ¼ cups of water
- 1 can of tuna fish in water; drained
- Crumpled feta cheese
- Fresh chopped parsley or dried
- 1/4 tsp. of salt
- 1/8 tsp. of pepper

Instructions:
1. Sauté the red onion for about 2 minutes. Add the dry noodles, tomatoes, water, salt and pepper
2. High pressure for 10 minutes. Lock the lid on the Ninja Foodi Multi-cooker and then cook for 10 minutes.

3. To get 10 minutes' cook time, press *Pressure* button and adjust the time
4. Pressure Release. Release the pressure using natural release method
5. Turn off the warm setting. Add tuna, artichokes and your reserved liquid from the artichokes and sauté on normal while stirring for about 4 more minutes till hot, top with a feta cheese to your liking
6. Close crisping lid and select Broil, set time to 7 minutes. Press Start/Stop button. Serve

Salmon with Bok Choy

(Ready in about: 15 minutes | **Servings:** 4)

Ingredients:
- 4 frozen skinless salmon fillets (4-ounces, 1-inch thick each)
- 1 cup jasmine rice, rinsed
- 3/4 cup water
- 2 heads baby bok choy, stems on, rinsed, cut in half
- 1/4 cup mirin
- 1 tsp. sesame oil
- 1 tsp. kosher salt
- 2 tbsp. red miso paste
- 2 tbsp. butter, softened
- Sesame seeds, for garnish

Instructions:
1. Place rice and water into the pot. Stir to combine. Place reversible rack in pot, making sure rack is in the higher position
2. Season salmon with salt, then place on rack. Assemble pressure lid, making sure the PRESSURE RELEASE valve is in the SEAL position. Select PRESSURE and set to HIGH. Set time to 2 minutes. Select START/STOP to begin
3. While salmon and rice are cooking, stir together miso and butter to form a paste. Toss bok choy with mirin and sesame oil
4. When pressure cooking is complete, quick release the pressure by moving the PRESSURE RELEASE valve to the VENT position. Carefully remove lid when unit has finished releasing pressure
5. Gently pat salmon dry with paper towel, then spread miso butter evenly on top of the fillets. Add bok choy to the rack. Close crisping lid. Select BROIL and set time to 7 minutes. Select START/STOP to begin, checking for doneness after 5 minutes
6. When cooking is complete, remove salmon from rack and serve with bok choy and rice. Garnish with sesame seeds, if desired

Pasta with Tuna

(Ready in about: 5 minutes | **Servings:** 2 to 4)

Ingredients:
- 16-ounce fusilli pasta
- 2 (5.5-ounce cans) Tuna packed in olive oil water to cover
- 3 anchovies
- 1 tbsp. olive oil
- 1 garlic clove
- 2 tbsp. capers
- 2 cups tomato puree
- 1 ½ tsp. salt

Instructions:
1. In the pre-heated Ninja Foodi Multi-cookeron *Sauté* mode, add the oil, garlic and anchovies.
2. Sauté until the anchovies begin to disintegrate and the garlic cloves are just starting to turn golden.
3. Add the tomato puree and salt and mix together
4. Pour in the uncooked pasta and the contents of one tuna can (5 oz.) mixing to coat the dry pasta evenly.
5. Flatten the pasta in an even layer and pour in just enough water to cover
6. High pressure for 3 minutes. Lock the lid on the Ninja Foodi Multi-cooker and then cook for 3 minutes.
7. To get 3 minutes' cook time, press *Pressure* button and use the Time Adjustment button to adjust the cook time to 3 minutes
8. Pressure Release. When time is up, open the cooker by releasing the pressure.
9. Finish the dish. Mix in the last 5-ounce of tuna. Close crisping lid and select Broil, set time to 7 minutes. Sprinkle with capers before serving

Lime Saucy Salmon Recipe

(Ready in about: 15 minutes | **Servings:** 4)

Ingredients:
- 4 (5 oz) Salmon Filets
- 1 cup Water
- 1 ½ tsp. Paprika
- 2 tbsp. chopped Parsley
- 2 tbsp. Olive Oil
- 1 tbsp. Maple Syrup
- 2 cloves Garlic, minced
- 2 tsp. Cumin Powder
- 2 tbsp. Hot Water
- 1 Lime, juiced
- Salt and Black Pepper to taste

Instructions:
1. In a bowl, add cumin, paprika, parsley, olive oil, hot water, maple syrup, garlic, and lime juice. Mix with a whisk. Set aside
2. Open the Ninja Foodi and pour the water in. Then, fit the rack. Season the salmon with pepper and salt; and place them on the rack
3. Close the lid, secure the pressure valve, and select Steam mode on High pressure for 3 minutes. Press Start/Stop.
4. Once the timer has ended, do a quick pressure release, and open the pot
5. Close the crisping lid and cook on Air Crisp mode for 3 minutes at 300 °F. Use a set of tongs to transfer the salmon to a serving plate and drizzle the lime sauce all over it. Serve with steamed swiss chard

Tasty Mahi Mahi Recipe

(Ready in about: 15 minutes | **Servings:** 4)

Ingredients:
- 4 Mahi Mahi Fillets, fresh
- 4 cloves Garlic, minced
- 1 tbsp. Sriracha Sauce
- 1 ½ tbsp. Maple Syrup
- 1 Lime, juiced
- 1 ¼ -inch Ginger, grated
- Salt and Black Pepper
- 2 tbsp. Chili Powder
- 1 cup Water

Instructions:
1. Place mahi mahi on a plate and season with salt and pepper on both sides
2. In a bowl, add garlic, ginger, chili powder, sriracha sauce, maple syrup, and lime juice. Use a spoon to mix it.
3. With a brush, apply the hot sauce mixture on the fillet
4. Then, open the Ninja Foodi's lid, pour the water it and fit the rack at the bottom of the pot. Put the fillets on the trivet.
5. Close the lid, secure the pressure valve, and select Steam mode on High pressure for 5 minutes. Press Start/Stop to start cooking
6. Once the timer has ended, do a quick pressure release, and open the lid
7. Use a set of tongs to remove the mahi mahi onto serving plates. Serve with steamed or braised asparagus.
8. For a crispier taste, cook them for 2 minutes on Air Crisp mode, at 300 °F

Tomatillo and Shrimp Casserole

(Ready in about: 30 minutes | **Servings:** 4)

Ingredients:
- 1 ½ lb. medium shrimp (about 30 per pound); peeled and deveined
- 1/4 cup loosely packed fresh cilantro leaves; chopped.
- 1 ½ lb. fresh tomatillos; husked and chopped.
- 1/2 cup bottled clam juice
- 1 cup shredded Monterey jack cheese (about 4-ounces)
- 2 tbsp. olive oil
- 1 medium yellow onion; chopped.
- 1 small fresh jalapeño chile; stemmed; seeded and minced
- 2 tsp. minced garlic
- 2 tbsp. fresh lime juice

Instructions:
1. Heat the oil in the Ninja Foodi Multi-cooker turned to the *Browning* function. Add the onion and cook, often stirring, until translucent, about 3 minutes
2. Add the jalapeño and garlic; cook until aromatic, stirring all the while, less than a minute.
3. Stir in the tomatillos, clam juice and lime juice
4. High pressure for 9 minutes. Lock the lid on the Ninja Foodi Multi-cooker and then cook for 9 minutes.
5. To get 9 minutes' cook time, press *Pressure* button and use the Time Adjustment button to adjust the cook time to 9 minutes.
6. Pressure Release Use the quick release method
7. Finish the dish. Unlock and open the pot. Turn the Ninja Foodi Multi-cooker to its *Sauté* function. Stir in the shrimp and cilantro; cook for 2 minutes, stirring frequently

8. Sprinkle the cheese over the top of the casserole. Close crisping lid and select Broil, set time to 5 minutes. Press Start/Stop button to begin. Serve and enjoy

Creamy Garlicky Oyster Stew Recipe

(Ready in about: 15 minutes | **Servings:** 4)

Ingredients:
- 2 cups Heavy Cream
- 3 (10 oz) jars Shucked Oysters in Liqueur
- 2 cups chopped Celery
- 2 cups Bone Broth
- 3 cloves Garlic, minced
- 3 tbsp. chopped Parsley
- 3 Shallots, minced
- 3 tbsp. Olive Oil
- Salt and White Pepper to taste

Instructions:
1. Add oil, garlic, shallot, and celery. Stir-fry them for 2 minutes on Sear/Sauté mode, and add the heavy cream, broth, and oysters. Stir once or twice
2. Close the lid, secure the pressure valve, and select Steam mode on High pressure for 3 minutes. Press Start/Stop
3. Once the timer has stopped, do a quick pressure release, and open the lid.
4. Season with salt and white pepper. Close the crisping lid and cook for 5 minutes on Broil mode. Stir and dish the oyster stew into serving bowls. Garnish with parsley and top with some croutons

Monk Fish with Power Greens

(Ready in about: 25 minutes | **Servings:** 4)

Ingredients:
- 4 (8 oz) Monk Fish Fillets, cut in 2 pieces each
- 1/2 lb Baby Bok Choy, stems removed and chopped largely
- 2 tbsp. Olive Oil
- 1 cup Kale Leaves
- 1 Lemon, zested and juiced
- 1/2 cup chopped Green Beans
- 2 cloves Garlic, sliced
- Lemon Wedges to serve
- Salt and White Pepper to taste

Instructions:
1. Pour in the coconut oil, garlic, red chili, and green beans. Stir fry for 5 minutes on Sear/Sauté mode. Add the kale leaves, and cook them to wilt, about 3 minutes
2. Meanwhile, place the fish on a plate and season with salt, white pepper, and lemon zest. After, remove the green beans and kale into a plate and set aside
3. Back to the pot, add the olive oil and fish. Brown the fillets on each side for about 2 minutes and then add the bok choy in
4. Pour the lemon juice over the fish and gently stir. Cook for 2 minutes and then press Start/Stop to stop cooking
5. Spoon the fish with bok choy over the green beans and kale. Serve with a side of lemon wedges and there, you have a complete meal

Shrimp with Risotto Primavera

(Ready in about: 40 minutes | **Servings:** 5)

Ingredients:
- 2 tbsp. olive oil, divided.
- 16 uncooked jumbo shrimp (fresh or defrosted), peeled, deveined
- 1 small onion, peeled, finely diced
- 5 ½ cups chicken or vegetable stock
- 2 cups Arborio rice
- 4 cloves garlic, peeled, minced, divided.
- 3 tsp. kosher salt, divided.
- 1 tsp. ground black pepper
- 2 tsp. garlic powder
- 2 tbsp. butter
- 1 ½ cups grated Parmesan cheese, plus more for serving
- Juice of 1 lemon
- 1 bunch asparagus, trimmed, cut in 1-inch pieces
- 1/2 tsp. crushed red pepper (optional)

Instructions:
1. Select SEAR/SAUTÉ and set to MD:HI. Select START/STOP to begin. Allow to preheat for 5 minutes.
2. Add 1 tbsp. oil and onion to pot. SAUTÉ until softened, about 5 minutes. Add half the garlic and cook until fragrant, about 1 minute. Season with 2 tsp. salt
3. Add stock and rice to pot. Assemble pressure lid, making sure the PRESSURE RELEASE valve is in the SEAL position
4. Select PRESSURE and set to HIGH. Set time to 7 minutes. Select START/STOP to begin. While rice is cooking, toss shrimp in the remaining oil, garlic, salt, garlic powder, black pepper, and crushed red pepper in a mixing bowl
5. When pressure cooking is complete, allow pressure to natural release for 10 minutes. After 10 minutes, quick release remaining pressure by moving the PRESSURE RELEASE valve to the VENT position. Carefully remove lid when unit has finished releasing pressure
6. Stir butter, lemon juice, and asparagus into the rice until evenly incorporated
7. Place reversible rack inside pot over risotto, making sure rack is in the higher position. Place shrimp on rack. Close crisping lid. Select BROIL and set time to 8 minutes. Select START/STOP to begin
8. When cooking is complete, remove rack from pot. Stir Parmesan into the risotto. Top with shrimp and Parmesan and serve immediately

Scallops with Butter Caper Sauce

(Ready in about: 15 minutes | **Servings:** 6)

Ingredients:
- 2 lb Sea Scallops, foot removed
- 4 tbsp. Capers, drained
- 4 tbsp. Olive Oil
- 10 tbsp. Butter, unsalted
- 1 cup Dry White Wine
- 3 tsp. lemon Zest

Instructions:
1. Melt the butter to caramel brown on Sear/Sauté. Use a soup spook to fetch the butter out into a bowl.
2. Next, heat the oil in the pot, once heated add the scallops and sear them on both sides to golden brown which is about 5 minutes
3. Remove to a plate and set aside

4. Pour the white wine in the pot to deglaze the bottom while using a spoon to scrape the bottom of the pot of any scallop bits
5. Add the capers, butter, and lemon zest. Use a spoon to gently stir the mixture once. After 40 seconds, spoon the sauce with capers over the scallops. Serve with a side of braised asparagus

Lemon and Dill Fish

(Ready in about: 15 minutes | Servings: 2)

Ingredients:
- 2 tilapia or cod fillets
- 2 tbsp. butter
- 2 sprigs fresh dill
- 4 slices lemon
- Salt, pepper and garlic powder

Instructions:
1. Layout 2 large squares of parchment paper. Place a fillet in the center of each parchment square and then season with a generous amount of salt, pepper and garlic powder
2. On each fillet, place in order: 1 sprig of dill, 2 lemon slices and 1 tbsp. of butter
3. For best results, place the rack or trivet at the bottom of your Ninja Foodi Multi-cooker
4. Pour 1 cup of water into the cooker to create a water bath.
5. Close up parchment paper around the fillets, folding to seal and then place both packets on metal rack inside cooker.
6. High pressure for 5 minutes. Lock the lid on the Ninja Foodi Multi-cooker and then cook for 5 minutes.
7. To get 5 minutes' cook time, press *Pressure* button and then adjust the time
8. Pressure Release. Perform a quick release to release the cooker's pressure. Unwrap packets and serve.
9. There is no need to remove the fish from the packets before serving. In fact, it makes a really nice presentation

Alaskan Cod with Pinto Beans

(Ready in about: 30 minutes | Servings: 4)

Ingredients:
- 2 (18 oz) Alaskan Cod, cut into 4 pieces each
- 2 cloves Garlic, minced
- 1/2 cup Olive Brine
- 3 cups Chicken Broth
- Salt and Black Pepper to taste
- 2 small Onions, chopped.
- 1 head Fennel, quartered
- 1 cup Pinto Beans, soaked, drained and rinsed
- 1 cup Green Olives, pitted and crushed
- 1/2 cup Basil Leaves
- 1/2 cup Tomato Puree
- 4 tbsp. Olive Oil
- Lemon Slices to garnish

Instructions:
1. Heat the olive oil and add the garlic and onion. Stir-fry on Sear/Sauté mode until the onion softens. Pour in chicken broth and tomato puree. Let simmer for about 3 minutes
2. Add fennel, olives, beans, salt, and pepper. Seal the lid and select Steam mode on High pressure for 10 minutes. Press Start/Stop to start cooking

3. Once the timer has stopped, do a quick pressure release, and open the lid. Transfer the beans to a plate with a slotted spoon. Adjust broth's taste with salt and pepper and add the cod pieces to the cooker.
4. Close the lid again, secure the pressure valve, and select Steam mode on Low pressure for 3 minutes. Press Start/Stop.
5. Once the timer has ended, do a quick pressure release, and open the lid
6. Remove the cod into soup plates, top with the beans and basil leaves, and spoon the broth over them. Serve with a side of crusted bread

Pernod Mackerel and Vegetables Recipe

(**Ready in about:** 25 minutes + 2 hours for marinating | **Servings:** 6)

Ingredients:
- 1 lb. Asparagus, trimmed
- 3 large Whole Mackerel, cut into 2 pieces
- 1 Carrot, cut into sticks
- 1 Orange Bell Pepper, seeded and cut into sticks
- 1 Celery stalk, cut into sticks
- 1/2 cup Butter, at room temperature
- 6 medium Tomatoes, quartered
- 1 large Brown Onion, sliced thinly
- 2 ½ tbsp. Pernod
- 3 cloves Garlic, minced
- 2 Lemons, cut into wedges
- 1 ½ cups Water
- Salt and Black Pepper to taste

Instructions:
1. Cut out 6 pieces of parchment paper a little longer and wider than a piece of fish with kitchen scissors. Then, cut out 6 pieces of foil slightly longer than the parchment papers
2. Lay the foil wraps on a flat surface and place each parchment paper on each aluminium foil.
3. In a bowl, add tomatoes, onions, garlic, bell pepper, Pernod, butter, asparagus, carrot, celery, salt, and pepper. Use a spoon to mix them
4. Place each fish piece on the layer of parchment and foil wraps. Spoon the vegetable mixture on each fish. Then, wrap the fish and place the fish packets in the refrigerator to marinate for 2 hours. Remove the fish to a flat surface
5. Open the Ninja Foodi, pour the water in, and fit the reversible rack at the bottom of the pot. Put the packets on the trivet. Seal the lid and select Steam mode on High pressure for 3 minutes. Press Start/Stop to start cooking
6. Once the timer has ended, do a quick pressure release, and open the lid. Remove the trivet with the fish packets onto a flat surface. Carefully open the foil and using a spatula. Return the packets to the pot, on top of the rack
7. Close the crisping lid and cook on Air Crisp for 3 minutes at 300°F. Then, remove to serving plates. Serve with lemon wedges

Carolina Crab Soup Recipe

(Ready in about: 45 minutes | **Servings:** 4)

Ingredients:
- 2 lb Crabmeat Lumps
- 2 Celery Stalk, diced
- 1 ½ cup Chicken Broth
- 3/4 cup Heavy Cream
- 6 tbsp. Butter
- 6 tbsp. All-purpose Flour
- Salt to taste
- 1 White Onion, chopped.
- 3 tsp. Worcestershire Sauce
- 3 tsp. Old Bay Seasoning
- 3/4 cup Muscadet
- 3 tsp. minced Garlic
- 1/2 cup Half and Half Cream
- 2 tsp. Hot Sauce
- Lemon Juice, Chopped Dill for serving

Instructions:
1. Melt the butter on Sear/Sauté mode, and mix in the all-purpose flour, in a fast motion to make a rue. Add celery, onion, and garlic. Stir and cook until soft and crispy, for 3 minutes
2. While stirring, gradually add the half and half cream, heavy cream, and broth.
3. Let simmer for 2 minutes. Add Worcestershire sauce, old bay seasoning, Muscadet, and hot sauce.
4. Stir and let simmer for 15 minutes. Add the crabmeat and mix it well into the sauce
5. Close the crisping lid and cook on Broil mode for 10 minutes to soften the meat. Dish into serving bowls, garnish with dill and drizzle squirts of lemon juice over
6. Serve with a side of garlic crusted bread

Potato Beer Fish

(Ready in about: 1 hour | **Servings:** 4)

Ingredients:
- 1 lb. fish fillet
- 4 medium size potatoes; peeled and diced
- 1 red pepper sliced
- 1 cup beer
- 1 tbsp. oyster flavored sauce
- 1 tbsp. rock candy
- 1 tbsp. oil
- 1 tsp. salt

Instructions:
1. Put all ingredients into your Ninja Foodi Multi-cooker. High pressure for 40 minutes. Lock the lid on the Ninja Foodi Multi-cooker and then cook for 40 minutes
2. To get 40 minutes' cook time, press *Pressure* button and use the Time Adjustment button to adjust the cook time to 40 minutes
3. Pressure Release. Release the pressure using natural release method.
4. Finish the dish. Close the crisping lid. Select "BROIL" and set the time to 5 minutes. Select START/STOP to begin. Cook until top is browned
5. Then that is it! Simple, fast, delicious, retaining flavour and nutrition, consistent results all the time. Serve and Enjoy!

Vegetable Recipes

Buffalo Cauliflower Bites

(Ready in about: 1 hour 20 minutes | **Servings:** 6)

Ingredients:
- 2 heads cauliflower, trimmed, cut in 2-inch florets
- 1 ½ cups water, divided.
- 1 tsp. garlic powder
- 1 tsp. onion powder
- 1 tsp. kosher salt
- 1 ½ cups cornstarch
- 1 tsp. black pepper
- 2 eggs
- 1/2 cup all-purpose flour
- 2 tsp. baking powder
- 1/3 cup buffalo wing sauce

Instructions:
1. Place cauliflower and 1/2 cup water into the pot. Assemble pressure lid, making sure the PRESSURE RELEASE valve is in the SEAL position. Select PRESSURE and set to LOW. Set time to 2 minutes. Select START/STOP to begin
2. When pressure cooking is complete, quick release the pressure by turning the PRESSURE RELEASE valve to the VENT position. Carefully remove lid when unit has finished releasing pressure. Drain cauliflower and chill in refrigerator until cooled, about 10 minutes
3. Whisk together cornstarch, flour, baking powder, garlic powder, onion powder, salt, and pepper. Whisk in eggs and 1 cup water until batter is smooth
4. Add chilled cauliflower to bowl with batter and gently toss until well coated. Transfer coated cauliflower to baking sheet and chill in freezer for 20 minutes
5. Close crisping lid. Preheat the unit by selecting AIR CRISP, setting the temperature to 360°F, and setting the time to 5 minutes
6. Meanwhile, arrange half the cauliflower in an even layer in the bottom of the Cook & Crisp Basket. After 5 minutes, place basket into the pot
7. Close crisping lid. Select AIR CRISP, set temperature to 360°F, and set time to 20 minutes. Select START/STOP to begin. When first batch of cauliflower is crisp and golden, transfer to a bowl. Repeat with remaining chilled cauliflower
8. When cooking is complete, microwave hot sauce for 30 seconds, then toss with cooked cauliflower. Serve immediately

One Pot Pasta Puttanesca

(Ready in about: 14 minutes | **Servings:** 4)

Ingredients:
- 8-ounces dried whole wheat ziti
- 1 small red onion; chopped.
- 1 tbsp. drained and rinsed capers; minced
- 1 tbsp. minced garlic
- 1 lb. eggplant (about 1 large); stemmed and diced (no need to peel)
- 1 (28-ounce) can diced tomatoes (about 3 ½ cups)
- 2 medium yellow bell peppers; stemmed, cored and chopped.
- 2 tbsp. olive oil
- 1 ¼ cups vegetable broth
- 2 tbsp. canned tomato paste
- 2 tsp. dried rosemary
- 1 tsp. dried thyme
- 1/2 tsp. ground black pepper

Instructions:
1. Heat the oil in the Ninja Foodi Multi-cooker turned to the *Sauté* function. Add the onion, capers and garlic; cook, often stirring, just until the onion first begins to soften, about 2 minutes
2. Add the eggplant and bell peppers; cook, often stirring, for 1 minute. Mix in the tomatoes, broth, tomato paste, rosemary, thyme and pepper, stirring until the tomato paste coats everything. Stir in the ziti until coated
3. High pressure for 8 minutes. Lock the lid on the Ninja Foodi Multi-cooker and then cook for 8 minutes.
4. To get 8 minutes' cook time, press *Pressure* button and use the Time Adjustment button to adjust the cook time to 8 minutes
5. Pressure Release. Use the quick release method to drop the pressure in the pot back to normal. Unlock and open the cooker. Stir well before serving

Rye Berry and Celery Root Salad

(Ready in about: 45 minutes | **Servings:** 4)

Ingredients:
- 1 medium celeriac (celery root); peeled and shredded through the large holes of a box grater
- 3/4 cup rye berries
- 2 tbsp. honey
- 2 tbsp. apple cider vinegar
- 2 tbsp. unsalted butter
- 1/2 tsp. salt
- 1/2 tsp. ground black pepper

Instructions:
1. Place the rye berries in the Ninja Foodi Multi-cooker; pour in enough cold tap water, so the grains are submerged by 2 inches
2. High pressure for 40 minutes. Lock the lid on the Ninja Foodi Multi-cooker and then cook for 40 minutes.
3. To get 40 minutes' cook time, press *Pressure* button and use the Time Adjustment button to adjust the cook time to 40 minutes
4. Pressure Release. Use the quick release method to bring the pot's pressure back to normal
5. Finish the dish. Unlock and open the cooker. Stir in the shredded celeriac. Cover the pot without locking it and set aside for 1 minute. Drain the pot into a large colander set in the sink. Wipe out the cooker
6. Melt the butter in the Ninja Foodi Multi-cooker; turned to it sauté function. Add the honey and cook for 1 minute, constantly stirring
7. Add the drained rye berries and celeriac; cook, constantly stirring, for 1 minute. Stir in the vinegar, salt and pepper to serve

Chickpea Stew with Carrots

(Ready in about: 18 minutes | **Servings:** 4)

Ingredients:
- 1 (9-ounce) box frozen artichoke heart quarters; thawed and squeezed of excess moisture
- 1 (14-ounce) can diced tomatoes (about 1 ¾ cups)
- 1 lb. baby-carrots; cut into 1-inch pieces
- 6 pitted dates; preferably Medjool, chopped.
- 1 medium red onion; halved and sliced into thin half-moons
- 1 ½ cups dried chickpeas
- 2 cups chicken broth
- 2 tbsp. all purpose flour
- 2 ½ tbsp. olive oil
- 2 tsp. minced garlic
- 1/2 tsp. ground cinnamon
- 1/2 tsp. ground coriander
- 1/2 tsp. ground cumin
- 1/2 tsp. salt
- 1 tbsp. sweet paprika

Instructions:
1. Soak the chickpeas in a big bowl of water for at least 12 hours or up to 16 hours
2. Drain the chickpeas in a colander set in the sink. Whisk the broth and flour in a medium bowl until the flour dissolves
3. Heat 1 ½ tbsp. oil in the Ninja Foodi Multi-cooker turned to the Sauté function. Add the onion and cook, often stirring, until softened, about 4 minutes
4. Stir in the garlic, paprika, cinnamon, coriander, cumin and salt until aromatic, about 30 seconds. Pour in the tomatoes as well as the broth mixture. Stir well, then add the carrots, dates and drained chickpeas.
5. High pressure for 12 minutes. Lock the lid on the Ninja Foodi Multi-cooker and then cook for 12 minutes.
6. To get 12 minutes' cook time, press *Pressure* button and use the Time Adjustment button to adjust the cook time to 12 minutes
7. Pressure Release. Use the quick release method to drop the pot's pressure back to normal.
8. Finish the dish. Unlock and open the cooker. Heat the remaining tbsp. oil in a large nonstick skillet set over medium-high heat
9. Add the artichoke heart quarters; fry until brown and crisp, stirring and occasionally turning about 10 minutes. Dish up the chickpea mixture into big bowls and top with the crisp artichoke bits

Crispy Ratatouille Recipe

(**Ready in about:** 14 minutes | **Servings:** 4)

Ingredients:

- 1 (14.5-ounce) can diced tomatoes; undrained
- 1 small red bell pepper; cut into ½-inch chunks (about 1 cup)
- 1 small green bell pepper; cut into ½-inch chunks (about 1 cup)
- 1 rib celery; sliced (about 1 cup)
- Kosher salt; for salting and seasoning
- 1 small eggplant; peeled and sliced 1/2-inch thick
- 1 medium zucchini; sliced 1/2-inch thick
- 2 tbsp. olive oil
- 1 cup chopped onion
- 3 garlic cloves; minced or pressed
- 1/2 tsp. dried oregano
- 1/4 tsp. freshly ground black pepper
- 2 tbsp. minced fresh basil
- 1/4 cup water
- 1/4 cup pitted green or black olives (optional)

Instructions:

1. Place a rack on a baking sheet. With kosher salt, very liberally salt one side of the eggplant and zucchini slices and place them, salted-side down, on the rack. Salt the other side
2. Let the slices sit for 15 to 20 minutes or until they start to exude water (you'll see it beading up on the surface of the slices and dripping into the sheet pan). Rinse the slices and blot them dry. Cut the zucchini slices into quarters and the eggplant slices into eighths
3. Turn the Ninja Foodi Multi-cooker to *Sauté*, heat the olive oil until it shimmers and flows like water. Add the onion and garlic and sprinkle with a pinch or two of kosher salt. Cook for about 3 minutes, stirring until the onions just begin to brown
4. Add the eggplant, zucchini, green bell pepper, red bell pepper, celery and tomatoes with their juice, water and oregano
5. High pressure for 4 minutes. Lock the lid on the Ninja Foodi Multi-cooker and then cook for 4 minutes.
6. To get 4 minutes' cook time, press *Pressure* button and use the Time Adjustment button to adjust the cook time to 4 minutes.
7. Pressure Release. Use the quick release method
8. Finish the dish. Unlock and remove the lid. Close the crisping lid. Select "BROIL" and set the time to 5 minutes. Select START/STOP to begin. Cook until top is browned
9. Stir in the pepper, basil and olives (if using). Taste, adjust the seasoning as needed and serve.
10. While this vegetable dish is usually served on its own, it's great tossed with cooked pasta or served over polenta

Greens and Beets with Horseradish Sauce

(**Ready in about:** 15 minutes | **Servings:** 4)

Ingredients:
- 2 large or 3 small beets with greens; scrubbed and root ends trimmed
- 2 tsp. unsalted butter
- 1 tbsp. minced fresh chives
- 1 cup water; for steaming
- 1 tbsp. whole milk
- 2 tbsp. sour cream
- 1 tsp. prepared horseradish
- 1/4 tsp. lemon zest
- 1/8 tsp. kosher salt; divided.

Instructions:
1. Trim off the beet greens and set aside. If the beets are very large (3 inches or more in diameter), quarter them; otherwise, halve them
2. Add the water and insert the steamer basket or trivet. Place the beets on the steamer insert.
3. High pressure for 10 minutes. Lock the lid on the Ninja Foodi Multi-cooker and then cook for 10 minutes.
4. To get 10 minutes' cook time, press *Pressure* button and use the Time Adjustment button to adjust the cook time to 10 minutes
5. When the timer goes off, turn the cooker off. (Warm* setting, turn off)
6. Pressure Release. Let the pressure to come down naturally.
7. While the beets are cooking and the pressure is releasing, wash the greens and slice them into 1/2-inch-thick ribbons, removing any tough stems. In a small bowl, whisk together the sour cream, milk, horseradish, lemon zest and $1/16$ tsp. of kosher salt
8. Finish the dish. When the pressure has released completely, unlock and remove the lid. Remove the beets and cool slightly; then use a paring knife or peeler to peel them. Slice them into large bite-size pieces and set aside
9. Remove the steamer from the Ninja Foodi Multi-cooker and pour out the water. Turn the Ninja Foodi Multi-cooker to *Sauté*. Add the butter to melt. When the butter stops foaming, add the beet greens and sprinkle with the remaining $1/16$ tsp. of kosher salt. Cook for 3 to 4 minutes, stirring until wilted
10. Return the beets to the Ninja Foodi Multi-cooker and heat for 1 or 2 minutes, stirring. Transfer the beets and greens to a platter and drizzle with the sour cream mixture. Sprinkle with the chives and serve
11. It may be tempting to cool the beets entirely before you peel them, but that would be a mistake. Beets are easiest to peel when they're just cool enough to handle; if they get too cold the skins tend to stick

Zucchini Fries with Marinara Sauce

(Ready in about: 1 hour and 20 minutes | **Servings:** 4)

Ingredients:
- 2 large zucchini, cut in sticks 3-inches long and 1/4-inch thick
- 2 tsp. kosher salt
- 2 cups all-purpose flour
- 3 eggs, beaten
- 3 cups seasoned bread crumbs
- 1/4 cup grated Parmesan cheese
- 1 tbsp. garlic powder
- 2 tsp. onion powder
- Marinara sauce, for serving

Instructions:
1. Place the zucchini sticks onto a plate and sprinkle with salt. Allow for 15 minutes to remove excess liquid. Pat dry
2. Place flour into a bowl. Place beaten eggs in another bowl. Combine bread crumbs, Parmesan, garlic powder, and onion powder in a third bowl
3. First, dredge fries in the flour, then shake off any excess and coat in the egg. Then coat in bread crumb mixture and return to a clean plate. Repeat with remaining zucchini. Cover plate with plastic wrap and place in the freezer for 30 to 40 minutes
4. Once coating has hardened, place the Cook & Crisp Basket in the pot. Close crisping lid. Preheat the unit by selecting AIR CRISP, setting the temperature to 360°F, and setting the time to 5 minutes. Press START/STOP to begin.
5. After 5 minutes, open lid and add zucchini fries to basket. Close lid. Select AIR CRISP, set temperature to 360°F, and set time to 24 minutes. Press START/STOP to begin
6. After 12 minutes, open lid, then lift basket and shake zucchini fries or toss them with silicone-tipped tongs. Lower basket back into pot and close lid to resume cooking
7. After 20 minutes, check fries for desired doneness. Cook for up to 5 more minutes for crispier results. When cooking is complete, serve fries immediately with marinara sauce

Smooth Carrots with Pancetta

(Ready in about: 18 minutes | **Servings:** 4)

Ingredients:
- 1 lb. baby carrots
- 4-ounces pancetta; diced
- 1/4 cup moderately sweet white wine; such as a dry Riesling
- 1 medium leek; white and pale green parts only, sliced lengthwise, washed and thinly sliced
- 1/2 tsp. ground black pepper
- 2 tbsp. unsalted butter; cut into small bits

Instructions:
1. Put the pancetta in the Ninja Foodi turned to the *Air crisp* function and use the Time Adjustment button to adjust the cook time to 5 minutes
2. Add the leek; cook, often stirring, until softened. Pour in the wine and scrape up any browned bits at the bottom of the pot as it comes to a simmer
3. Add the carrots and pepper; stir well. Scrape and pour the contents of the Ninja Foodi Multi-cooker into a 1-quart, round, high-sided soufflé or baking dish
4. Dot with the bits of butter. Lay a piece of parchment paper on top of the dish, then a piece of aluminum foil. Seal the foil tightly over the baking dish.

5. Set the Ninja Foodi Multi-cooker rack inside and pour in 2 cups water. Use aluminum foil to build a sling for the baking dish; lower the baking dish into the cooker
6. High pressure for 7 minutes. Lock the lid on the Ninja Foodi Multi-cooker and then cook for 7 minutes.
7. To get 7 minutes' cook time, press *Pressure* button and use the Time Adjustment button to adjust the cook time to 7 minutes
8. Pressure Release. Use the quick release method to return the pot's pressure to normal.
9. Finish the dish. Close the crisping lid. Select "BROIL" and set the time to 5 minutes. Select START/STOP to begin. Cook until top is browned
10. Unlock and open the pot. Use the foil sling to lift the baking dish out of the cooker. Uncover, stir well and serve

Braised Red Cabbage and Apples

(Ready in about: 18 minutes | **Servings:** 4)

Ingredients:
- 1 medium red cabbage (about 2 lb.); cored and thinly sliced
- 1 medium tart green apple; such as Granny Smith; peeled, cored and chopped.
- 4 thin bacon slices; chopped.
- 1/2 cup chicken broth
- 1 small red onion; chopped.
- 1 tsp. dried thyme
- 1/4 tsp. ground allspice
- 1/4 tsp. ground mace
- 1 tbsp. balsamic vinegar
- 1 tbsp. packed dark brown sugar

Instructions:
1. Fry the bacon in the Ninja Foodi turned to the *air crisp* function, until crisp, about 4 minutes
2. Add the onion to the pot; cook, often stirring, until soft, about 4 minutes. Add the apple, thyme, allspice and mace. Cook about 1 minute, stirring all the while, until fragrant.
3. Stir in the brown sugar and vinegar; keep stirring until bubbling, about 1 minute
4. Add the cabbage; toss well to mix evenly with the other ingredients. Drizzle the broth over the cabbage mixture.
5. High pressure for 13 minutes. Lock the lid on the Ninja Foodi Multi-cooker and then cook for 13 minutes.
6. To get 13 minutes' cook time, press *Pressure* button and use the Time Adjustment button to adjust the cook time to 13 minutes.
7. Pressure Release. Use the quick release method to return the pot to normal pressure
8. Unlock and open the pot. Close the crisping lid. Select "BROIL" and set the time to 5 minutes. Select START/STOP to begin. Cook until top is browned. Serve

Quinoa and Potato Salad

(Ready in about: 20 minutes | **Servings:** 4)

Ingredients:
- 1 ½ lb. tiny white potatoes; halved
- 1/4 cup white balsamic vinegar
- 1 cup blond (white) quinoa
- 1 medium shallot; minced
- 2 medium celery stalks; thinly sliced
- 1 large dill pickle; diced
- 1 tbsp. Dijon mustard
- 1 tsp. sweet paprika
- 1/2 tsp. ground black pepper
- 1/4 tsp. celery seeds
- 1/4 tsp. salt
- 1/4 cup olive oil

Instructions:
1. Whisk the vinegar, mustard, paprika, pepper, celery seeds and salt in a large serving bowl until smooth; whisk in the olive oil in a thin, steady stream until the dressing is fairly creamy
2. Place the potatoes and quinoa in the Ninja Foodi Multi-cooker; add enough cold tap water so that the ingredients are submerged by 3 inches (some of the quinoa may float)
3. High pressure for 10 minutes. Lock the lid on the Ninja Foodi Multi-cooker and then cook for 10 minutes.
4. To get 10 minutes' cook time, press *Pressure* button and use the Time Adjustment button to adjust the cook time to 10 minutes
5. Pressure Release. Use the quick release method to bring the pot's pressure back to normal.
6. Finish the dish. Unlock and open the pot. Close the crisping lid. Select "BROIL" and set the time to 5 minutes. Select START/STOP to begin
7. Cook until top is browned. Drain the contents of the pot into a colander lined with paper towels or into a fine-mesh sieve in the sink. Do not rinse
8. Transfer the potatoes and quinoa to the large bowl with the dressing. Add the shallot, celery and pickle; toss gently and set aside for a minute or two to warm up the vegetables.

Simple Potato Wedges

(Ready in about: 45 minutes | **Servings:** 4)

Ingredients:
- 4 Idaho potatoes, cut in 2-inch wedges
- 1 tbsp. fresh oregano leaves, minced
- 4 cloves garlic, peeled, minced
- Juice of 1 lemon
- 2 tbsp. extra virgin olive oil, divided.
- 2 tsp. kosher salt
- 1/2 cup water
- 1 tsp. ground black pepper

Instructions:
1. Pour water into the pot. Place potatoes into the Cook & Crisp Basket and place basket into pot.
2. Assemble pressure lid, making sure the PRESSURE RELEASE valve is in the SEAL position. Select PRESSURE and set to LOW. Set time to 3 minutes. Select START/STOP to begin
3. While potatoes are cooking, stir together 1 tbsp. olive oil with oregano, garlic, lemon juice, salt, and pepper in a small bowl. Set aside
4. When pressure cooking is complete, quick release the pressure by moving the PRESSURE RELEASE valve to the VENT position. Carefully remove lid when unit has finished releasing pressure
5. Pour remaining olive oil over the potatoes in the basket, shaking to coat evenly
6. Close the crisping lid. Select AIR CRISP, set temperature to 400°F, and set time to 18 minutes

7. Select START/STOP to begin. Check potatoes after 12 minutes. Continue cooking for up to 18 minutes for desired crispiness. When cooking is complete, remove potatoes from basket. Toss with oregano dressing and serve

Spaghetti Squash and Spinach Walnut Pesto

(**Ready in about:** 15 minutes | **Servings:** 4)

Ingredients:
- 1 cup Water
- 4 lb. Spaghetti Squash

For the Pesto
- 1/2 cup spinach, chopped
- 1/3 cup extra virgin olive oil
- 2 Garlic Cloves, minced
- 2 tbsp. Walnuts
- Salt and ground pepper, to taste
- Zest and juice from ½ lemon

Instructions:
1. In a food processor put all the pesto ingredients and blend until everything is well incorporated. Season to taste and set aside
2. Put the squash on a flat surface and use a knife to slice in half lengthwise. Scoop out all seeds and discard them.
3. Next, open the Ninja Foodi, pour the water into it and fit the reversible rack at the bottom. Place the squash halves on the rack, close the lid, secure the pressure valve, and select Steam on High pressure for 5 minutes. Press Start/Stop
4. Once the timer has ended, do a quick pressure release, and open the lid.
5. Remove the squash halves onto a cutting board and use a fork to separate the pulp strands into spaghetti-like pieces. Return to the pot and close the crisping lid. Cook for 2 minutes on Broil mode
6. Scoop the spaghetti squash into serving plates and drizzle over the spinach pesto

Vegetable Stew Recipe

(**Ready in about:** 55 minutes | **Servings:** 6)

Ingredients:
- 6 cups vegetable stock (or beef/chicken stock)
- 1/2 cup red wine or rice wine (red wine is preferred)
- 2 large carrots; cut into bite size pieces
- 3 potatoes cut into chunks
- 4 celery stalks cut into bite size pieces
- 2 cups of sliced white mushrooms
- 1 large onion; diced
- 6 tomatoes; diced
- 3 gloves garlic; minced
- 1 cup pearl barley
- 1 tbsp. dried parsley flakes
- 1 tbsp. dried thyme
- 1 bay leaf

Instructions:
1. In a nonstick pan add a drizzle of olive oil and quickly sauté the white mushrooms with the minced garlic and onions until golden brown (2 - 3 minutes on medium heat) then add in the red wine and cook for another minute. Set aside
2. In the Ninja Foodi Multi-cooker add the rest of the ingredients not including the barley
3. High pressure for 20 minutes. Lock the lid on the Ninja Foodi Multi-cooker and then cook for 20 minutes.
4. To get 20 minutes' cook time, press *Pressure* button and adjust the time.

5. Pressure Release. Use the quick release method to bring the pot's pressure back to normal
6. Add the mushrooms and barley, give it a good stir and add 2 pinches of salt and pepper
7. High pressure for 10 minutes. Lock the lid on the Ninja Foodi Multi-cooker and then cook for 10 minutes.
8. To get 10 minutes' cook time, press *Pressure* button and use the Time Adjustment button to adjust the cook time to 10 minutes
9. Pressure Release. Use the quick release method to bring the pot's pressure back to normal.
10. Finish the dish. At this point the potatoes and carrots should have softened. Add salt and pepper to taste.
11. Serve with your favorite pasta dish fresh baked biscuits

Butter Spaghetti Squash

(**Ready in about:** 18 minutes | **Servings:** 6)

Ingredients:
- 1 (3- to 3½ lb) spaghetti squash; halved lengthwise and seeded
- 1/2 cup finely grated Parmesan cheese (about 1-ounce)
- 2 tbsp. packed fresh sage leaves; minced
- 6 tbsp. unsalted butter
- 1/2 tsp. salt
- 1/2 tsp. ground black pepper

Instructions:
1. Put the squash cut side up in the cooker; add 1 cup water
2. High pressure for 12 minutes. Lock the lid on the Ninja Foodi Multi-cooker and then cook for 12 minutes.
3. To get 12 minutes' cook time, press *Pressure* button and use the Time Adjustment button to adjust the cook time to 12 minutes
4. Pressure Release. Use the quick release method to bring the pot's pressure back to normal
5. Finish the dish. Unlock and open the cooker. Transfer the squash halves to a cutting board; cool for 10 minutes. Discard the liquid in the cooker. Use a fork to scrape the spaghetti-like flesh off the skin and onto the cutting board; discard the skins
6. Melt the butter in the electric cooker turned to its browning function. Stir in the sage, salt and pepper, then add all of the squash. Stir and toss over the heat until well combined and heated through about 2 minutes. Add the cheese, toss well
7. Close the crisping lid. Select "BROIL" and set the time to 5 minutes. Select START/STOP to begin. Cook until top is browned. Serve

Soups

Colombian Style Chicken Soup Recipe

(Ready in about: 11 minutes | **Servings:** 4)

Ingredients:
- 3 bone in chicken breasts (about 2 lb. or 907 g)
- 5 cups (1.2 L) water
- 1 ½ tsp. kosher salt
- 1 ½ lb. Yukon gold potatoes, cut into 1/2-inch (13 mm) pieces
- 1 ear corn, cut into 4 pieces
- 1 medium yellow onion, cut in half
- 2 medium carrots, cut in half crosswise
- 2 ribs celery, cut in half crosswise
- 1/4 cup sour cream
- 1 tbsp. capers, rinsed
- 1/4 tsp. freshly ground black pepper
- 1 avocado
- 1 tsp. dried oregano
- 1 lime; quartered
- 8 sprigs fresh cilantro

Instructions:
1. To the Ninja Foodi Multi-cooker, add the onion, carrots, celery, chicken, water and salt
2. High pressure for 15 minutes. Lock the lid on the Ninja Foodi Multi-cooker and then cook for 15 minutes.
3. To get 15 minutes' cook time, press *Pressure* Button and then adjust the time
4. Pressure Release. Use the *Quick Release* method to vent the steam, then open the lid. Transfer the chicken to a large bowl. When cool enough to handle, shred into pieces, discarding the skin and bones
5. Discard the onion, carrots and celery. Add the potatoes and corn to the broth
6. High pressure for 2 minutes. Lock the lid on the Ninja Foodi Multi-cooker and then cook for 2 minutes
7. To get 2 minutes' cook time, press *Pressure* button and use the Time Adjustment button to adjust the cook time to 2 minutes.
8. Pressure Release. Use the *Quick Release* method to vent the steam, then open the lid
9. Finish the dish. Stir in the chicken and pepper
10. Divide the soup among bowls. Peel, pit and slice the avocado. Top the soup with the avocado, sour cream, capers, oregano and cilantro.
11. Serve with the lime quarters for squeezing

Butternut Squash Soup with Chicken

(Ready in about: 11 minutes | **Servings:** 6)

Ingredients:
- 1 ½ lb. of fresh baked butternut squash; peeled and cubed
- 1 cup chicken breast; seasoned, cooked and diced
- 1 onion; diced
- 1 garlic clove; minced
- 2 cans chicken broth
- 1 cup orzo; cooked
- 1/2 cup celery; diced
- 1/2 cup carrots; diced
- 2 tbsp. red pepper flakes
- 2 tbsp. dried parsley flakes
- 1 tomato diced
- 3 tbsp. butter
- 1/4 tsp. freshly ground black pepper

Instructions:
1. Set the Ninja Foodi Multi-cooker to sauté and melt butter to sauté the onion, garlic clove, celery and carrots
2. Then add the chicken broth, red pepper flakes, dried parsley flakes, black pepper, baked butternut squash and tomato diced to the Ninja Foodi Multi-cooker
3. High pressure for 15 minutes. Lock the lid on the Ninja Foodi Multi-cooker and then cook for 15 minutes.
4. To get 15 minutes' cook time, press *Pressure* Button
5. Pressure Release. Use the quick release method
6. Blend/puree until mixture is smooth.
7. High pressure for 5 minutes. Then add it back to your Ninja Foodi Multi-cooker along with the chicken breast and orzo and cook for another 5 minutes
8. To get 5 minutes' cook time, press *Pressure* button and adjust the time
9. Pressure Release. Use the quick release method. Serve with fresh dinner rolls and butter on the side

Chicken Noodle Soup Recipe

(**Ready in about:** 11 minutes | **Servings:** 6)

Ingredients:
- 2 large bone in skinless chicken breasts (about 1 lb. each)
- 1 medium red onion; halved
- 6 cups chicken broth
- 2 medium carrots
- 2 fresh thyme sprigs
- 2 fresh sage sprigs
- 2 medium garlic cloves; peeled
- 4-ounces wide egg noodles
- 1 tbsp. minced fresh dill fronds
- 2 tbsp. olive oil
- 1/2 tsp. salt

Instructions:
1. Heat the oil in the Ninja Foodi Multi-cooker, turned to the sauté function. Add the chicken and brown well on both sides, about 4 minutes in all, turning once
2. Pour in the broth; add the onion, carrots, salt, thyme, sage and garlic
3. High pressure for 18 minutes. Lock the lid on the Ninja Foodi Multi-cooker and then cook for 18 minutes.
4. To get 18 minutes' cook time, press *Pressure* button and use the Time Adjustment button to adjust the cook time to 18 minutes.
5. Pressure Release. Use the quick release method to return the pot's pressure to normal
6. Unlock and open the cooker. Transfer the chicken to a cutting board. Cool for a few minutes, then debone and chop the meat into bite size bits; set aside.
7. Discard the onion, carrots, thyme, sage and garlic from the pot. Stir in the noodles and dill
8. High pressure for 4 minutes. Lock the lid on the Ninja Foodi Multi-cooker and then cook for 4 minutes.
9. To get 4 minutes' cook time, press *pressure* button and use the Time Adjustment button to adjust the cook time to 4 minutes.
10. Pressure Release. Use the quick release method to return the pot's pressure to normal
11. Finish the dish. Unlock and open the cooker. Stir in the chopped chicken. Cover loosely and set aside for a couple of minutes to warm through

French Onion Soup Recipe

(Ready in about: 40 minutes | **Servings:** 4)

Ingredients:

- 1-ounce Gruyère or other Swiss-style cheese; coarsely grated (about 1/3 cup)
- 1/4 cup dry sherry
- 2 cups low sodium chicken broth
- 1/2 cup Beef Stock; Mushroom Stock or low sodium broth
- 4 cups thinly sliced white or yellow onions; divided.
- 2 thin slices French or Italian bread
- 1/2 tsp. kosher salt; plus additional for seasoning
- 1/2 tsp. Worcestershire sauce
- 2 tbsp. unsalted butter; divided.
- 1/4 tsp. dried thyme
- 1 tsp. sherry vinegar or red wine vinegar; plus additional as needed

Instructions:

1. Set the Ninja Foodi Multi-cooker to *Sauté*, heat 1 tbsp. of butter until it stops foaming and then add 1 cup of onions. Sprinkle with a pinch or two of kosher salt and stir to coat with the butter. Cook the onions in a single layer for about 4 minutes or until browned
2. Resist the urge to stir them until you see them browning. Stir them to expose the other side to the heat and cook for 4 minutes more. The onions should be quite browned but still slightly firm. Remove the onions from the pan and set aside
3. Pour the sherry into the pot and stir to scrape up the browned bits from the bottom. When the sherry has mostly evaporated, add the remaining 1 tbsp. of butter and let it melt
4. Stir in the remaining 3 cups of onions and sprinkle with 1/2 tsp. of kosher salt
5. High pressure for 25 minutes. Lock the lid on the Ninja Foodi Multi-cooker and then cook for 25 minutes.
6. To get 25 minutes' cook time, press *Pressure* button and use the Time Adjustment button to adjust the cook time to 25 minutes.
7. Pressure Release Use the quick release method
8. Unlock and remove the lid.
9. The onions should be pale and very soft, with a lot of liquid in the pot. Add the chicken broth, Beef Stock, Worcestershire sauce and thyme
10. High pressure for 10 minutes. Lock the lid on the Ninja Foodi Multi-cooker and then cook for 10 minutes.
11. To get 10 minutes' cook time, press *Pressure* button and use the Time Adjustment button to adjust the cook time to 10 minutes
12. Pressure Release Use the quick release method
13. Finish the dish. Unlock and remove the lid. Stir in the sherry vinegar and taste. The soup should be balanced between the sweetness of the onions the savory stock and the acid from the vinegar. If it seems bland, add a pinch or two of kosher salt or a little more vinegar
14. Stir in the reserved cup of onions and keep warm while you prepare the cheese toasts
15. Preheat the broiler. Reserve 2 tbsp. of the cheese and sprinkle the remaining cheese evenly over the 2 bread slices. Place the bread slices on a sheet pan under the broiler for 2 to 3 minutes or until the cheese melts
16. Place 1 tbsp. of the reserved cheese in each of 2 bowls. Ladle the soup into the bowls, float a toast slice on top of each and serve.

Tasty Chicken Soup

(Ready in about: 45 minutes | **Servings:** 8)

Ingredients:
- 3 peeled carrots chopped into similar size as potatoes for even cooking time
- 4 cups of water and chicken concentrate/bullion of your choice to equal 32-ounces – or if you have it, use chicken stock
- 2 frozen boneless skinless chicken breasts
- 4 washed medium size diced potatoes (I did not peel you can if you want)
- 1/2 large onion diced
- Salt and pepper to taste (flavors will intensify while under pressure)

Instructions:
1. Mix the broth, chicken, potatoes, onion, carrots, salt and pepper in the Ninja Foodi Multi-cooker
2. High pressure for 35 minutes. Lock the lid on the Ninja Foodi Multi-cooker and then cook for 35 minutes
3. To get 35 minutes' cook time, press *pressure* button and use the Time Adjustment button to adjust the cook time to 35 minutes
4. Pressure Release Let the pressure to come down naturally for at least 15 minutes, then quick release any pressure left in the pot. Open when all pressure is released stir and enjoy

Potato, Carrot and Leek Soup Recipe

(Ready in about: 11 minutes | **Servings:** 4)

Ingredients:
- 1 lb. carrots; coarsely chopped.
- 1 bouquet garni (parsley sprigs; bay leaf, a sprig of thyme, tied tightly with string or in cheesecloth)
- 1 large potato; peeled and coarsely chopped.
- 1 medium leek; white and pale green parts only, coarsely chopped.
- 1 tbsp. olive oil
- 2 tbsp. unsalted butter
- 2 tsp. salt
- 4 cups salt free Chicken Stock
- Freshly ground black pepper
- 1/4 cup heavy cream
- 1/8 tsp. freshly grated nutmeg
- Fresh thyme sprigs or chopped fresh chives; for serving

Instructions:
1. Heat the Ninja Foodi Multi-cooker using the *Sauté* function, add the oil and butter and cook until the butter has melted. Stir in the chopped leeks and salt and sauté, infrequently stirring, until the leeks have softened about 5 minutes
2. Add the carrots and cook, infrequently stirring, until they are golden on one side, about 5 more minutes. Add the potato, stock, pepper to taste and the bouquet garni
3. High pressure for 10 minutes. Lock the lid on Ninja Foodi Multi-cooker and then cook for 10 minutes.
4. To get 10 minutes' cook time, press *Pressure* button and use the Time Adjustment button to adjust the cook time to 10 minutes
5. Pressure Release When the time is up, open the cooker with the Normal Release method.
6. Finish the dish. Fish out and discard the bouquet garni. Using an immersion blender, puree the soup in the cooker

7. Stir in the cream and nutmeg. Ladle into bowls and dot each serving with a thyme sprig or a few chopped chives

Beef Stock Recipe

(Ready in about: 11 minutes | **Servings:** 6)

Ingredients:
- 2 lb beef soup bones
- 1 large onion; quartered, skin on
- 2 tsp. ground pepper
- 1 tsp. ground Himalayan salt
- 2 tbsp. garlic; minced
- 3 tbsp. apple cider vinegar
- 3 large carrots
- 1 bay leaf
- 3 celery sticks
- Handful fresh parsley
- Water

Instructions:
1. Ideally, baking the bones at 375°F (190°C) for 30 minutes prior to pressure cooking them helps draw out the marrow, but if you only have access to your Multi-cooker, it will still get the job done
2. To start the stock, place the bones, veggies and seasonings into the Ninja Foodi Multi-cooker
3. Pour in the apple cider vinegar and cover with water. The amount of water will vary based on the size and quantities of your vegetables. You can add in extra greens if you want
4. High pressure for 90 minutes. Lock the lid on the Ninja Foodi Multi-cooker and then cook for 90 minutes
5. To get 90 minutes' cook time, press *Pressure* button and use the time adjustment button to adjust the cook time to 90 minutes
6. Pressure Release. Once complete, quick release the pressure valve, allowing the steam to escape

Chicken Stock Recipe

(Ready in about: 1 hour 10 minutes | **Servings:** 10 cups)

Ingredients:
- 2 ½ lb. chicken carcasses
- 2 carrots; diced
- 2 bay leaves
- 4 garlic cloves; crushed
- 1 tsp. whole peppercorn
- 2 celery stalks; diced
- 2 onions (keep the outer layers too); diced
- 1 tbsp. apple cider vinegar (optional)
- 10 cups water
- Your favorite fresh herbs

Instructions:
1. Optional step: Brown the chicken carcasses in your Ninja Foodi Multi-cooker with 1 tbsp. of oil. This will slightly elevate the flavors and result in a brown stock. Then, add water to deglaze the pot with 1/2 Cup (100 ml) of water
2. Add all ingredients in the Ninja Foodi Multi-cooker
3. High pressure for 60 minutes. Lock the lid on the Ninja Foodi Multi-cooker and then cook for 60 minutes.
4. To get 60 minutes' cook time, press *Pressure* button and use the Time Adjustment button to adjust the cook time to 60 minutes.
5. Pressure Release. When the time is up, open the cooker with the Natural Release method

6. Finish the dish. Open the lid. Strain the stock through a colander discarding the solids and set aside to cool. Let the stock sit in the fridge until the fat rises to the top and form a layer of gel. Then, skim off the fat on the surface.
7. You can use the stock immediately, keep it in the fridge or freeze it for future use

Storage: Silicone Mold – We love freezing our chicken stock with this mold!! After they freeze in the mold, we pop them out and store them in Ziploc freezer bags. It's a great portion for many recipes, thaws quickly and super convenient

Creamy Asparagus Soup

(Ready in about: 11 minutes | **Servings:** 4)

Ingredients:
- 1 lb. asparagus; tough ends removed, cut into 1-inch pieces
- 3 green onions; sliced crosswise into 1/4-inch pieces
- 1 tbsp. olive oil
- 4 cups salt-free Chicken Stock
- 1 tsp. ground white pepper; plus more as needed
- 1/2 cup heavy cream
- 1 tbsp. unsalted butter
- 1 tbsp. all-purpose flour
- 2 tsp. salt

Instructions:
1. Heat the Ninja Foodi Multi-cooker using the *Sauté* function, add the oil, green onions and a pinch of salt. Sauté the green onions for a few minutes, then add the asparagus and stock
2. High pressure for 5 minutes. Lock the lid on the Ninja Foodi Multi-cooker and then cook for 5 minutes.
3. To get 5 minutes' cook time, press *Pressure* button and use the Time Adjustment button to adjust the cook time to 5 minutes
4. Meanwhile, make a blond roux: In a small saucepan over low heat, mix the butter and flour and cook, constantly stirring, until the butter has melted and the mixture foams and begins to turn golden beige. Remove from the heat.
5. Pressure Release. When the time is up, open the cooker with the Natural Release method
6. Finish the dish. Add the roux, salt and pepper to the soup and puree with an immersion blender until smooth. Taste and season with more pepper if you wish. Swirl in the cream just before serving. Serve and Enjoy!

Tomato Soup Recipe

(Ready in about: 11 minutes | **Servings:** 2 to 4)

Ingredients:
- 1 (14.5-ounce) can fire roasted tomatoes
- 1 small roasted red bell pepper; cut into chunks (about 1/4 cup)
- 1/2 cup sliced onion
- 3/4 cup Chicken Stock or low sodium broth
- 1/4 cup dry or medium dry sherry
- 3 tbsp. olive oil
- 1 tbsp. heavy (whipping) cream (optional)
- 1 medium garlic clove; sliced or minced
- 1/8 tsp. ground cumin
- 1/8 tsp. freshly ground black pepper
- Kosher salt

Instructions:
1. Set the Ninja Foodi Multi-cooker to sauté, heat the olive oil until it shimmers and flows like water. Add the onions and sprinkle with a pinch or two of kosher salt. Cook for about 5 minutes, stirring until the onions just begin to brown. Add the garlic and cook for 1 to 2 minutes more or until fragrant
2. Pour in the sherry and simmer for 1 to 2 minutes or until the sherry is reduced by half, scraping up any browned bits from the bottom of the pan. Add the tomatoes, roasted red bell pepper and Chicken Stock to the Ninja Foodi Multi-cooker
3. High pressure for 10 minutes. Lock the lid on the Ninja Foodi Multi-cooker and then cook for 10 minutes.
4. To get 10 minutes' cook time, press *Pressure* button and use the Time Adjustment button to adjust the cook time to 10 minutes
5. Pressure Release. Use the quick release method. Finish the dish. For a smooth soup, blend using an immersion or standard blender. Add the cumin and pepper and adjust the salt, if necessary. If you like a creamier soup, stir in the heavy cream
6. If using a standard blender, be careful. Steam can build up and blow the lid off if the soup is very hot. Hold the lid on with a towel and blend in batches, if necessary; don't fill the jar more than halfway full

Vegetable Stock Recipe

(Ready in about: 11 minutes | **Servings:** 6)

Ingredients:
- 2 large unpeeled yellow onions; sliced lengthwise in half, root ends removed
- 1 bunch fresh flat leaf parsley; tied with string (so it's easy to remove)
- 2 medium tomatoes (fresh or canned)
- 2 unpeeled garlic
- 2 medium carrots; snapped in half
- 2 celery stalks; snapped in half
- 1 tbsp. whole black peppercorns
- 2 bay leaves
- Cold water; as needed

Instructions:
1. Add the vegetables, herbs and spices to the Multi-cooker base. Pour in cold water to just cover these ingredients
2. High pressure for 10 minutes. Lock the lid on the Ninja Foodi Multi-cooker and then cook for 10 minutes.
3. To get 10 minutes' cook time, press *Pressure* button and use the Time Adjustment button to adjust the cook time to 10 minutes
4. Pressure Release Let the pressure to come down naturally for at least 20 to 30 minutes, then quick release any pressure left in the pot
5. Finish the dish. Carefully strain the contents of the cooker into a stainless steel bowl and let cool to room temperature. Reserve the solids or discard them. Freeze the stock if not using in the next couple of days

Cream of Sweet Potato Soup Recipe

(Ready in about: 11 minutes | **Servings:** 6)

Ingredients:
- 2 lb. sweet potatoes (about 2 large); peeled and cut into 2-inch pieces
- 8 tbsp. (1 stick) unsalted butter; cut into small pieces
- 1/2 tsp. ground cinnamon
- 1/2 tsp. ground ginger
- 1/4 tsp. baking soda
- 2 ½ cups chicken broth
- 1/2 cup heavy cream
- 1 tsp. salt

Instructions:
1. Melt the butter in a Ninja Foodi Multi-cooker turned to the browning function. Stir in the sweet potatoes, salt, cinnamon, ginger and baking soda. Pour 1/2 cup water over everything
2. High pressure for 15 minutes. Lock the lid on the Ninja Foodi Multi-cooker and then cook for 15 minutes.
3. To get 15 minutes' cook time, press *Pressure* button and then adjust the time
4. Pressure Release. Use the quick release method to bring the pot's pressure back to normal
5. Finish the dish. Unlock and open the pot. Stir in the broth and cream. Use an immersion blender to puree the soup in the pot or ladle the soup in batches into a blender, remove the knob from the blender's lid, cover the hole with a clean kitchen towel and blend until smooth

Rice Recipes

Rice Pilaf with Cashews

(Ready in about: 40 minutes | **Servings:** 4)

Ingredients:
- 1 ½ cups long-grain brown rice; such as brown basmati
- 1 large leek; white and pale green parts only, halved lengthwise, washed and thinly sliced
- 3 cups vegetable or chicken broth
- 1/2 cup chopped roasted unsalted cashews
- 3 tbsp. unsalted butter
- 1/8 tsp. ground turmeric
- 1/2 tsp. dried thyme
- 1/2 tsp. salt

Instructions:
1. Melt the butter in the Ninja Foodi Multi-cooker turned to the *Sauté* function. Add the leek and cook, often stirring, until softened, about 2 minutes
2. Stir in the thyme, salt and turmeric until fragrant, less than half a minute. Add the rice and cook for 1 minute, stirring all the while
3. Pour in the broth and stir well to get any browned bits off the bottom of the cooker
4. High pressure for 33 minutes. Lock the lid on the Ninja Foodi Multi-cooker and then cook for 33 minutes.
5. To get 33 minutes' cook time, press *Pressure* button and use the Time Adjustment button to adjust the cook time to 33 minutes
6. Pressure Release. Use the quick release method to return the pot's pressure to normal but do not open the cooker
7. Set aside for 10 minutes to steam the rice. Unlock and open the pot. Stir in the chopped cashews before serving

Seafood Risotto Recipe

(Ready in about: 16 minutes | **Servings:** 4)

Ingredients:
- 3 cups mixed seafood (calamari, shrimp, clams, etc.)
- 3 oil-packed anchovies
- 2 cups Arborio or Carnaroli rice
- 2 tbsp. olive oil; plus more to finish
- 3 garlic cloves; chopped.
- Freshly squeezed juice of 1 lemon
- 1 bunch flat-leaf parsley; chopped.
- Lemon wedges; for serving
- Water; as needed
- 2 tsp. salt
- 1/4 tsp. ground white pepper

Instructions:
1. Separate the shellfish from the other seafood and set the shellfish aside. Add the remaining seafood to a 4-cup measuring cup and add water to just over the 4-cup mark
2. Heat the Ninja Foodi Multi-cooker using the *Sauté* mode, add the oil and heat briefly. Stir in the garlic and anchovies and sauté until the garlic is golden and the anchovies are broken up
3. Add the rice, stirring to coat well. While you continue to stir, look carefully at the rice, it will first become wet and look slightly transparent and pearly; then it will slowly begin to look dry and solid white again. At that point pour in the lemon juice
4. Scrape the bottom of the Ninja Foodi Multi-cooker gently and keep stirring until all of the juice has evaporated. Stir in the seafood and water and the salt and pepper. Place the shellfish on top without stirring any further
5. High pressure for 6 minutes. Lock the lid on the Ninja Foodi Multi-cooker and then cook for 6 minutes.
6. To get 6 minutes' cook time, press *Pressure* button and use the Time Adjustment button to adjust the cook time to 6 minutes
7. Pressure Release. When the time is up, open the Ninja Foodi Multi-cooker with the Natural Release method.
8. Stir the risotto. Swirl some oil over the top and sprinkle with parsley. Serve with lemon wedges

Rice Salad with Apples

(Ready in about: 24 minutes | **Servings:** 4)

Ingredients:
- 2 or 3 celery stalks; thinly sliced (about 1 cup)
- 1 medium Gala; Fuji or Braeburn apple, cored and cut into 1/2-inch pieces
- 1 ¼ tsp. kosher salt; divided.
- 4 cups water
- 1 cup wild rice
- 1/3 cup walnut or olive oil
- 3 tbsp. cider vinegar
- 1/8 tsp. freshly ground black pepper
- 1/4 tsp. celery seed
- Pinch granulated sugar
- 1/2 cup walnut pieces; toasted

Instructions:
1. Add the water into the Ninja Foodi Multi-cooker and 1 tsp. of kosher salt. Stir in the wild rice
2. High pressure for 18 minutes. Lock the lid on the Ninja Foodi Multi-cooker and then cook for 18 minutes.
3. To get 18 minutes' cook time, press *Pressure* button and use the Time Adjustment button to adjust the cook time to 18 minutes

4. Pressure Release. Use the natural release method. Finish the dish. Unlock and remove the lid. The rice grains should be mostly split open. If not, simmer the rice for several minutes more, in the Ninja Foodi Multi-cooker set to *Sauté*, until at least half the grains have split. Drain and cool slightly
5. To a small jar with a tight-fitting lid, add the walnut oil, cider vinegar, celery seed the remaining 1/4 tsp. of kosher salt the pepper and the sugar and shake until well combined.
6. In a medium bowl, add the cooled rice, walnuts, celery and apple. Pour half of the dressing over the salad and toss gently to coat, adding more dressing as desired. Serve

Risotto with Butternut Squash

(**Ready in about:** 15 minutes | **Servings:** 6)

Ingredients:
- 2 cups seeded; peeled and finely chopped butternut squash
- 1/2-ounce dried porcini mushrooms; crumbled
- 1/2 cup finely grated Parmesan cheese (about 1-ounce)
- 2 tbsp. unsalted butter
- 1 medium leek; white and pale green parts only, halved lengthwise, washed and thinly sliced
- 1 ½ cups white Arborio rice
- 1/4 cup dry vermouth
- 4 cups (1 quart) vegetable broth
- 1 tsp. dried thyme
- 1/4 tsp. saffron threads

Instructions:
1. Melt the butter in the Ninja Foodi Multi-cooker turned to the *Sauté* function. Add the leek and cook, often stirring, until softened, about 2 minutes
2. Add the rice; stir until coated in the butter. Pour in the vermouth; stir over the heat until fully absorbed into the grains, 1 to 2 minutes. Add the broth, squash, dried porcini, thyme and saffron.
3. High pressure for 10 minutes. Lock the lid on the Ninja Foodi Multi-cooker and then cook for 10 minutes.
4. To get 10 minutes' cook time, press *Pressure* button and use the Time Adjustment button to adjust the cook time to 10 minutes
5. Pressure Release. Use the quick release method
6. Finish the dish. Unlock and open the cooker. Turn the Ninja Foodi Multi-cooker to its *Sauté* function. Bring to a simmer, stirring until thickened, about 2 minutes
7. Stir in the cheese. Put the lid on the cooker without locking it in place. Set aside for 5 minutes to melt the cheese and blend the flavors. Stir again before serving. Serve and Enjoy!

Simple White Rice

(**Ready in about:** 28 minutes | **Servings:** 4)

Ingredients:
- 1 ½ cups long-grain white rice
- 1 tsp. vegetable oil or unsalted butter
- 3 cups water
- 1/2 tsp. salt

Instructions:
1. Place the rice, water, salt and oil in the Ninja Foodi Multi-cooker base
2. High pressure for 3 minutes. Lock the lid on the Ninja Foodi Multi-cooker and then cook for 4 minutes.

3. To get 3 minutes' cook time, press *Pressure* button and adjust the time
4. Pressure Release. When the time is up, open the Ninja Foodi Multi-cooker with the 10-Minute Natural Release method
5. Fluff the rice with a fork and serve

Simple Brown Rice

(**Ready in about:** 28 minutes | **Servings:** 4)

Ingredients:
- 1 ½ cups brown rice
- 1/2 tsp. salt
- 2 ½ cups water
- 1 tsp. olive oil

Instructions:
1. Place the rice, water, salt and oil in the Ninja Foodi Multi-cooker base
2. High pressure for 20 minutes. Lock the lid on the Ninja Foodi Multi-cooker and then cook for 20 minutes.
3. To get 20 minutes' cook time, press *pressure* button and use the Time Adjustment button to adjust the cook time to 20 minutes
4. Pressure Release. When the time is up, open the Ninja Foodi Multi-cooker with the 10-Minute Natural Release method. Fluff the rice with a fork and serve

Brown Rice Pilaf

(**Ready in about:** 33 minutes | **Servings:** 4)

Ingredients:
- 1/2 cup brown rice
- 3/4 cup low sodium vegetable broth
- 1/4 cup dry white wine
- 3/4 cup diced onion
- 1/2 tsp. kosher salt; divided., plus additional for seasoning
- 1 fresh thyme sprig or 1/4 tsp. dried thyme
- 2 tbsp. chopped fresh parsley
- 1 tbsp. olive oil
- 1 garlic clove; minced
- 1/3 cup wild rice
- 2/3 cup water
- 1 bay leaf

Instructions:
1. Set the Ninja Foodi Multi-cooker to *Sauté*, heat the olive oil until it shimmers and flows like water. Add the onion and garlic and cook for about 3 minutes, stirring until the garlic is fragrant and the onions soften and separate
2. Add the wild rice, water and 1/4 tsp. of kosher salt and stir
3. High pressure for 15 minutes. Lock the lid on the Ninja Foodi Multi-cooker and then cook for 15 minutes.
4. To get 15 minutes' cook time, press *Pressure* Button and then adjust the time.
5. Pressure Release. Use the quick release method
6. Unlock and remove the lid. Stir in the brown rice, vegetable broth, remaining 1/4 tsp. of kosher salt, white wine, bay leaf and thyme
7. High pressure for 12 minutes. Lock the lid on the Ninja Foodi Multi-cooker and then cook for 12 minutes.
8. To get 12 minutes' cook time, press *Pressure* button and adjust the time.
9. When the timer goes off, turn the cooker off. (Warm* setting, turn off).

10. Pressure Release. After cooking, use the natural method to release pressure for 12 minutes, then the quick method to release the remaining pressure
11. Finish the dish. Unlock and remove the lid. Remove the bay leaf and thyme sprig and stir in the parsley. Taste and adjust the seasoning, as needed
12. Replace but do not lock the lid. Let the rice steam for about 4 minutes, fluff gently with a fork and serve.

Quinoa Risotto with Bacon

(Ready in about: 16 minutes | **Servings:** 4)

Ingredients:
- 1 ½ cups white or red quinoa; rinsed if necessary
- 3-ounces slab bacon; diced
- 1/4 cup finely grated Parmesan cheese (about 1/2-ounce)
- 6 medium scallions; thinly sliced
- 12 cherry tomatoes; halved
- 1/4 cup dry vermouth
- 3 ½ cups chicken broth
- 3 fresh thyme sprigs
- 1/2 tsp. ground black pepper

Instructions:
1. Place the bacon in the Ninja Foodi turned to the *Air crisp* function and adjust the time to 4 minutes.
2. Add the scallions; stir over the heat until softened, about 1 minute. Put in the tomatoes; cook just until they begin to break down, about 2 minutes, occasionally stirring
3. Pour in the vermouth; as it comes to a simmer, scrape up any browned bits in the bottom of the cooker.
4. Stir in the broth, quinoa and thyme sprigs. High pressure for 9 minutes. Lock the lid on the Ninja Foodi Multi-cooker and then cook for 9 minutes
5. To get 9 minutes' cook time, press *Pressure* button and use the Time Adjustment button to adjust the cook time to 9 minutes
6. Pressure Release. Return the pot's pressure to normal with the quick release method.
7. Finish the dish. Unlock and open the cooker. Turn the Ninja Foodi Multi-cooker to its *Sauté* function. Discard the thyme sprigs.
8. Bring the mixture in the pot to a simmer; cook, often stirring, until thickened, 2 to 3 minutes. Stir in the cheese and pepper to serve

Armenian Style Rice Pilaf

(Ready in about: 10 minutes | **Servings:** 4)

Ingredients:
- 2 cups long-grain white or basmati rice
- 1/2 cup vermicelli or angel hair pasta; broken into 1-inch pieces
- 4 cups salt-free Chicken Stock; preferably double-strength
- 2 tbsp. unsalted butter
- 1 tbsp. olive oil
- 2 tsp. salt

Instructions:
1. Heat the Ninja Foodi Multi-cooker using the *Sauté* Function. Add the butter and oil and cook until the butter has melted
2. Add the vermicelli and stir well to coat. Sauté until the pieces just begin to turn golden.

3. Add the rice; stir well to coat and toast for about 1 minute. Add the chicken stock and salt
4. High pressure for 3 minutes. Lock the lid on the Ninja Foodi Multi-cooker and then cook for 3 minutes.
5. To get 3 minutes' cook time, press *Pressure* button and use the Time Adjustment button to adjust the cook time to 3 minutes
6. Pressure Release. When the time is up, open the Ninja Foodi Multi-cooker with the 10-Minute Natural Release method.
7. Mix the pilaf well, pulling up the rice from the bottom of the Ninja Foodi Multi-cooker to the top before serving

Prawn Risotto

(Ready in about: 40 minutes | **Servings:** 2 to 4)

Ingredients:
- 1/2 lb. frozen tiger prawns; thawed and peeled
- 2 stalk green onions; thinly sliced
- 2 cups Arborio rice
- 3/4 cup cooking sake
- 2 tsp. soy sauce
- 4 cups fish stock or Japanese Dashi
- 3 tbsp. olive oil
- 4 tbsp. butter
- 1 shallot; minced
- 1/4 cup (about 20 grams) Parmesan cheese; finely grated
- 3 cloves garlic; minced
- 1 tsp. salt
- 1 tsp. white pepper

Instructions:
1. In mixing bowl season the prawns with salt and white pepper. Set the Ninja Foodi Multi-cooker on brown and add the olive oil and butter and sauté prawns for 5 - 10 minutes with the shallot and garlic the prawns should be about 80% cooked
2. Remove and set aside. Add the Arborio rice, cooking sake, soy sauce and fish stock into Ninja Foodi Multi-cooker with a swirl of olive oil. Stir and combine, make sure the rice is coated with the liquids or Japanese Dashi
3. High pressure for 25 minutes. Lock the lid on the Ninja Foodi Multi-cooker and then cook for 25 minutes.
4. To get 25 minutes' cook time, press *Pressure* button and use the Time Adjustment button to adjust the cook time to 25 minutes.
5. Pressure Release. Use the quick release method to return the pot's pressure to normal
6. Place the prawns on top of the risotto and sprinkle the Parmesan cheese over the prawns and risotto.
7. High pressure for 5 minutes. Cover and lock the lid again and cook on High for another 5 minutes
8. To get 5 minutes' cook time, press *Pressure* button and use the Time Adjustment button to adjust the cook time to 5 minutes.
9. Pressure Release. Use the quick release method to return the pot's pressure to normal. Garnish with the sliced green onions

Rice with Sweet Potatoes

(Ready in about: 50 minutes | **Servings:** 4)

Ingredients:
- 1 large sweet potato (about 1 lb.); peeled and diced
- 2 medium celery stalks; chopped.
- 1 medium yellow onion; chopped.
- 1 tbsp. packed fresh sage leaves; minced
- 2 tsp. fresh thyme leaves
- 2 tbsp. olive oil
- 3 cups vegetable or chicken broth
- 1/4 cup dried cranberries
- 1 ½ cups black wild rice (about 8-ounces)
- 1/2 tsp. salt
- 1/2 tsp. ground black pepper

Instructions:
1. Heat the olive oil in the Ninja Foodi Multi-cooker turned to the *Sauté* function. Add the onion and celery; cook, often stirring, until the onion softens, about 4 minutes
2. Mix in the sage and thyme; cook until fragrant, about 30 seconds. Stir in the rice and toss well to coat. Pour in the broth; stir well to get up any browned bits in the bottom of the pot
3. High pressure for 30 minutes. Lock the lid on the Ninja Foodi Multi-cooker and then cook for 30 minutes.
4. To get 30 minutes' cook time, press *Pressure* button and adjust the time.
5. Pressure Release. Use the quick release method to return the pot's pressure to normal
6. Unlock and open the cooker. Stir in the sweet potato, cranberries, salt and pepper
7. High pressure for 15 minutes. Lock the lid back on the Ninja Foodi Multi-cooker and then cook for 15 minutes. To get 15 minutes' cook time, press *Pressure* Button and then adjust the time.
8. Pressure Release. Use the quick release method to return the pot's pressure to normal. Unlock and open the cooker. Stir well before serving

Risotto with Shrimp and Peas

(Ready in about: 11 minutes | **Servings:** 4)

Ingredients:
- 1/2 lb. raw medium shrimp; shelled and deveined
- 1/2 cup frozen peas; thawed
- 2 3/4 cups Chicken Stock or low sodium broth; divided.
- 1/4 cup grated Parmigiano-Reggiano or similar cheese
- 1 tbsp. unsalted butter
- 1/2 cup chopped onion
- 1 cup Arborio rice
- 1/3 cup white wine

Instructions:
1. Turn the Ninja Foodi Multi-cooker to *Sauté*, heat the butter until it stops foaming. Add the onion and cook for about 2 minutes, stirring until soft
Add the rice and stir to coat with the butter. Cook for 1 minute, stirring. Stir in the white wine and cook for 1 to 2 minutes or until it's almost evaporated. Add 2 ½ cups of Chicken Stock and stir to make sure no rice is sticking to the bottom of the cooker.
2. High pressure for 6 minutes. Lock the lid on the Ninja Foodi Multi-cooker and then cook for 6 minutes.
3. To get 6 minutes' cook time, press *Pressure* button and use the Time Adjustment button to adjust the cook time to 6 minutes
4. Pressure Release. Use the quick release method.

5. Finish the dish. Unlock and remove the lid. Turn the Ninja Foodi Multi-cooker to *brown*, Continue to cook the rice, stirring for 1 to 2 minutes more or until the rice is firm just in the very center of the grain and the liquid has thickened slightly
6. Add the shrimp and peas and continue to cook for about 4 minutes more or until the shrimp are cooked. Stir in the Parmigiano-Reggiano. If the risotto is too thick, stir in a little of the remaining 1/4 cup of Chicken Stock to loosen it up. Serve immediately
7. Risotto is one of those dishes that lend themselves to almost endless variation. Leftover ham is a great addition, as is smoked salmon or trout or go vegetarian with *Sauté* Mushrooms, roasted peppers or even beets

Barley Risotto with Spinach

(**Ready in about:** 28 minutes | **Servings:** 4)

Ingredients:
- 1 cup pearled barley
- 4 cups baby spinach
- 4 cups chicken stock or broth
- 1/4 cup grated Parmesan cheese
- 1 tbsp. olive oil
- 1 tbsp. light margarine
- 1 yellow onion; diced
- Juice of 1 lemon
- 1 tbsp. minced garlic
- Salt and pepper

Instructions:
1. With the cooker's lid off, heat oil and margarine on *brown*, until oil is sizzling and margarine is melted.
2. Place diced onion in the cooker and sauté until translucent, 5 minutes
3. Stir in barley and sauté 1 additional minute. Add the chicken broth, lemon juice and minced garlic.
4. High pressure for 25 minutes. Lock the lid on the Ninja Foodi Multi-cooker and then cook for 25 minutes.
5. To get 25 minutes' cook time, press *Pressure* button and use the Time Adjustment button to adjust the cook time to 25 minutes.
6. Pressure Release. Let the Pressure Release naturally 5 minutes before performing a quick release for any remaining pressure
7. With the cooker's lid off, set to sauté and stir in spinach and Parmesan cheese, simmering until spinach cooks down. Season with salt and pepper to taste before serving

Rice with Lentils

(**Ready in about:** 40 minutes | **Servings:** 4)

Ingredients:
- 2 cups long-grain brown rice; preferably basmati
- 3 large onions; halved through the root (flatter) end, then sliced into thin half-moons
- 5 tbsp. olive oil
- 4 ½ cups vegetable or chicken broth
- 1/2 cup green lentils (French lentils or lentils de Puy)
- 1 tsp. coriander seeds
- 1 tsp. cumin seeds
- 1/2 tsp. ground turmeric
- 1/2 tsp. ground allspice
- 1/2 tsp. ground cinnamon
- 1 tsp. sugar
- 1 tsp. ground black pepper
- 1/2 tsp. salt

Instructions:
1. Heat 1 ½ tbsp. oil in the Ninja Foodi Multi-cooker turned to the *Sauté* function. Add half the onions and cook until well browned and crisp at the edges, at least 10 minutes, occasionally stirring
2. Transfer the cooked onions to a large bowl; repeat with 1 ½ tbsp. more oil and the rest of the onions.
3. Add the remaining 2 tbsp. oil to the cooker; stir in the coriander, cumin, turmeric, allspice and cinnamon until aromatic, about 1 minute.
4. Add the rice, sugar, pepper and salt; stir for 1 minute. Stir in the broth, scraping up any brown bits in the cooker. Stir in the lentils
5. High pressure for 35 minutes. Lock the lid on the Ninja Foodi Multi-cooker and then cook for 35 minutes.
6. To get 35 minutes' cook time, press *pressure* button and use the Time Adjustment button to adjust the cook time to 35 minutes
7. Pressure Release. Turn off the Ninja Foodi Multi-cooker or unplug it, so it doesn't flip to the keep-warm setting. Let its pressure return normal naturally, 14 to 20 minutes.
8. Finish the dish. Unlock and open the cooker. Spoon the caramelized onions on top of the rice; set the lid back on the cooker without locking it in place and set aside for 10 minutes to warm the onions
9. Serve by scooping up big spoonfuls with onions and rice in each

Desserts

Chocolate Pudding Recipe

(Ready in about: 20 minutes | **Servings:** 4)

Ingredients:
- 6-ounces semisweet or bittersweet chocolate; chopped.
- 1 ½ cups light cream
- 4 large egg yolks; at room temperature and whisked in a small bowl
- 1 tbsp. vanilla extract
- 1/2-ounce unsweetened chocolate; chopped.
- 6 tbsp. sugar
- 1/4 tsp. salt

Instructions:
1. Place all the chopped chocolate and the sugar in a large bowl. Heat the cream in a saucepan over low heat until small bubbles fizz around the inside edge of the pan
2. Pour the warmed cream over the chocolate; whisk until the chocolate has completely melted. Cool a minute or two, then whisk in the yolks, vanilla and salt.
3. Pour the mixture into six 1/2-cup heat-safe ramekins, filling each about three-quarters full. Cover each with foil
4. Set the rack in the Ninja Foodi Multi-cooker; pour in 2 cups water
5. Set the ramekins on the rack, stacking them as necessary without anyone ramekin sitting directly on top of another.
6. High pressure for 15 minutes. Lock the lid on the Ninja Foodi Multi-cooker and then cook for 15 minutes.
7. To get 15 minutes' cook time, press *Pressure* button and then adjust button
8. Pressure Release. Turn off the Ninja Foodi Multi-cooker or unplug it, so it doesn't flip to its keep-warm setting. Let its pressure return to normal naturally, 10 to 14 minutes
9. Finish the dish. Unlock and open the cooker. Transfer the hot ramekins to a cooling rack, uncover and cool for 10 minutes before serving or chill in the refrigerator for up to 3 days, covering again once the puddings have chilled

Awesome Donuts

(Ready in about: 10 minutes | **Servings:** 6)

Ingredients:
- 1 can of biscuits
- 1/3 cup granulated sweetener
- Pinch of allspice
- 4 tbsp. dark brown sugar
- 1/2 to 1 tsp. cinnamon
- 3 tbsp. melted coconut oil

Instructions:
1. Preparing the ingredients. Preheat the unit by selecting Bake/Roast, setting the temperature to 300°F and setting the time to 5 minutes. Press Start/Stop to begin
2. Mix allspice, sugar, sweetener and cinnamon together
3. Take out biscuits from can and with a circle cookie cutter, cut holes from centers and place into Ninja Foodi.
4. Air Frying the Dish. Close the Crisping Lid. Select Bake/Roast, set the temperature to 350°F and set the time to 5 minutes

5. Select Start/Stop to begin. As batches are cooked, use a brush to coat with melted coconut oil and dip each into sugar mixture. Serve warm!

Strawberry Jam Recipe

(**Ready in about:** 18 minutes | **Servings:** 4 cups)

Ingredients:
- 1 lb. strawberries (fresh or frozen)
- 1 /2 to 1 lb. granulated sugar
- 1 tbsp. butter (optional: vegans can omit)
- 1 navel orange

Instructions:
1. If you are using fresh berries, remove the stems, leaves and any bruised spots from the strawberries, lightly wash them and cut into halves or quarters, depending on size
2. For frozen berries, defrost before use, cut them up if necessary
3. Peel the navel orange, removing the bitter white pith and any white connective tissues. I do this by slicing a bit off the top, so I can see how thick the peel is. I then take the knife and cut slices of peel down the sides of the orange. It is better to remove a little of the orange than to leave the bitter pith on the orange
4. Once you have removed all the peel and any pith attached to the outside of the orange, break it apart into segments, remove any white pithy connective tissues inside and roughly chop the segments. Reserve the chopped segments and any juice
5. For a very smooth jam, place the sliced strawberries and chopped orange segments and juice into a food processor or blender and puree until smooth, then add to the sugar.
6. If you would like your jam more like preserves (with small pieces of fruit mixed in), combine the sliced strawberries, orange pieces and orange juice into the sugar
7. Once mixed, use a potato masher to mash the strawberries roughly. The mixture should macerate in the refrigerator for at least an hour, but if you can let it set for 8 – 24 hours, that's even better
8. Once the mixture has macerated, add to the Ninja Foodi Multi-cooker. Using the *Sauté* setting, bring the jam up to a hard boil for 3 minutes to dissolve the sugar and reduce the excess water content. Stir frequently with the longest handled spatula you own
9. Stir in 1 tbsp. of butter. High pressure for 8 minutes. Lock the lid on the Ninja Foodi Multi-cooker and then cook for 8 minutes.
10. To get 8 minutes' cook time, press *Pressure* button and use the Time Adjustment button to adjust the cook time to 8 minutes.
11. Pressure Release. Let its pressure return to normal naturally, 8 to 12 minutes
12. Finish the dish. After pressure has released, unlock and remove the lid, tilting the front side down and the back side up to direct any residual heat and steam away from you
13. With the lid *OFF* and the *Sauté* setting, bring the mixture back to the boil for 3 minutes, stirring frequently.
14. Turn the unit off after the 3 minutes are up. Allow mixture to cool to room temperature, stirring periodically. Once cooled, put the jam in a container in the refrigerator to finish setting

Orange Cranberry Sauce

(Ready in about: 10 minutes | **Servings:** 6)

Ingredients:
- 1 lb. Fresh Cranberries
- 1/2 cup Demerara Sugar; maple syrup or sugar; to taste
- 1 cup Orange Juice
- 1 tsp. Cinnamon; ground
- 1 tsp. True Orange Ginger
- 1 Cinnamon Stick
- Zest from one Large Orange

Instructions:
1. Rinse and drain cranberries and set aside
2. Whisk together orange juice, sugar, cinnamon and True Orange Ginger (or grated ginger)
3. Add cranberries and juice to the Ninja Foodi Multi-cooker cooking pot. Add cinnamon stick.
4. High pressure for 4 minutes. Lock the lid on the Ninja Foodi Multi-cooker and then cook for 4 minutes.
5. To get 4 minutes' cook time, press *Pressure* button and use the Time Adjustment button to adjust the cook time to 4 minutes
6. Pressure Release. When beep sounds, allow a full Natural Pressure Release.
7. For a thicker Sauce, simmer until desired consistency. Open the lid and add Orange Zest

Chocolate Chip Skillet Cookie

(Ready in about: 35 minutes | **Servings:** 6)

Ingredients:
- 1 cup + 2 tbsp. all-purpose flour
- 1 stick (1/2 cup) unsalted butter, softened, plus more for greasing
- 1/2 tsp. baking soda
- 1/2 tsp. vanilla extract
- 1 large egg
- 1 cup semi-sweet chocolate chips
- 1/2 tsp. kosher salt
- 6 tbsp. granulated sugar
- 6 tbsp. packed brown sugar
- 1/2 cup chopped walnuts, pecans, or almonds, if desired

Instructions:
1. Close crisping lid. Preheat the unit by selecting BAKE/ROAST, setting the temperature to 325°F, and setting the time to 5 minutes. Select START/STOP to begin
2. While unit is preheating, whisk together flour, baking soda, and salt in a mixing bowl.
3. In a separate mixing bowl, beat together the butter, sugars, and vanilla until creamy. Add egg and beat until smooth and fully incorporated
4. Slowly add the dry ingredients to the egg mixture, about 1/3 at a time. Use a rubber spatula to scrape down the sides so all dry ingredients get incorporated. Make sure not to over-mix, or the cookie will become dense when baked.
5. Fold the chocolate chips and nuts into the cookie dough until they are evenly distributed.
6. Generously grease the bottom of the 8-inch baking pan. Add the cookie dough to the pan, making sure it is evenly distributed
7. Once unit has preheated, place the pan onto the reversible rack, making sure rack is in the lower position. Place rack with pan in pot. Close crisping lid. Select BAKE/ROAST, set temperature to 325°F, and set time to 23 minutes. Select START/STOP to begin
8. When cooking is complete, allow cookie to cool for 5 minutes. Then serve warm with toppings of your choice.

Cinnamon Rolls

(Ready in about: 25 minutes | **Servings:** 6)

Ingredients:
- 1 lb. frozen bread dough; thawed
- 1/4 cup melted coconut oil
- 3/4 cup brown sugar
- 1 ½ tbsp. cinnamon

Glaze:
- 1 ¼ cup powdered erythritol
- 4-ounces softened cream cheese
- 1/2 tsp. vanilla
- 2 tbsp. softened ghee

Instructions:
1. Preparing the ingredients. Preheat the unit by selecting Bake/Roast, setting the temperature to 300°F and setting the time to 5 minutes.
2. Press Start/Stop to begin. Lay out bread dough and roll out into a rectangle. Brush melted ghee over dough and leave a 1-inch border along edges
3. Mix cinnamon and sweetener together and then sprinkle over dough. Roll dough tightly and slice into 8 pieces. Let sit 1 - 2 hours to rise. To make the glaze, simply mix ingredients together till smooth
4. Once rolls rise, place into the Ninja Foodi. Select Bake/Roast, set the temperature to 350°F and set the time to 5 minutes. Select Start/Stop to begin
5. Serve rolls drizzled in cream cheese glaze. Enjoy!

Chocolate Lemon Pudding

(Ready in about: 20 minutes | **Servings:** 6)

Ingredients:
- 6-ounces white chocolate; chopped.
- 4 large egg yolks; at room temperature and whisked in a small bowl
- 1 tbsp. sugar
- 1 tbsp. finely grated lemon zest (about 1 medium lemon)
- 1 cup heavy cream
- 1 cup half-and-half
- 1/4 tsp. lemon extract

Instructions:
1. Put the chopped white chocolate in a large bowl. Mix the cream and half-and-half in a small saucepan and warm over low heat until bubbles fizz around the edges of the pan
2. Pour the warm mixture over the white chocolate and whisk until melted. Whisk in the egg yolks, sugar, zest and extract. Pour the mixture into six 1/2-cup heat-safe ramekins; cover each tightly with aluminum foil.
3. Set the Ninja Foodi Multi-cooker rack in the Ninja Foodi Multi-cooker; pour in 2 cups water. Set the ramekins on the rack, stacking them as necessary without anyone ramekin sitting directly on top of another
4. High pressure for 15 minutes. Lock the lid on the Ninja Foodi Multi-cooker and then cook for 15 minutes.
5. To get 15 minutes' cook time, press *Pressure* button and then adjust the time.
6. Pressure Release. Turn off the Ninja Foodi Multi-cooker or unplug it, so it doesn't jump to its keep-warm setting. Let its pressure return to normal naturally, 10 to 14 minutes
7. Finish the dish. Unlock and open the cooker. Transfer the (hot!) ramekins to a cooling rack; uncover each and cool for a few minutes before serving or store in the refrigerator for up to 3 days, covering the ramekins again after they have chilled

Mamma's Molten Gingerbread Cake

(Ready in about: 20 minutes | **Servings:** 2)

Ingredients:
- 3 tbsp. boiling water
- 2/3 cup all-purpose flour
- 1/4 cup vegetable oil
- 1/4 cup molasses
- 1/4 cup packed brown sugar
- 1/4 tsp. baking powder
- 1/4 tsp. baking soda
- 3/4 tsp. ground ginger
- 1/2 tsp. ground cinnamon
- 1/4 tsp. kosher salt
- 1 large egg
- 1 cup water, for steaming (double-check the Ninja Foodi Multi-cooker manual to confirm the amount and follow the manual if there is a discrepancy)

Instructions:
1. In a small bowl, using a hand mixer, mix the hot water, vegetable oil, brown sugar, molasses and egg. In another small bowl, sift together the flour, ground ginger, cinnamon, kosher salt, baking powder and baking soda. Add the dry ingredients to the liquid mixture
2. Mix on medium speed until the ingredients are thoroughly combined, with no lumps. Pour the batter into a nonstick mini (3 by 5-inch) loaf pan. Cover the pan with aluminum foil, making a dome over the pan.
3. Add the water and insert the steamer basket or trivet. Carefully place the loaf pan on the steamer insert.
4. High pressure for 15 minutes. Lock the lid on the Ninja Foodi Multi-cooker and then cook for 15 minutes.
5. To get 15 minutes' cook time, press *Pressure* button and use the Time Adjustment button to adjust the cook time to 15 minutes
6. When the timer goes off, turn the cooker off. (Keep Warm* setting, turn off).
7. Pressure Release. After cooking, use the natural method to release pressure for 5 minutes, then the quick method to release the remaining pressure
8. Finish the dish. Unlock and remove the lid. Using tongs, carefully remove the pan from the Ninja Foodi Multi-cooker.
9. Let the cake rest for 2 to 3 minutes; remove the foil, slice and serve.
10. To sift the dry ingredients, place a medium-coarse sieve over a small bowl or on a sheet of wax paper or parchment paper. Measure the dry ingredients in the sieve
11. Tap the side of the sieve to move the contents through the sieve to the bowl or parchment paper; then transfer the sifted ingredients to the wet ingredients

Yummy Blackberry Swirl Cheesecake

(Ready in about: 30 minutes | **Servings:** 6)

Ingredients:
- 1 cup fresh blackberries
- 4 tbsp. unsalted butter
- 1/2 cup powdered sugar
- Freshly grated zest from 1 lemon
- Freshly grated zest from half an orange
- 2 large eggs
- 1/2 cup granulated sugar
- 1 cup crushed graham crackers
- 14-ounces cream cheese (one 8-ounce and two 3-ounce packages)

Instructions:
1. Add 2 cups of water to the Ninja Foodi Multi-cooker base; insert the steamer basket and set aside. Cut a piece of wax paper to fit the bottom of a wide, flat-bottomed 4-cup baking dish; also cut a strip sized to fit the sides of the dish
2. Line the dish with the paper. Puree the blackberries and powdered sugar in a blender and set aside.
3. Melt the butter in a medium saucepan over medium heat. Remove the pan from the heat and mix in the crushed crackers
4. Scoop the mixture into the prepared baking dish and, using the back of your hand, push it into a flat, thin, even layer that covers the bottom of the dish, and, if there is enough, partway up the sides. Put the dish in the refrigerator to chill, uncovered, while you prepare the filling
5. In a medium bowl, using an electric mixer on medium speed, mix the cream cheese, granulated sugar and lemon and orange zests. Add the eggs and mix into a smooth batter, about 5 minutes.
6. Remove the dish with the crust from the refrigerator. Slowly pour the batter over the crust, spreading level. To add the blackberry swirl, pour the puree into a squirt bottle (or food storage bag with one corner clipped off) and with it draw a spiral from the center out on top of the batter. Then use a toothpick or skewer to drag radiating lines from the center to the edge of the dish. Using a foil sling, lower the dish into the Ninja Foodi Multi-cooker; do not cover the dish
7. High pressure for 20 minutes. Lock the lid on the Ninja Foodi Multi-cooker and then cook for 20 minutes.
8. To get 20 minutes' cook time, press *Pressure* button and use the Time Adjustment button to adjust the cook time to 20 minutes
9. Pressure Release. When the time is up, open the Ninja Foodi Multi-cooker using the 10-Minute Natural Release method.
10. Finish the dish. Lift the dish out of the Ninja Foodi Multi-cooker and check the cake for doneness, transfer the dish to a wire rack.
11. Let the cake cool, uncovered, for about 30 minutes. Then cover the dish with plastic wrap and refrigerate until ready to serve, for at least 4 hours
12. Work quickly and delicately to unmold the chilled cake: Invert a plate over the dish and flip the dish and plate over together. Lift the dish off the cake and then peel off the wax paper circle on the base and the strip on the sides
13. Then invert a serving plate on the cake and gently flip all three components over together; lift off the top plate. Serve the cake cold, cut into wedges

Apple Pies

(**Ready in about:** 35 minutes | **Servings:** 6)

Ingredients:
- 2 apples; cored and diced
- 4 frozen piecrusts; thawed if frozen hard
- 1/8 tsp. nutmeg
- 2 tsp. cornstarch
- 1/4 cup honey
- 1 tsp. cinnamon
- 1 tsp. vanilla extract
- 1 tsp. water
- Cooking oil

Instructions:
1. Preheat the unit by selecting Bake/Roast, setting the temperature to 300°F and setting the time to 5 minutes. Press Start/Stop to begin
2. Place a saucepan over medium-high heat. Add the apples, honey, cinnamon, vanilla and nutmeg. Stir and cook for 2 to 3 minutes, until the apples are soft. In a small bowl, mix the cornstarch and water.
3. Add to the pan and stir. Cook for 30 seconds. Cut each piecrust into two 4-inch circles. You should have 8 circles of crust total. Lay the piecrusts on a flat work surface. Mound 1/3 cup of apple filling on the center of each
4. Fold each piecrust over so that the top layer of crust is about an inch short of the bottom layer.
5. Using your fingers, tap along the edges of the top layer to seal. Use the back of a fork to press lines into the edges.
6. Air Frying the Dish. Place the hand pies in the Ninja Foodi. I do not recommend stacking the hand pies. They will stick together if stacked
7. Close the Crisping Lid. Select Bake/Roast, set the temperature to 300°F and set the time to 10 minutes. Select Start/Stop to begin.
8. Finish the Dish. Allow the hand pies to cool fully before removing from the Ninja Foodi

Awesome Strawberry Cheesecake Rolls

(Ready in about: 30 minutes | **Servings:** 6)

Ingredients:
- 1 (8-ounce) can crescent rolls
- 1/3 cup sliced fresh strawberries
- 4-ounces cream cheese
- Cooking oil
- 1 tbsp. strawberry preserves

Instructions:
1. Preparing the ingredients. Preheat the unit by selecting Bake/Roast, setting the temperature to 300°F and setting the time to 5 minutes. Press Start/Stop to begin. On a flat work surface, roll out the dough into a large rectangle
2. Cut the dough into 12 rectangles by making 3 cuts crosswise and 2 cuts lengthwise. Place the cream cheese in a small, microwave-safe bowl. Microwave for 15 seconds to soften
3. In a medium bowl, combine the cream cheese and strawberry preserves and stir. Scoop 2 tsp. of the cream cheese and strawberry mixture onto each piece of dough. Spread, but avoid the edges of the dough. Add 2 tsp. of fresh strawberries to each.
4. Roll up each of the rectangles to create a roll.
5. Air Frying. Spray the Ninja Foodi basket with cooking oil. Place the rolls in the basket. Do not stack. Cook in batches. Spray the rolls with cooking oil. Close the Crisping Lid. Select Bake/Roast, set the temperature to 350°F and set the time to 8 minutes. Select Start/Stop to begin
6. Finish the dish. Allow the rolls to cool for 2 to 3 minutes, then remove from the Ninja Foodi. Repeat steps for the remaining rolls. Cool before serving

Lemon Ricotta Cheesecake with Strawberries

(Ready in about: 35 minutes | **Servings:** 6)

Ingredients:
- 10-ounce Cream Cheese
- 1/4 cup Sugar
- 1/2 cup Ricotta Cheese
- 1 ½ cups Water
- 10 Strawberries, halved to decorate
- 2 Eggs, cracked into a bowl
- 1 tsp. Lemon Extract
- 3 tbsp. Sour Cream
- One Lemon, zested and juiced

Instructions:
1. In the electric mixer, add the cream cheese, quarter cup of sugar, ricotta cheese, lemon zest, lemon juice, and lemon extract. Turn on the mixer and mix the ingredients until a smooth consistency is formed. Adjust the sweet taste to liking with more sugar
2. Reduce the speed of the mixer and add the eggs. Fold it in at low speed until it is fully incorporated. Make sure not to fold the eggs in high speed to prevent a cracked crust
3. Grease the spring form pan with cooking spray and use a spatula to spoon the mixture into the pan. Level the top with the spatula and cover it with foil
4. Open the Ninja Foodi, fit in the reversible rack, and pour in the water. Place the cake pan on the rack. Close the lid, secure the pressure valve, and select Pressure mode on High pressure for 15 minutes. Press Start/Stop.
5. Meanwhile, mix the sour cream and one tbsp. of sugar. Set aside
6. Once the timer has gone off, do a natural pressure release for 10 minutes, then a quick pressure release to let out any extra steam, and open the lid.
7. Remove the rack with pan, place the spring form pan on a flat surface, and open it. Use a spatula to spread the sour cream mixture on the warm cake. Refrigerate the cake for 8 hours
8. Top with strawberries; slice it into 6 pieces and serve while firm

Vanilla Pudding with Berries

(Ready in about: 35 minutes 6h for refrigeration | **Servings:** 4)

Ingredients:
- 1 cup Heavy Cream
- 4 Egg Yolks
- 1/2 cup Sugar
- 4 Raspberries
- 4 Blueberries
- 1/2 cup Milk
- 1 tsp. Vanilla
- 4 tbsp. Water + 1 ½ cups Water

Instructions:
1. Turn on your Ninja Foodi and select Sear/Sauté mode on Medium(MD)
2. Add 4 tbsp. for water and the sugar. Stir it constantly until it dissolves. Press Stop. Add milk, heavy cream, and vanilla. Stir it with a whisk until evenly combined
3. Crack the eggs into a bowl and add a tablespoon of the cream mixture. Whisk it and then very slowly add the remaining cream mixture while whisking.
4. Fit the reversible rack at the bottom of the pot, and pour one and a half cup of water in it. Pour the mixture into four ramekins and place them on the rack
5. Close the lid of the pot, secure the pressure valve, and select Pressure mode on High Pressure for 4 minutes. Press Start/Stop

6. Once the timer has gone off, do a quick pressure release, and open the lid. With a napkin in hand, carefully remove the ramekins onto a flat surface. Let them cool for about 15 minutes and then refrigerate them for 6 hours.
7. After 6 hours, remove them from the refrigerator and garnish them with the raspberries and blueberries. Enjoy immediately or refrigerate further until dessert time is ready

Delicious Lava Cake

(Ready in about: 40 minutes | **Servings:** 8)

Ingredients:
- 1 cup Butter
- 4 tsp. Vanilla Extract
- 4 tbsp. Milk
- 7 tbsp. All-purpose Flour
- 5 Eggs
- 1 ½ cups Chocolate Chips
- 1 ½ cups Sugar
- Powdered sugar to garnish
- 1 cup Water

Instructions:
1. Grease the cake pan with cooking spray and set aside. Open the Ninja Foodi, fit the reversible rack at the bottom of it, and pour in the water
2. In a medium heatproof bowl, add the butter and chocolate and melt them in the microwave for about 2 minutes. Remove it from the microwave
3. Add sugar and use a spatula to stir it well. Add the eggs, milk, and vanilla extract and stir again. Finally, add the flour and stir it until even and smooth
4. Pour the batter into the greased cake pan and use the spatula to level it.
5. Place the pan on the trivet in the pot, close the lid, secure the pressure valve, and select Pressure on High for 15 minutes. Press Start/Stop
6. Once the timer has gone off, do a natural pressure release for 10 minutes, then a quick pressure release, and open the lid.
7. Remove the rack with the pan on it and place the pan on a flat surface. Put a plate over the pan and flip the cake over into the plate. Pour the powdered sugar in a fine sieve and sift it over the cake.
8. Use a knife to cut the cake into 8 slices and serve immediately (while warm)

Poached Peach Cups

(**Ready in about:** 10 minutes | **Servings:** 4)

Ingredients:
- 4 peaches; cut in half and pitted
- 1 cup part-skim ricotta cheese
- 1/4 cup apple juice
- 1/4 tsp. vanilla extract
- 3 tbsp. light brown sugar
- 1/8 tsp. ground cinnamon
- 1/4 cup water
- 2 tbsp. honey

Instructions:
1. Add peaches, apple juice, water, brown sugar and cinnamon in the cooker
2. High pressure for 5 minutes. Lock the lid on the Ninja Foodi Multi-cooker and then cook for 5 minutes.
3. To get 5 minutes' cook time, press *Pressure* button and use the Time Adjustment button to adjust the cook time to 5 minutes
4. Pressure Release. Perform a quick release to release the cooker's pressure
5. Remove peaches from cooking liquid and set aside.
6. Finish the dish. Combine ricotta cheese, honey and vanilla extract and serve spooned into the center of each peach half

Tasty Crème Brulee

(**Ready in about:** 35 minutes 6h for refrigeration | **Servings:** 4)

Ingredients:
- 3 cups Heavy Whipping Cream
- 2 tbsp. Vanilla Extract
- 2 cups Water
- 6 tbsp. Sugar
- 7 large Egg Yolks

Instructions:
1. In a mixing bowl, add the yolks, vanilla, whipping cream, and half of the swerve sugar. Use a whisk to mix them until they are well combined
2. Pour the mixture into the ramekins and cover them with aluminium foil
3. Open the Ninja Foodi, fit the reversible rack into the pot, and pour in the water. Place 3 ramekins on the rack and place the remaining ramekins to sit on the edges of the ramekins below
4. Close the lid, secure the pressure valve, and select Pressure mode on High for 8 minutes. Press Start/Stop.
5. Once the timer has stopped, do a natural pressure release for 10 minutes, then a quick pressure release to let out the remaining pressure
6. With a napkin in hand, remove the ramekins onto a flat surface and then into a refrigerator to chill for at least 6 hours
7. After refrigeration, remove the ramekins and remove the aluminium foil
8. Equally, sprinkle the remaining sugar on it and return to the pot. Close the crisping lid, select Bake/Roast mode, set the timer to 4 minutes on 380 ° F. Serve the crème brulee chilled with wiped cream.

Made in the USA
San Bernardino, CA
11 January 2019